The editor gratefully acknowledges permission to reprint the following:

Chapter 6: From "The Rabbi as Caregiver: A Clerical Model" in *Tradition* 23:3 (Spring 1988). Reprinted by permission of the Rabbinical Council of America.

Chapter 18: From "Children of Rabbis" in *Tradition* 23:2 (Winter 1988). Reprinted by permission of the Rabbinical Council of America.

Chapter 21: From a lecture delivered at the Institute of Judaism and Contemporary Jewish Thought at Bar Ilan University, July 6, 1979. Published as "The Challenge of Jewish Spiritual Leaders" in the publication of the Institute of Judaism and Contemporary Jewish Thought. Reprinted by permission of the Institute and Rabbi Immanuel Jakobovits.

Chapter 22: From "New Directions and Challenges in the Contemporary Rabbinate" in *Sh'ma* 20 (Jan. 19, 1990). Reprinted by permission of *Sh'ma*.

Chapter 23: Reprinted from *Yearbook of Religious Zionism* (1985/1986), pp. 14–28. Reprinted by permission of *Mesilot*, the Society for the Advancement of Religious Zionism.

Library of Congress Cataloguing-in-Publication Data

The rabbinate as calling and vocation: models of rabbinic leadership / edited by Basil Herring.
    p. m.
   Includes bibliographical references and index.
   ISBN 0-87668-735-4
   1. Rabbis—United States—Office. 2. Orthodox Judaism—United
States. I. Herring, Basil.
   BM652.R33 1991
   296.6'1—dc20   90-1247

Manufactured in the United States of America. Jason Aronson Inc. Offers books and cassettes. For information and catalog write to Jason Aronson Inc., 230 Livingston Street, Northvale, New Jersey 07647.

Contents

Part II
THE RABBI'S PERSONAL AND PROFESSIONAL LIFE

Part III
VISION AND PERSPECTIVE

Contents v

Foreword

Rabbis live in a world of two geographies—one a visible landscape of material prosperity, the other a metaphysical atlas that lies embedded in memory.

The first world is that of public, congregational life—rich in potential for growth and abounding in programs of study and chesed. The second world is the old, inwardly sensed *rabbanishe velt*—where the rabbi inhabits the "Rav" gestalt of the collective unconscious of our people—a commitment to the books and ideas of the wise, an intimate involvement with the Master of the Universe, and an involvement with those personal areas where he is presumed to be a paragon— meticulous care for family, and heightened personal sensitivity about matters of honor and shame, decency, and boorishness.

The first landscape has many highroads and intricate pathways down which many have trod, and the turf is well known—such as synagogue goals and community structures that are known to all; newspapers display them constantly and they are the subjects of numerous meetings and forums. The metaphysical atlas is only rarely intuited, few laymen actually having been there—most only imagine it, and the human imagination is notably impoverished.

Who helps the rabbi to live in this other landscape, the one embedded in memory and hopes? How many understand his rabbinic predilections, its fragilities and needs? How many recognize that *velt* or even believe he is entitled to it? How does the rabbi go about balancing his classical learned scholar role with the ever-increasing demands on him to administer efficiently, guide, counsel, reach out, and reach in to his congregation and community? Finally, how can the rabbi be an accessible husband and father and provide the necessary time for family and personal needs?

It is the goal of this volume to give the reader an inside look into the thinking of a wide range of leading rabbis, most of whom were ordained at the Rabbi Isaac Elchanan Theological Seminary (RIETS), an affiliate of Yeshiva University, to gain an understanding of their priorities and perspectives on the contemporary rabbinate.

The publication and dissemination of the volume is supported by the Gindi Family Professional Enhancement Program of RIETS, created to assist congregational rabbis and rebbitzins, some of whom serve in isolated and conflicted communities, by providing opportunities for collegiality, guidance, and encouragement by senior colleagues and mentors.

Rabbi Basil Herring, who is one of RIETS's most distinguished and scholarly graduates, has edited this volume with insight. The writers he has chosen to include are rabbis who know well the congregational world, from years of dedicated experience. The book was initiated, in great measure, because of the imaginative efforts of Rabbi Robert S. Hirt, Vice President for Administration and Professional Education at RIETS.

Perhaps if rabbis and lay leaders more fully understand the visible landscape of the rabbinate and its veiled underpinnings, we will merit achieving the sanctified geography that we long to occupy.

Rabbi Maurice Lamm
Chair in Professional Rabbinics
Director, Gindi Family Program for the
Enhancement of Professional Rabbinics

Introduction

This volume is a modest attempt to address the many challenges of the Orthodox rabbinate as it finds itself in the closing decade of the twentieth century, a time of flux and change in Jewish life, given the evolving realities affecting the Jewish people in our time. The contemporary rabbi faces significant demands as well as opportunities—and this manual attempts to encapsulate the attitudes and the approaches, the methods and the modalities, that some of the most effective, or promising, Orthodox rabbis of our generation have used with real success.

WHAT IS THE CONDITION OF THE ORTHODOX RABBINATE TODAY?

On the one hand rabbis are much better off than they were yesteryear, financially and professionally. Twenty or thirty years ago rabbis were for the most part lonely souls, fighting a rear-guard action against a widespread attitude that belittled religion and Judaism. This was especially true of Orthodox rabbis, whose faith and practices were written off as a relic doomed to disappear. Today there is a new respect for tradition and faith, and Orthodoxy has demonstrated unexpected vitality in the Jewish community.

Notwithstanding all this, it is also true that many pulpit rabbanim have become disenchanted and burned out, with a good number leaving the field for greener pastures. In smaller communities there are many empty pulpits; in larger communities good positions are increasingly difficult to find. Many of the most talented have developed new or parallel careers, because of what they see as the limitations and frustrations of the rabbinate. And most disturbing, many men who have great promise choose not to enter the rabbinate in the first place, choosing more lucrative, and often more satisfying vocations instead.

The truth is that there are significant pleasures and benefits in the rabbinate. It is not a "nine-to-five" job, and not limited to sitting in an office; it is people-oriented and therefore never dull; and it affords endless opportunities for helping people on the most fundamental level, as they experience the fullness of life, from the cradle to the grave. Without question there is much satisfaction in the knowledge of having helped and shared in the ups and the downs, the joys and the travails, of a fellow human being. Another plus is the opportunity for Torah study as part of one's daily routine. If one's "work" involves the pleasures of Talmud and Codes, philosophical thought and social comment, studying them and teaching them, reviewing them and even adding to them—such pleasures are a rare privilege for any Jew. There is also the deep satisfaction garnered in seeing one's efforts sometimes result in other Jews coming closer to the practice of Judaism, or the strengthening of the fabric of one's Jewish community as a result of one's efforts. And as a rabbi, one constantly senses the spirit of *Klal Yisrael*, the totality of the Jewish people. There is a sense of rootedness in the past and an identification with corporate Israel around the globe, in a sense representing one's larger constituency as a rabbi. Finally, in enumerating the major benefits of the rabbinate, there is the matter of *kavod*, or respect and recognition usually accorded most rabbis, at least, that is, to start with.

But there is also a negative side to the rabbinate. Often the rabbi is viewed as an employee whose boss is every dues-paying member of the synagogue. His income is usually less than that of his average *balebos*. Hence his standard of living suffers by comparison—even though he often provides leadership and services that in the professional or business world would receive vastly greater remuneration. Additionally there is the question of his responsibilities. He is always on call, having no partner to pick up when he is off duty. He makes house calls and he must be available from early morning till late at night. His weekends are usually taken up with synagogue and communal business, his evenings occupied with classes, meetings, and phone calls, because that is when his congregants are free. Shabbat and Yom Tov are his "busy period," hence they are times of stress and pressure for him, and for his family.

And during normal work hours what does he do? While every congregation is different, a short list for many rabbis might include most of the following: he runs the synagogue office, carries on correspondence, keeps an eye on the Hebrew School, the nursery, the youth programs, and the synagogue building. He visits the sick and comforts the bereaved, he counsels those who are troubled, and he officiates at family events, both happy and sad. He prepares lectures and discussion groups for adults and children, writes articles, messages, and editorials. He assists charitable causes within the community and beyond it; he participates in regional and national organizations in the larger Jewish community that ask him to lecture or attend their meetings. He must work with Sisterhood and Men's Club, synagogue officers and personnel, consulting and supervising, with grace and with fortitude, to deal with the 101 little crises that crop up on a daily basis. He officiates at funerals and bar mizvahs, weddings and dinners, fund-raisers and cocktail parties, always ready with a bon mot, and a dvar Torah. He is at all times expected to be an ambassador of good will to unaffiliated Jews, to the Gentile world, to other synagogues.

Of course it is assumed that the rabbi spends much of his time studying. And so he does—with Torah and Talmud, the *parshah* and the *Shulchan Arukh*. But that is not enough, for in addition he must be current on the state of the world through his reading of newspapers, magazines, popular books, and journals. After all, how else will he be able to get up on the pulpit week after week, month after month, year in year out, to make insightful pronouncements on the perplexing issues of the day, in fields as disparate as politics and family life, religion and society, Zionism and theology? Imagine the challenge of creating fifty or sixty such sermons a year, Shabbat and Yom Tov, to speak with intelligence and charm, humor and learning—never sure how his words will be received or commented on, or whether they will be totally ignored.

These, then, are but a few of the pros and the cons, the positive and the negative, that make up the rabbinic portfolio, the rabbi's business. Looked at in these terms, many would say that he is not in a very good line of work at all. It would appear that there are many more liabilities than there are assets in dealing full-time with synagogues, *balebatim*, and communal demands. If so, we must ask the obvious question: why should a young man choose to enter the rabbinate today, and if he is already in the rabbinate, why should he choose to remain, when there are so many other things he could be doing?

WHAT MAKES THE RABBINIC CALLING WORTHWHILE?

One answer to this question is found in a beautiful and inspiring, even if familiar, midrash relating to authentic Jewish leadership:

> Once when Moshe Rabbeinu was attending the flock of Yitro in the desert, a young lamb ran away. He ran after it . . . and found it drinking at a pool of water. When he saw this sight, he said "I did not know that you ran away because you were thirsty; you must be tired." He put the lamb on his shoulders and carried it home. Said God: "If you are so compassionate to treat dumb animals thus, by your life you shall tend my flock, the people of Israel." [Exodus *Rabbah* 2:2]

This midrash, says the great Rabbi Yehiel Ya'akov Weinberg of Montreaux in his volume entitled *la-Perakim*, articulates the real meaning of Jewish leadership, as immortalized by Moshe Rabbeinu. The lost lamb is the symbol of the errant Jew, and Moshe represents the servant of God, compassionate and loving, who reaches out and runs after those who have strayed from God's ways. To the casual eye, when Jews wander far and wide from traditional pastures, it appears to be a form of rebellion and disenchantment. Not so to Moshe. He follows his precious lambs step by step, knowing that it is not rebellion at all, not a lack of love, but rather a real thirst and genuine confusion that drives them in new directions, far from home, the result of a hostile environment, a world inimical to God's ways. Like Moshe, the true leader of Israel seeks out his lambs wherever they are, he runs after them to bring them back, if necessary to carry them on his shoulders, bearing their weight with dignity and strength, alternately diminishing their pain and their burdens, and multiplying their moments of exultation, lifting them on high, so that they can see beyond the spiritual horizon. Like Moshe, a rabbi must be filled with compassion and love for each one, keeping them together, shepherding them on the right path, providing them with sustenance and faithful support through thick and thin, leading the way, building the flock, creating a sense of togetherness.

Those were the qualities of Moshe. And these are the qualities that must drive today's rabbi, as pastor and as visionary, as teacher and as an inspirer of men and women of all ages. Like Moshe, to understand the deep spiritual thirst that compels so many of our people to graze in foreign pastures and drink at alien fountains; to assume the burdens of their troubles and disappointments and losses—but in so doing to lift them on high to see a better path and a clearer perspective on life. Like Moshe our teacher, to be a *melamed*, to uncover and project the life-giving waters of Torah and tradition, in each generation.

This then is the answer to our questions: What makes the rabbinic calling worthwhile? What makes the sacrifices bearable? It is the promise and the reality of bringing Jews home to where they belong, of building a Torah community, of raising up on high religious standards and spiritual expectations. Merely to leave things at status quo, not to challenge the comfortable assumptions of the community, to be thwarted in the attempt at creating something new—frankly, under such circumstances it is simply not worth it. But to be able to go forward together, under the flag of the Torah and tradition, makes all the difference in the world. That is why the creative rabbinate is a vocation for none but the brave, those who are willing to assume a challenge against many odds, to give up some of the conventional rewards for the sake of a greater good, to be a selfless idealist and visionary in an oft-cynical and materialistic world. For individuals such as this, the rewards and the satisfactions of such a life are immeasurable, and profoundly satisfying, in many, many ways.

CREATING AN EFFECTIVE RABBINIC LIFE

Even so, vision and dedicated commitment by themselves are not enough to make for a successful and effective rabbinic life. It is necessary to acquire and formulate specific tools and techniques, ideas and programmatics that will translate such high sentiment into concrete results. And that is no easy task.

Hence the present volume. It is neither ideological nor moralizing in substance or tone. And it does not claim to cover every area of rabbinic activity. What it does attempt is a somewhat comprehensive description of the multifaceted responsibilities, activities, and challenges of the Orthodox rabbinate. Moreover it does so with the help of eminently successful, in many ways model pulpit rabbis, each writing in an area in which he has achieved recognition and expertise.

Our authors are many and varied—in geographical location, in age, in outlook, and in specialization. Moreover, in their presentations here they do not always agree in their approaches and methodologies. There is both overlap and inconsistency, and it is not our intention in bringing them together in one volume to imply that any one rabbi could ever possibly embrace all of the perspectives and specialties presented in these pages. Every rabbi brings his own personality, special talents, interests, and inclinations to his calling. And the reader of these pages will perforce need to approach each essay with a keen awareness of his own abilities and priorities, not to speak of the particular circumstances that prevail in a given community. Yet our authors do have in common a deep commitment to what is sometimes known as centrist, or modern, Orthodoxy, mostly as graduates of Yeshiva University and its affiliate Rabbi Isaac Elchanan Theological Seminary (RIETS).

And so, what they have done in these pages is a rare and beautiful thing: they have shared the secrets of their own success, in the hope of inspiring others to learn from, or follow in, their footsteps. What has taken them years, if not decades, of effort, hardship, trial and error, accomplished through great personal courage, they here present "on a platter," for the benefit and edification of their colleagues, present and future, and the greater good of the Torah. For this chesed we are profoundly in their debt.

It is our hope that not only the neophyte or the *semikhah* student will benefit from these pages—but that even many seasoned rabbanim of every stripe will reap a rich harvest as well. For it is often true that only after we have been out in the field on our own can we truly appreciate and understand the significance of what our teachers and fellows have had to say to us. In addition, it is to be hoped that not only rabbis, but laymen of all kinds who share an interest in and commitment to strengthening synagogue and communal life will find new insight on the rabbinic role so as to lead to a higher level of mutual understanding—and enrichment.

May our combined efforts serve to raise the banner of Torah ever higher, to give succor to a parched generation, and to bring closer the fullest redemption of our people Israel, under a renewed and invigorated rabbinic leadership.

I

RABBINIC
MODELS
AND
METHODS

1

The Rabbi as Halakhic Authority

Rabbi Hershel Billet

The Orthodox rabbi is, in the first place, the embodiment of halakhah, in his actions and in his teachings, public and private. He is called upon to represent and communicate Jewish law on a daily basis, a responsibility that he shoulders with care and precision. Rabbi Hershel Billet carefully describes the many halakhic decisions that the Rav must deal with and some of the resources available to him.

There is no profession serving the Jewish community which makes as many varied demands upon its practitioner as the contemporary Orthodox rabbinate. The classical role of the rabbi as teacher and halakhic authority, and primary religious role model in the community, has been extended to encompass all facets of life. The rabbi has become as well a social worker for all stages of life, an advisor in making difficult choices, an advocate on local and general communal issues, and a key figure in many other areas affecting the life of each member of his community. As such the rabbinate is an exciting, multifaceted, and ever challenging profession which makes unprecedented demands upon the time of the rabbi.

The classical image of the Rav, as one whose "Torah is his profession," who interrupts his studies only to tend to the halakhic needs of his constituents, is no longer a realistic model—except in rare circumstances. The demands of *"Yiftach be'doro ki-Shmuel be'doro"* require the modern-day Rav to adjust to the demands of his profession and uphold at the same time his traditional calling as the halakhic authority for his community.

How does the modern-day rabbi maintain the same high standards of halakhic competence that his title of *Moreh Hora'ah* implies, in light of the extraordinary extracurricular demands on his time made by his communal role? Rav Moshe Feinstein wrote of the awesome burden of one who is called upon to be responsible for the halakhic life of the Jewish community. On the one hand he acknowledges the trepidation with which one must approach the task, and on the other hand he recognizes the obligation of those whose calling it is to meet the challenge and bear the burden. In this sense the modern-day Orthodox rabbi is no different from the classical Rav of the proverbial *kehilah kedoshah*. Only time and circumstances have changed and we, the bearers of the most sacred and noble Jewish profession begun by Moshe at Sinai, must adjust to the challenges of contemporary times.

The purpose of this chapter is twofold: to suggest some formulae which address the "halakhic condition" of a contemporary Rav, and to share with the reader a basic bibliography of suggested texts and sefarim that I have found useful in given areas of halakhic concern. The ideas presented within this essay are of necessity limited by the demands of space and by the perspective of their author. Nevertheless, it is my hope that they can be of use as a foundation for further discussion of this subject.

PREPARATION

Hakhanah, as a concept relative to Shabbat and Tefillah, implies respect for something important. Preparation is in fact a necessary prerequisite for anything important in life. In the context of the rabbinate we called that preparation in the early years *chinukh*, and in our more mature intellectual years "Talmud Torah."

The authors of the Avnei Nezer and the Bet ha-Levi both describe two types of Torah study. One is studying Torah in order to fulfill the mizvah of Talmud Torah. The other is studying Torah for the sake of fulfilling the practical demands of the halakhah. One who selects the rabbinate as his life's calling must prepare himself by striking a delicate balance between the more general Torah study for

Torah's sake, and the more focused studying demanded by the daily responsibilities of the rabbinate. A rabbi should be a talmid chakham in general, but he must surely be a talmid chakham in numerous practical areas. Of course, one's obligation and commitment to all forms of Talmud Torah must continue even after achieving Semikhah. Nevertheless, it would be most beneficial to a young Rav if he entered the rabbinate with a heavy dosage of practical knowledge.

Practical knowledge is achieved in two ways, both of which are necessary. First, there must be a thorough examination of the sources; and second, there must be some shimush with a more experienced colleague. Such a colleague is clearly wiser to the realities of the world where theory and circumstance do not always blend together as smoothly as one would expect when sitting "between the walls" of the Bet ha-Midrash.

PRACTICAL STUDY

To prepare for the rabbinate and to function in the rabbinate it is necessary to set specific goals to be achieved. The practicing Rav will always be on call to answer questions as they are presented by his constituents. Some of the answers will be readily accessible to him because of his extensive study of halakhah. Others will require research and at times a consultation with a posek.

We can now deal with a number of specific issues relative to the role of the Rav as halakhic authority for his community.

AREAS OF HALAKHAH REQUIRING SPECIALIZED STUDY

The following is a list of subjects that a Rav should master to some degree. Different positions and differing circumstances may demand more knowledge in some of these areas and less in others. Undoubtedly, there are other subjects which I may have omitted by oversight or by the constraints of space.

Laws Pertaining to the Synagogue

The laws of prayer in general. Frequently raised issues include the repetition of words by the chazzan, the inclusion and omission of certain prayers, who is obligated and who may not lead services, the rules of kaddish, etc.

Prayers and customs relating to specific calendar days. This includes the order of services on Shabbat and Yom Tov, when certain prayers are omitted, etc.

The laws of Torah reading. Some common questions are: What is called an error by the reader? When does a mistake in the Sefer Torah render it *passul?* When and where is one eligible for an aliyah? What are the rules of carrying the Torah in the synagogue? What are the rules of a *siyum Sefer Torah* and *hakhnasat Sefer Torah?*

How the synagogue building and sanctuary are used. This applies both during times of prayer and study and at other times. The rules of mechitzah and of kedushat Bet ha-Knesset are essential. If there is a caterer in the building who rents the social hall and has rights to the sanctuary, specific guidelines must be established. May the synagogue building be used, albeit by outsiders who pay rent, for nonhalakhic or antihalakhic events? The use of the synagogue for religious nonprayer and Torah study events such as funerals and weddings is an important issue.

The use of non-Jewish help. Their role and responsibilities in the synagogue on Shabbat and Yom Tov should be clarified. An area directly related to this one is the kitchen of non-Jewish domestic help, that is, what they may and may not do in the home on Shabbat and Yom Tov.

Laws Pertaining to Kashrut

Kashering dishes. Kashrut questions abound concerning sundry problems that arise in the home. Questions about kashering dishes, utensils, and dishwashers are common during the year and for Pesach.

Shechitah. In running local communal kashrut organizations, all of the above apply. Also, a practical working knowledge of *shechitah* and *nikur* and *melichah* are essential. Here *shimush* plays a very important role.

Miscellaneous. There is interplay in kashrut with the rules of Shabbat, *cbishul akum, pat akum, chalav yisrael, stam yainam, chalah, terumot* and *maasrot, ne'emanut, basar she-nitalem min ha'ayin, simanei dagim,* etc. *Shimush* and consultations with respected individuals in the field of kashrut are essential. Good general knowledge of the various kosher symbols, agencies, and practices in the *hashgachah* field is important. Familiarity with caterers, restaurants, sources of supply, slaughterhouses, and distributors is essential.

Laws Pertaining to Yom Tov

Each holiday calls upon the Rav to set policies and standards for services in the synagogue. Each holiday as well brings its own unique set of questions from the members of the synagogue as to their personal conduct at home. Here too, it is worthwhile to spell out the most common Yom Tov rules in a bulletin. This will limit questions to more specific and less obvious areas. Following are some of the issues which arise most frequently during each festival.

Rosh Hashanah and Yom Kippur. The length and quality of shofar blowing; shofar blowing for individual men and women confined to home; the chazzanim and how they conduct the services; what liturgy to omit; repetition of words; who does not fast on Yom Kippur and how to eat on Yom Kippur.

Sukkot. Sundry construction problems for the sukkah, e.g., under trees, the types of *skhakh*, support for the *skhakh*; rain on the first two nights; *arba minim*; the rules of Chol ha-Moed; Hoshannah Rabbah services; eating in the sukkah on Shmini Azeret; and Simchat Torah festivities.

Hanukkah candle lighting. The rules of lighting candles in the synagogue and at home; rules pertaining to people with erratic time schedules, guests, and travelers.

Purim. The fulfillment of *matanot le'evyonim; mishloach manot* for mourners; Megillah reading in noisy synagogues with a microphone; Megillah reading for individual men and women confined to home; Parshat Zakhor on the Shabbat of a bar mitzvah.

Pesach products. Medicine; cosmetics; kashering; Bedikat chametz for travelers; laws of mekhirat chametz for people staying home and those traveling to different time zones; laws of the Seder.

Sefirat ha-Omer. Scheduling of parties in the context of varying customs; attending dinners; haircuts; shaving; rules regarding Yom Hashoah, Yom Ha-Atzmaut, and Yom Yerushalayim.

Shavuot. Conduct of those who stay up all night concerning certain berakhot, and *talit katan* in the morning and after they awaken from their morning sleep.

The fast days. Rules concerning personal hygiene on the different fast days; who does not or may not fast; conduct during the Three Weeks, the Nine Days, *shavua she-chal bo*, and Tisha B'Av.

Laws Pertaining to Eruvin

Many communities today demand or need an eruv for a number of reasons: to attract young couples with babies, or to avoid *chilul Shabbat*, which would otherwise take place. It is essential for a Rav to know the rules of eruvin, the practical requirements for a properly constructed eruv, and the problems that must often be overcome in constructing an eruv. Here shimush and a consultation with a respected expert in chilkhot eruvin to review the community's eruv would be appropriate procedure.

I believe that a Rav who constructs an eruv should use it himself. If, however, he personally is uncomfortable using an eruv for whatever reason, he should not condemn others who do—as long as the eruv conforms to the stipulations of a reliable authority.

Laws Pertaining to Aveilut

The circumstance of death is one that calls upon the skills, compassion, and halakhic knowledge of the rabbi. There are questions common to all situations concerning the general observances of mourning. But the rabbi must be prepared as well for unique circumstances in each situation. A good practical working knowledge of the Laws of Mourning is a sine qua non for the community rabbi.

If the community is able to maintain it, the rabbi should involve himself and his members in setting up a Chevra Kadisha. Classes should be taught and the practical aspects of all matters of *kavod ha-met* must be examined. The organization of all details of the Chevra from the moment that death takes place through the burial must be studied. Even the functions of the Chevra in the house of mourning must be covered. It is helpful to review the practices of other Chevrot Kadisha both past and present.

Laws Pertaining to Mikvah

This area of the practical rabbinate involves itself in several areas of communal life.

Construction of a mikvah. The basic laws of Mikvaot, the proper choice of a reliable Rav ha-Makhshir, and the choice of the right builder all should be matters of concern to the community rabbi.

Taharat ha-Mishpachah. Formal policies should be set for the use of the mikvah. Common situations which need consideration are the use of the mikvah by day on the seventh or eighth day after the count of the seven clean days began; questions of chatzitzah; use of the mikvah by unmarried women; and long nails both natural and artificial. The role of the mikvah attendant and her approach to the clientele who use the mikvah should be of concern to the rabbi. Other matters of importance which should not be overlooked are upkeep, appearance, and halakhic and cosmetic maintenance of the mikvah.

Geirut. A raging issue today is the one regarding who may or may not use the mikvah for conversion. The question is whether non-Orthodox or nonhalakhic conversions ought to be allowed in the local mikvah.

Tevilat Kelim. This is one of the most overlooked mitzvot. A full knowledge of the rules of what has to be immersed and how to do it properly is important.

Laws Pertaining to Geirut

The basic criteria for halakhic conversion is an area which demands increased involvement by the local Orthodox rabbi. Conversion of adopted children is a common occurrence. What does one do when the parents are not observant? The local yeshivah may seek advice on admission policies concerning converted children, and the children of converts. Conversions for the sake of marriage and converts joining the synagogue might also raise questions for the rabbi.

Laws Pertaining to Kiddushin and the Family

Chuppah-Kiddushin. Essential to any rabbi's activities is a good working knowledge of the laws of chuppah-kiddushin. The rabbi has to counsel a couple about all details of the marriage. Each step has to be explained. The meaning of the ketubah and how to fill it out properly are important areas of knowledge.

Taharat ha-Mishpachah. The practical aspects of these laws are important to be able to instruct every bride and groom and to subsequently respond to questions from all people who uphold these important laws.

Marital problems. Halakhic ramifications sometimes arise in this context. These problems may require a Rav to advise on contraception or fertility problems. Fidelity is an issue which a Rav might also be called upon to confront.

Laws Pertaining to the Child–Parent Relationship

This area also challenges the Rav as a posek. What are the parameters of *kibud av ve'eim?* Dealing with the delicate balance of shalom bayit and halakhic requirements are common questions which require knowledge and sensitivity.

Laws Pertaining to Gittin

It is not necessary to know how to write a get. But it is necessary to know the procedure of the Bet Din and to have a proper Bet Din to which one will refer people. A Rav also has to be prepared to convince recalcitrant spouses not to impede the get process in an unfair manner. At times it becomes the Rav's responsibility to intercede actively in a difficult situation.

Laws Pertaining to Kiruv

The growth of the *Ba'al Teshuvah* movement has given rise to many questions. If the Rav serves a community which calls for kiruv, a very active part of the rabbinate, then there are many areas which may challenge the Rav. Questions of *yichus*, means and ends, mixed marriages, and the like will confront the rabbi.

The Rav will also have to be prepared to advise a *Ba'al Teshuvah* about his relationship to parents, relatives, and rabbis who may be affiliated with non-Orthodox branches of Judaism.

Laws Relating to Everyday Situations

As much as I have tried to deal with common categories, the halakhic challenges of the Rav are as complex as life itself. The Rav will confront questions of business ethics, confidentiality, and medical ethics very frequently.

In the areas of business there will be questions of partnerships and their impact on Shabbat and Yom Tov, as well as questions concerning litigation with other Jews in rabbinical as well as secular courts. Questions of interest, loans, and contracts will arise.

In the field of medicine, life-and-death questions, such as whether or not to resuscitate someone or to what degree heroic measures must be taken to treat a gravely ill patient, often come up.

Confidential information will be borne by the rabbi, who will have to determine the parameters of *lashon hara* versus other obligations as he ponders the questions that affect people's lives.

METHODOLOGY IN RESPONDING TO HALAKHIC QUESTIONS

Besides being asked questions on many different subjects, a synagogue Rav is called upon to respond to different types of questions. The simpler questions require only a consultation with one or several primary or secondary sources where the answer can be found explicitly or implicitly. The more complex questions require more research and are not always easily solved in the sources.

When a recognized posek responds to such a question he is called upon not only for the simple decisive answer but also for an exposition and elucidation of the sources which lead to his response. On the other hand, a synagogue Rav is more often called for the answer, and not for the analysis. Of course that does not mean that the Rav should free himself of the obligation to do the research or at the very least to understand the background to the answer he receives from the halakhic authority he consults.

Answering the simple questions is not always so easy. The Rav should have at hand a good library of halakhic literature. This includes the basic primary sources of Shas, *Shulchan Arukh*, and responsa literature. There is also a vast collection of organized anthologies with footnotes in all of the areas outlined and described earlier. One should never lose sight of the fact that the *Shulchan Arukh* and the poskim must be the ultimate authority to respond to a halakhic inquiry. But as long as the secondary sources such as the anthologies (at times organized in ways better suited to the Rav's immediate need) are not used to replace the primary sources, the Rav should make good use of them. There are also indices to the responsa literature that can be most useful to a Rav.

The more complex questions often call for insight not readily found in the available literature. In such circumstances, the Rav has to seek guidance from a recognized halakhic authority. There are several qualifications which a Rav should consider prior to choosing a favorite consultant on halakhic matters. First, the person has to be objectively a bona fide authority whose competence and erudition is respected in the greater community. Second, he should be someone who is readily available and accessible to the Rav. Third, he should be a person with a broader perspective who understands that each problem which must be resolved has to be evaluated not only in the context of the subjective reality.

It is generally advisable to consult with one authority to maintain consistency in one's answers and not to become a shopper for *kulot* or *chumrot*. Nevertheless, there may be circumstances which call for a Rav consulting with more than one authority. There may be times when the primary authority is not available. Or there may be an individual beside the primary posek who has a special expertise in a specific area of halakhah such as eruv, kashrut, mikvah, taharat ha-mishpachah, or medical ethics. There may be a complex situation where the Rav has to hear the opinions of several authorities, and only after understanding all of the opinions will he be able to render the best answer for the particular situation at hand. In such a circumstance the Rav should inform the posek that he is seeking his advice along with the advice of others.

In the end, the Rav should understand that he and he alone is responsible for the answer that is given. It is the responsibility of the Rav to learn to research, to consult, to evaluate, and then to decide. As *Mara De'Atra* for his synagogue he must be the one who is accountable for the answer he conveys.

A BASIC LIBRARY FOR PRACTICAL HALAKHAH

What follows is a short list of suggested titles that might be useful for a synagogue rabbi to own in order to facilitate his role as *Mara De'Atra*. It is by no means an exhaustive accounting of what is available.

Basic Works

Mishneh Torah (*Yad*)
Tur Shulchan Arukh
Shulchan Arukh
Arukh ha-Shulchan
Chayyei Adam, Chokhmat Adam
Kitzur Shulchan Arukh (with *She'arim ha-Metzuyanim be'Halakhah*)
Mishnah Berurah
Pe'at ha-Shulchan

Specific Topics

On specific topics there are many works, some recently published, that are very useful. One should never lose sight of the fact that the answer to all questions emanate from an exhaustive process of analyzing Shas and poskim. The anthologies should not become the primary source for answers. Nevertheless, they are often well organized with excellent indices and footnotes that refer one to the primary sources.

Shabbat

Sefer Hilkhot Shabbat (Eider)
Shemirat Shabbat ke'Hilkhatah (Neuwirth)
Piskei Hilkhot Shabbat (Padawer)

Yom Tov

Shemirat Shabbat ke'Hilkhatah (Neuwirth)
Piskei Hilkhot Yomtov (Padawer)
Arba'at ha-Minim (Weisfish)
Sukkah ke'Hilkhatah (Schwartz)
Halakhot of Hanukkah (Eider)
Hilkhot Ner Ish u-Beito (Shlesinger)
Purim ve'Hodesh Adar (Cohen)
Sefer Hilkhot Pesach (Eider)
Seder Mekhirat Chametz ke'Hilkhatah (Stern)
Sefirat ha-Omer (Cohen)

Bein Pesach le'Shavuot (Cohen)
Summary of Halakhot of the Three Weeks (Eider)
Yomtov Sheini ke'Hilkhatah (Fried)
Chol ha-Mo'ed (Zuker/Francis)
Mo'adim be'Halakhah (Zevin)
Muktzah (Bodner)

Aveilut

Gesher ha-Chayyim (Tucazinski)
Yesodei Semakhot (Felder)
Kol Bo (Greenwald)
Pnei Barukh (Goldberg)
Zikhron Meir (Levine)

Niddah

Badei ha-Shulchan (Cohen)
Taharat Bat Yisrael (Kahana)
Pardes Rimonim (Tendler)
Sefer Hilkhot Niddah (Eider)

Marriage

Nachalat Shivah (Shmuel b. David ha-Levi)
Sefer ha-Nisuim ke'Hilkhatah (Adler)
Sefer Halakhot ve'Halikhot Bar Mitzvah (Adler)
Halikhot Beitah (Auerbach)
Ha-Ishah ve'Ha-Mitzvot; Hatznea Lekhet; Ish ve'Ishto (Ellinson)
Kedoshim Tiheyu (Katz)

Kashrut

Ohalei Yeshurun (Felder)
Hagalat Keilim (Cohen)
Tevilat Keilim (Cohen)

Brit Milah

Sefer ha-Brit (Peretinsky)
Otzar ha-Brit (Weisberg)

Sefer Torah

Dinei Sefer Torah she-Nimtza Bo Ta'ut (Steiner/Goldstein)

Medicine

Nishmat Avraham (Abraham)
Jewish Bioethics (Bleich and Rosner)
Bikkur Cholim ke'Hilkhatah (Cohen)

Technology

Ha-Chashmal be'Halakhah (Makhon Mada'ei Tekhnologia)
Kashrut ve'Shabbat be'Mitbach ha-Moderni (Halperin)

General Anthologies and Responsa Literature

Responsa

Chatam Sofer
Noda bi'Yehudah
Binyan Zion
Seridei Eish
Melamed le'Ho'il
Mikra'ei Kodesh
Iggerot Moshe
Yabia Omer
Yechaveh Da'at
Yesodei Yeshurun
Ziz Eliezer
Chazon Ish

Anthologies and Journals on Contemporary Issues

Encyclopedia Talmudit
Sdei Chemed

Contemporary Halakhic Problems
Journal of Halakhah and Contemporary Society
Tradition
Noam
Techumin
Halakhah u-Refuah
Yesodei Yeshurun (Felder)
Nachalat Zvi (Felder)
Taamei ha-Minhagim
Otzar ha-Dinim ve'ha-Minhagim

CONCLUSION

Clearly the rabbi's role as halakhic authority is one that demands care, sensitivity, and careful study of the halakhic literature. While this role is a challenging one, it is this function more than any other that distinguishes the Orthodox rabbinate in our time, and that sets the tone for all our other efforts and goals, as we go about the avodat ha-kodesh of strengthening the commitment of our congregations and communities to a life inspired and regulated by Torah and mitzvah. Certainly, given the realities of Orthodox life today, the role of halakhic authority is essential to the effectiveness, as well as satisfactions, of today's Orthodox Rav.

2

The Rabbi as Teacher

Rabbi A. Mark Levin

In a profound sense, the rabbi is essentially a teacher, or melamed, whose vocation is the dissemination of Torah knowledge
in all its forms. Everything he does is colored by this goal and
activity. To accomplish his teaching goals effectively he needs a
thorough knowledge of the sources and the literature, classic,
medieval, and modern. But he must also be imaginative in
projecting Torah knowledge in ever more effective ways. Rabbi
Levin shares some of the techniques and methods that have
worked well for him.

INTRODUCTION

Dr. Norman Lamm, teacher, mentor, and current president of
Yeshiva University, writes in *The Royal Reach*, "The real identifying
mark of Orthodoxy is not 'Glatt Kosher' and not the Mechitzah, but
the study of Torah. The Orthodox synagogue is a shul—a school."
Torah is, of course, one of three pillars on which the Jewish
world as a microcosm is balanced. Hence, it is imperative that the
synagogue assert its role, mission, and purpose as a Bet Midrash—a
central place of Torah learning in the community, *the* central address
for the study of Torah at every level. The synagogue cannot compete
(nor should it attempt to do so) with catering halls, Jewish Community Centers, Jewish Family Services, and other specialized agencies

17

within the Jewish community. In addition to "specializing" in tefillah, the synagogue can and should "specialize" in Torah!

In fact, the synagogue is ill equipped to compete with the variety of other institutions that have proliferated in the American Jewish community within the past fifty years, even in many areas of Jewish life which once may have been the province of the synagogue. Even so, the role of the synagogue as a Bet Midrash has not *yet* been usurped by other institutions.

Clearly, this means that the rabbi bears the responsibility of asserting the rightful place of the synagogue as *the* Bet Midrash in the community. In order to achieve this goal, he must exemplify the priority of Jewish learning as a continuous, ongoing, vital part of his daily routine. Only then does he stand a chance of successfully motivating greater efforts at Torah learning, and all forms of Jewish education in the congregation.

Invariably, it is the rabbi of the congregation who takes the initiative, and frequently teaches many of these programs, in the face of opposition and discouragement from members of the congregation, or even the leadership itself.

It is important for the rabbi to appreciate that "success" in Jewish-learning efforts and opportunities should be measured by different criteria than those generally associated with success. In our frame of reference, a successful shiur may have five regular, daily participants. A successful weekly Talmud shiur may attract a minyan. A popular lecture series may attract anywhere from 40 to 200 or more. A weekly discussion group can be regarded as successful with five to ten participants. The objective is to involve as many and as diverse a group of people as possible.

THE RABBI AS TEACHER OF TORAH

The rabbi of the congregation is the central figure in transforming the synagogue from being solely a Bet Knesset, a place of prayer, worship, and ritual life-cycle functions, into encompassing the role of Bet Midrash. In order to be effective in this capacity, the rabbi must serve as a *model*. It is imperative that his congregation and community perceive him to be a student of Torah, who is frequently engaged in the study of Torah. The rabbi must be in a state of

continual personal growth in Torah. When the congregation understands this priority in his life, it is more likely that they will be more
accepting of his leadership in transforming the Bet Knesset into a Bet
Midrash.

A MODEL OF THE SHUL AS BET MIDRASH

Obviously, any Bet Midrash program has to be tailored to the
specific needs of the constituency. Frequently those needs, like the
constituency, may be extremely diverse. What may be appropriate for
one constituency may be totally inapplicable to another. *Ha-kol lefi
ha-makom ve'ha-zeman.* Frequently, the rabbi will have to demonstrate
leadership, initiative, imagination, and ingenuity in bringing along
the tzibbur with him!

Examples of Daily Shiurim

Daily shiur before (or after) Shacharit and between Minchah
and Ma'ariv. A brief (10–20 minutes) shiur on self-contained units
that require no continuity since the participants may vary from day to
day.

Following is a list of sources and texts that can be extremely
helpful, either for use in shiurim or as handy review material for the
rabbi, who functions under many pressures and must be prepared for
the shiur.

Daily Halakhah shiur (10–20 minutes)

Mishnah Berurah
Kitzur Shulchan Arukh
The Concise Code of Jewish Law (Appel-Ktav/Yeshiva)
She'elot U'Teshuvot (Iggerot Moshe; Yabia Omer; Yehaveh Da'at)

Daily Torah shiur (10–20 minutes)

Mikra'ot Gedolot
Studies in Torah (Nechama Leibowitz)
Art Scroll Chumash

Daily Mishnah shiur (10–20 minutes)

Standard text with classical *mefarshim*
Mishnah, Kehati edition
Mishnah, Art Scroll edition

Particularly useful as a tool for teaching basic concepts, and out of which emerges practical halakhah, is Seder Mo'ed. However, it is also desirable to teach other sedarim, which can expose participants to a wide variety of Torah concepts.

Sefer Ha-Chinukh

This can be taught either on the basis of Parshat ha-Shavua, or on a consecutive basis. Careful thought to selection of the mitzvot is highly recommended.

Sefer ha-Chinukh (Mosad HaRav Kook or Menukad edition)
Sefer ha-Chinukh (Feldheim Hebrew/English edition)
The Mitzvot (Chill — Good quick review and overview of other *ta'amei ha-mitzvot* that can enrich the study of *Sefer ha-Chinukh*)

Rambam, Mishneh Torah

Sefer ha-Mada
Hilkhot Melakhim
Careful selections from other parts of the *Mishneh Torah*. These provide good opportunities for projecting Torah *hashkafah*.

Agadata

Selections from *Ein Ya'akov*

Halakhah Yomit Program

Daf Yomi program

Mishnah Yomit program

Examples of Weekly Shiurim/Classes

Talmud shiur. Preferably *Masekhtot* that are intrinsically useful and practical, particularly Seder Mo'ed.

Shabbat afternoon before Minchah
Sunday morning after Shacharit (in conjunction with breakfast)
Weekday evening
Lunch hour shiur in boardroom of densely populated Jewish
  constituency.

Talmud
Standard editions of Talmud, Rishonim, and knowledge of
  contemporary Responsa literature dealing with issues
  raised in the particular *masekhta*.
Steinsaltz edition, highly useful for review of *mefarshim* and
  halakhah.

Sisterhood shiur. Torah with *Mefarshim*; *Sefer ha-Chinukh*;
Rambam—*Sefer ha-Mada* and/or the thirteen principles; Halakhah;
Mishnah; *Pirkei Avot*; *Hashkafah*.
Lunch and learn. For specialized groups of doctors, lawyers,
business people.
Dvar Torah at Seudah Shelishit. A brief, sharp ethical idea
expressed from the Parshah. The following list is especially suitable for
Seudah Shelishit.

Divrei Torah/Vertelach resources

Itturei Torah
Parperaot la-Torah
Otzar Chayyim
Ma'ayanei shel Torah
Da'at Hakhamim
Torah Temimah
Hagachot be'Parshiyot ha-Torah

Examples of Monthly Programs

Lunch and learn. For specialized groups, e.g., lawyers, accountants, business people. Issues of particular concern to the participants,
e.g., Jewish medical ethics, Jewish business ethics.
Monthly Sisterhood home study circle. Sisterhood committee
selects theme for the year. Some examples are

Jewish ethics, using *Pirkei Avot*

Book reviews of best-sellers, preferably in paperback, with Jewish
   interest with the themes critically examined and evaluated
   from a Torah perspective

Sefer ha-Chinukh—carefully selected mitzvot with a contemporary flavor, expanded and elaborated upon

Five Megillot—carefully programmed for study before they are
   actually read in shul

Examples of Seasonal Programs

Spring/Summer Oneg Shabbat afternoon family programs.
During the long Shabbat days, expanded Torah learning sessions,
offering a greater variety and options from which participants may
choose, in conjunction with Family Seudah Shelishit.

Winter Oneg Shabbat Friday evening programs. During the
short winter days and long nights, with Shabbat being early, on
alternate Friday evenings, meeting in private homes, Chavurah sessions with the rabbi as resource person (*Reflections of the Rav*, a good
text; *Faith and Doubt*, by Dr. Norman Lamm, a good alternative).

**Institute of Adult Jewish Education/College of Jewish Stud-
ies.** Examples of three-, four-, or five-part Lecture Series follow.
Schedule two semesters during the year, selecting particular consecutive weekday evenings of a particular month (e.g., Mondays in
March). Divide the evening into two parts:

Jewish skill workshops: targeted at small groups of five to ten
participants each, to acquire specific Jewish skills.

Learning to Read Hebrew from Scratch, or Aleph Bet
Conversational Hebrew—Beginner and Intermediate
Learn to Read the Torah
Learn How to Chant a Haftarah
Learn How to Lead Minchah/Ma'ariv/Shacharit
How to Build a Sukkah
How to Set a Pesach Seder Table
Conducting the Seder
Jewish Crafts at Home for Your Children
Ritual, Ceremonies, and Everyday Judaism
The Structure of the Siddur and Analysis of Major Prayers

Discussion/debate/lecture series: covering themes of topical and contemporary interest and concern. Some examples are

Torah Judaism Faces Contemporary Crises in America Today

The Varieties of Jewish Religious Expression in the United States

Contemporary Israel, Challenges and Concerns

Mysteries of Life and After-Life (basically selections from the Thirteen Principles): useful issues include *Is There Life after Life?*, *We Want Mashiach Now*, *When Bad Things Happen to Good People — Reward and Punishment.*

Forty Years Later — A Generation Looks Back. Selected Holocaust issues, e.g., "The Variety of Religious Responses to the Holocaust — Jewish and non-Jewish." Useful films include "Genocide," "Shoah," "Night and Fog."

The Jewish State or the State of/for Jews. Some examples of issues which could be studied are: Who Is a Jew; Issues in Israel; Jews vs. Jews, the Potential for Civil War in Israel — Religion and State; The Return of Shomron and Yehudah to the Arabs.

Examples of Special Programs

Annual scholar-in-residence program. Carefully selected scholars/rabbis who will project/reinforce our Torah *hashkafah* and spend a Shabbat in the congregation, lecturing following Seudat Shabbat Friday evening (possibly occupying the pulpit Shabbat Morning); lecture/discussion, before Minchah Shabbat afternoon; informal question/dialogue with guest scholar motzei Shabbat (preferably in private home); concluding lecture/discussion Sunday morning after tefillah and breakfast.

Weekend retreat program. With or without scholar-in-residence; possibly at a state park location or motel resort; possibly and preferably in conjunction with another community. The Orthodox Union's Department of Rabbinic Services is helpful in making arrangements and supplying scholars.

Jewish music concerts. Contemporary Jewish Sound, "For the Kiddies," Cantor-in-Concert.

Halakhic shiurim. Try to select timely and specific topics. Shalosh Regalim and Rosh Hashanah have been good times meeting with good response for such shiurim. The bibliography (pp. 28–29) contains a list of useful resources for halakhic shiurim.

THE WRITTEN WORD AS AN EFFECTIVE TOOL OF TORAH TEACHING

In addition to the *spoken* word as the effective means of communication and teaching Torah, the *written* word represents an opportunity to confront the congregation (and, sometimes, entire Jewish and even general community) with Torah perspectives. There are a number of avenues which can be effectively utilized to put forward the best foot of Torah:

The congregation's bulletin/newsletter. This is an important means of communication with the congregation, reaching a wider audience than the spoken word (the Postal Service delivers it to every member's home, while many may choose not to attend services or shiurim). It is also the official record of the congregation, and reflects the congregation's priorities, goals, and self-image. As such, it is important that the bulletin/newsletter be well designed, written, and produced so that recipients will want to read it. In addition to announcements about forthcoming programs, personalia, and reports of past programs, the lead article should be penned by the rabbi, addressing an issue of interest, or attempting to teach an important value.

Local Jewish newspaper. Where such a newspaper exists in your community, it can be an important and effective means of communication, not only with your own members, but with the wider Jewish community. Frequently the local editor (with whom you should cultivate a good relationship) will be happy to feature the rabbi (after all, representing an important segment of the Jewish community, articulating specific perspectives) as a guest editorial writer or associate reporter. In addition, advertisements in such a newspaper about forthcoming Torah Study programs can reach a wider audience.

SYNAGOGUE LIBRARIES AS EDUCATION RESOURCES

Different libraries within the ynagogue complex can serve and meet different needs and purposes.

Rabbinical library. Usually located within the rabbi's study.

This is a permanent synagogue facility for the exclusive use of the rabbi for his own study and preparation for shiurim, lectures, sermons, divrei Torah, and articles. Since this library serves the rabbi, it will reflect his own personal interests. It will most likely include Torah with *mefarshim*, Mishnah, Talmud, Rishonim and Aharonim, *Sifrei Pesak*, Encyclopaedia Judaica, Encyclopedia Talmudit, *Sifrei Derush*, and sermonica.

Bet Midrash library. Within the Bet Midrash where daily services are held, it will be useful and helpful to develop a library containing Torah, Mishnah, Talmud, Halakhah, and Midrash, for the use of worshipers on a daily basis.

Congregational library. *Books.* The recommendation is to develop a Judaic library containing works of enduring Jewish value (as opposed to popular best-sellers of Jewish interest) and reflecting Torah *hashkafah*. It may be *the* one specialized place in the congregation, community, or even city, in which such volumes can be found. It will also be a handy and useful resource center for teaching *geirim*.

Audio tape library. The number and extent of cassette tapes on a wide variety of Torah Jewish topics recommend them to become an important part of the congregational library. The Yeshiva University Rabbinic Alumni maintain a valuable tape library that can be purchased; Chadish Media has produced a large volume of tapes; Rabbi Benjamin Yudin's tapes on Torah are popular; Daf Yomi tapes exist, and there are many others. These can be a useful and rich resource.

Video tapes. The video revolution has begun to spill over into the world of Torah learning, and many valuable films can either be purchased or rented. Recently, there has been a proliferation of quality Holocaust material. Such video tapes can lend diversity and enrichment to virtually any program where a suitable and appropriate tape can be incorporated into the shiur or lecture. Frequently, where financial resources are limited and guest lecturers cannot be brought into the community, video tapes can be a good alternative substitute.

Records, tapes, and discs. Tapes or records of classical cantorial compositions and cantors, and chasidic and neo-chasidic music can all enrich the congregational library.

PUBLIC RELATIONS

Without public knowledge and public awareness, the most superb shiurim, lectures, concerts, libraries, or any other facet or dimension of the most outstanding Adult Education program remain unappreciated and unknown. Following are some effective means of communicating what is taking place within the congregation.

Pulpit announcements. In the two weeks leading up to the shiur, lecture, or event, effective use can be made of the pulpit announcement. Announcements should be noted for their brevity, carefully worded for maximum attention-grabbing and impact. The person who actually makes the announcement should have some effective communication skills as well (voice projection and modulation, among others).

Shul newsletters/bulletins. Snappy announcements or attention-grabbing headlines and articles about specific forthcoming events should appear in the congregation's newsletter in the two weeks before the events are to occur. These should always appear in the front pages of the newsletter. It is frequently helpful for follow-up reports of the events which happened to appear in the same newsletter, this time in the back of the newsletter. This helps to shape the public awareness.

Mailings. *Special mailings.* Focusing on one particular shiur or imminent lecture series, an attractively designed special mailing can generate interest, serve as a reminder, and swell the number of participants.

Seasonal mailings. One or two general mailings throughout the year which describe the scope and range of Torah-learning opportunities on an ongoing basis within the congregation.

Newspapers. *Local Jewish newspapers.* In many medium-sized, and even small Jewish communities, there exists a local Jewish newspaper that circulates within the entire Jewish community, both affiliated and nonaffiliated. It can become a valuable tool in reaching not only the members, but the wider Jewish community as well.

General local newspapers. The rabbi might write an article or letter to the editor for the local, mass-circulation, general community newspaper. At times, it might even be desirable to place an advertisement. When *non-Jewish* clients, neighbors, business associates, and friends read about the activities of the congregation in the local newspaper and comment on them to a member, this can have the same positive effect—or even greater—than the local Jewish newspaper in reaching the Jewish community.

Radio and television. A significant handicap in using radio and television is the expense for advertisement. Some would question whether it is desirable or tasteful to utilize them at all. That is an individual question that the particular rabbi of the congregation must determine for himself. Another dimension of radio and television is to utilize the connections and clout of prominent members to have a local weekly radio program or television show, either alone or in conjunction with other clergy. These are generally "public service" programs which do not entail expense. Their value is in creating enormous public knowledge and awareness, not necessarily of a specific congregation's activities, but of Torah Judaism, for which the rabbi serves as a spokesperson.

Telephone calls. The use of a telephone committee to specifically solicit participation in upcoming programs can be another effective tool in reaching the community.

CONCLUDING REMARKS

The task of "positioning" the Bet Knesset as a Bet Midrash is a challenging, even formidable one. Those who have set for themselves the goal of asserting the role of the shul as *the* central place of Torah learning in the community have frequently encountered failure.

It takes a rabbi of great personal strength, patience, and courage to accept the failures, but more important, to learn and grow from them, always keeping in mind the goal of *harbatzat Torah*, disseminating Torah as far and as wide as humanly possible. The power of Torah to establish "soul-connections" between rebbe and talmid should not be underestimated or disparaged. The rebbe par excellence, Moshe Rabbeinu, experienced profound frustration, rejection, and disappointment from his talmidim, but he persevered, and bonded *Am Yisrael* to Torah and Hashem in unique and permanent ways. An even more powerful and inspiring model is that of Hashem Himself, depicted by Chazal as patiently teaching Torah, despite the frequent rejection He experienced, and the rebellions mounted against Him and His Torah.

The rabbi as rebbe/teacher walks in the footsteps of Hashem, emulating Him, the rebbe par excellence, and in so doing the rabbi fulfills the mizvah of *"ve'halakhta bi-derakhav"* — "and you shall walk in His Ways . . ." (Deuteronomy 28:9).

SELECTED BIBLIOGRAPHY

Useful Resources for Halakhic Shiurim

Ha-Mo'adim Be'Halakhah (Zevin)
Chikrei Zemanim (Hilewitz)
Shiurim L'Zekher Abba Mori (Soloveitchik)
Encyclopedia Talmudit
Journal of Halacha and Contemporary Society
Gesher ha-Chayyim; Kol Bo Al Aveilut; Yesodei Semakhot (all on aspects of mourning)
The Minhagim (Chill)
Reasons for Jewish Customs and Traditions (Sperling)
Encyclopaedia Judaica
Otzar ha-Minhagim

Useful Resources for Weekly or Monthly Shiurim

Hashkafah/Torah, Jewish philosophy
   With Perfect Faith (Bleich/Ktav)
   Torah Faith: The Thirteen Principles (Fendel)
Works by Rabbi Dr. J. B. Soloveitchik:
   Reflections of the Rav (Besdin)
   Five Addresses
   Halakhic Mind
   On Repentance
Tradition: A Journal of Orthodox Jewish Thought
Jewish medical ethics: the interface of halakhah and modern medicine
   Contemporary Halakhic Problems, vols. 1 and 2 (Bleich/Ktav/Yeshiva)
   Jewish Bioethics (Rosner and Bleich)
   Jewish Medical Ethics (Jakobovits)
   Modern Medicine and Jewish Law (Rosner/Ktav/Yeshiva)
   Practical Medical Halacha (Rosner/Tendler)
   Medical Halacha for Everyone (Abraham)

Contemporary Jewish ethical issues

   Jewish Ethics and Halakhah for Our Time (Herring/Ktav/
      Yeshiva)

   Journal of Halacha and Contemporary Society

   Economics and Jewish Law—Halakhic Perspectives (Levine/
      Ktav/Yeshiva)

   Modern Jewish Ethics (Fox)

   Jewish Woman in Jewish Law (Meiselman/Ktav/Yeshiva)

   Morality, Halakhah & the Jewish Tradition (Spero/Ktav/
      Yeshiva)

   Free Enterprise and Jewish Law: Aspects of Jewish Business Ethics
      (Levine/Ktav/Yeshiva)

   *Honor Thy Father and Mother: Filial Responsibility In Jewish Law
      and Ethics* (Blidstein/Ktav)

   Jewish Marriage (Bulka/Ktav)

   Articles from various journals/magazines, e.g., *Judaism, Mo-
      ment, Sh'ma*

3

The Rabbi as Outreach Practitioner

Rabbi Ephraim Buchwald

Reaching out to less committed Jews is central to the rabbinic calling. In recent years the *Ba'al Teshuvah* movement has grown in leaps and bounds, offering many exciting options and directions of teaching Torah on the most fundamental, yet far-reaching, basis. Rabbi Ephraim Buchwald has had extensive experience in the field, and his work reflects the growing impact of this newest trend in Jewish life.

BACKGROUND

The American Jewish community is currently experiencing the best of times and the worst of times. Tragically, most American Jews have little or no connection to Jewish life. In fact, more than 50 percent of the American Jewish community is unaffiliated, and only one third of American Jewish families contribute to the United Jewish Appeal, which is probably the lowest common denominator of Jewish identity. Marriages between Jews and Gentiles have become so commonplace that hardly an eyebrow is raised at what was once considered a major tragedy.

On the other hand, the foment for return has never been greater. The *Teshuvah* movement is nothing less than a revolution gaining momentum. Outreach is the call of the day. Traditionalism, particu-

31

larly traditional Judaism, is a hot media item, and the positive coverage which Orthodoxy has received in the last seven years has been nothing short of astounding.

OBJECTIVES

As much as we like the objective of a successful outreach program to be to produce fully observant Jews, this objective is not only fatuous, but probably counterproductive. Coming on too strong usually results in alienating Jews further, rather than drawing them closer. Most Jews who are unaffiliated, or defect from the Jewish community, do so not out of choice, but out of ignorance. The objective of a balanced outreach program should be to provide every adult Jew with the information and knowledge that will make it possible for that Jew to choose to affiliate or not affiliate. Sadly, most Jews have never been given that choice, and the most highly educated and richly cultured generation of Jews in all of Jewish history stands out as one of the most exceptional in its basic Jewish illiteracy.

On the other hand, our generation provides one of the most propitious opportunities to reach out to the American Jewish community, and the average Jew would value an embrace by a welcoming Jewish environment.

PRINCIPLES OF OUTREACH

Attitudinal Change

Probably the most important factor necessary to succeed in getting a Jew involved in Jewish life is "attitudinal change." Most Jews see Judaism as something irrelevant to their lives, and see traditional Judaism as something even worse: primitive, medieval, discriminatory. In order to engage a Jew in the outreach process, one has to develop a strategy to accomplish an attitudinal change. This can be effected through the use of media, positive articles on traditional Judaism in newspapers—a good example being the Sunday *New York Times Magazine* piece, "American Jews Rediscover Orthodoxy," which portrayed successful Jews who are traditional. Another effective method is a simple crash course in Hebrew reading that offers a nonthreatening opportunity for involvement in Jewish study. For some people an invitation to a Shabbat meal in a private home or a Shabbaton, or a "Turn Friday Night into Shabbat" experience, a Discovery Seminar, could help achieve attitudinal change, but these involve much more effort on the part of the outreach practitioner. Bear in mind that the average Jew is ready to be touched and that reaching out is the easy part, while follow-up is far more difficult.

Full-time Commitment

While an outreach program need not be a full-time program, the outreach practitioner must see it as a full-time commitment. An effective outreach worker must be concerned with the whole person, and not how many *neshamot* he has saved. Very often people who come looking for the spiritual have serious social, economic, and possibly psychological needs, which must be attended to. The development of a healthy *Ba'al Teshuvah* requires that these needs be addressed even before the spiritual needs. Frequently, people are attracted to a synagogue because they feel isolated and lonely, and integrating them into the synagogue community is a critical element in the success of any outreach program. A simple test of whether one is committed to the whole person or only to the spiritual agenda is whether one continues to care about them even after they have fallen out of traditional observance.

OUTREACH AS A PROCESS

Instant conversions do not work in Judaism. The faster they become religious, the faster they fall out. Some *Ba'alei Teshuvah* may get involved deeply and intensely rather quickly, and need to be slowed down. Probably the most important advice you can give a quick starter is to stress learning rather than observance. Similarly, a healthy *Ba'al Teshuvah* needs multiple religious exposures, learning from numerous teachers, and contact with numerous religious leaders. The initial outreach process is invariably very intense and *Ba'alei Teshuvah* often tend to become dependent upon their teachers. By exposing them to other teachers, they become less dependent upon their "rebbe," and when the time comes for healthy separation, they are able to handle it, rather than totally collapse. The fact that the teacher is prepared to expose them to other views and personalities also shows an intellectual integrity, which I believe leaves a deep impression on the searching Jew.

Outreach workers must be aware of their limitations. Not every teacher is suitable for every student, and vice versa. Experienced outreach workers can often successfully screen candidates for their programs, directing those who will not respond to their own particular program to one where they will be more successfully integrated. A good rule of thumb is to be aware of those outreach workers who profess to have "the way"—that is, the only way!

FOLLOW-UP: THE MOST CRUCIAL ELEMENT

Reaching out is easy, follow-up is most difficult. To a great extent, reaching out without a follow-up mechanism in place is immoral. Great disillusionment will result when a person is reached out to and not followed up. An experience of this type can be so shattering that it will often make it impossible to ever reach that disillusioned Jew again. An effective follow-up program must have both the cognitive and experiential elements, both study and spiritual experiences, as part of its program.

If we are to touch even a small percentage of the huge numbers of Jews who are unaffiliated, we must think boldly. We can no longer be satisfied with reaching out to the one Jew and thus "save a whole world." We are in a position to save thousands, and we must be convinced that we can accomplish just that.

PROGRAMMING

Adult Education

An effective outreach program must have an adult education program as an essential core of the outreach activities. Basic courses on all levels must be taught in Hebrew—Bible, Jewish law and practices, Jewish philosophy, and Talmud. The educational programming should be exciting, and should teach *it*—not *about* it! Basic courses should be skill-oriented, teaching students how to read and analyze texts. Biblical Hebrew, emphasizing rules of grammar, is often the most important tool for cognitive and intellectual advancement. One-on-one situations are a good way to start, but eventually classroom situations are healthier.

Most synagogues have huge reservoirs of marginally affiliated members. Make them an offer they cannot refuse. The telephone is the most important outreach tool at our disposal. Call the members. Ask them to suggest courses which they would like to see offered. Make it impossible for them to refuse. Make Torah study a part of your Yom Kippur appeal. Let everyone know that your synagogue is first and foremost an educational growth center.

Crash Courses

Crash courses in basic Jewish knowledge and/or skills are particularly effective outreach tools. Since respondents are called upon to make only a minimal commitment, and the promise of return is great, crash courses which are properly taught can result in large enrollments, and bring significant numbers of totally nonaffiliated Jews through the portals of local synagogues. Crash courses should be packaged in a nonthreatening, basic manner, and offered as a series of five 1-hour, or 1½-hour sessions.

Crash course in Hebrew reading. This course consists of five 1½-hour lessons, to teach mastery of the Hebrew alphabet and basic Hebrew vocabulary. The primer text should be based on the siddur. *Reishit Binah*, published by Bloch Publishing, is an effective and inexpensive text. Find a warm, caring teacher who will follow up with students, for example, with Shabbat invitations. Hebrew reading is a wonderful, innocuous way of introducing novice worshipers to Hebrew, the prayer book, synagogue life, and further religious growth. The National Jewish Outreach program offers Hebrew crash course programs three or four times a year, in many locations.

Crash course in basic Judaism. This course consists of five lessons introducing basic Jewish concepts and practices. The National Jewish Outreach program offers it as well several times a year. A full outline and curriculum, which is available, includes topics such as Belief in God, Prayer, Shabbat, Rituals, and Sexuality.

Street Outreach

Street outreach can be an effective project. It broadcasts the message to the community that if they don't come to the synagogue, the synagogue will come to them. Although there is very little immediate return on an investment in street outreach, the long-term results are quite profound.

Some basic ideas that every synagogue can undertake, depending of course on the community and environment, are as follows:

Holiday packets distributed before Jewish holidays are an inexpensive but effective way to get communal attention. A packet consists of a plastic storage bag containing the following: a letter of greeting from the rabbi, a postpaid return card for further information, and some sort of holiday gift. Suggested gifts and activities: samples of honey on Rosh Hashanah; lulav and etrog and/or Sukkah-mobile on Sukkot; outdoor Simchat Torah dancing; public Hanukkah menorah; samples of candles and dreidels; a "Feel Jewish" party on December 25th for elementary school Jewish students; shalach manos on Purim; a model seder on the street for Pesach; samples of shmurah matzah; literature on Yom Hashoah, Yom Ha-Atzmaut, Yom Yerushalayim; flowers for Shavuot.

Other effective street outreach activities include holiday banners posted on the facades of the synagogue; Jewish jogging events; Jewish "I.Q." Test; free High Holiday services, abridged and full length; "Ask the Rabbi" booths on the street.

Turn Friday Night into Shabbat

Once a year invite local residents for a traditional Friday night Shabbat experience, with abridged Beginner's Services, a full explanation of the Friday night Shabbat ritual, Kiddush, washing, Hamotzi, Zemirot, Divrei Torah, singing, dancing, and celebrating. Seat hosts at each table who will facilitate follow-up and invite the guests to their home on future Shabbatot, and/or to synagogue services and classes. A full handbook on how to "Turn Friday Night into Shabbos" is available through Lincoln Square Synagogue and the National Jewish Outreach Program.

Beginner's Services

A most effective method of reaching unaffiliated Jews is through a special service for people with little or no background. Participants in the beginner's service are urged to enroll in the free five-session crash course in Hebrew reading, which is conducted during the week (as described above). The service itself, which is conducted on Shabbat, is an abridged traditional Hebrew service. The service consists of the essential parts of Shacharit, read both in Hebrew and English at a slow pace, with opportunities to interrupt for questions at any time. Participants are taught Hebrew reading, nusach, and philosophy of prayer. A dvar Torah is delivered by a beginner, the Torah portion is read and analyzed in English, and musaf is recited. After Kiddush, participants who have no arrangements for Shabbat lunch are offered hospitality at the homes of synagogue members. In order to be truly effective, a beginner's service should be supplemented by a series of support activities such as monthly Shabbat lunches in the synagogue, a monthly "shmooze," weekly Shabbat hospitality, adopt-a-beginner program (in which regular members of the congregation guide beginners through their first months at the synagogue), a beginner's newsletter, personal counseling, two or three Shabbatonim a year, a home koshering service, special funds for buying tefillin and study in Israel. A full guide book for establishing a beginner's program is available through the National Jewish Outreach Program.

Inreach

Very often while looking outward to the nonaffiliated we neglect those who are members of our own synagogues. Some wonderful inreach programs can be developed.

Mitzvah day. An entire day devoted to the performance of the various mitzvot, mezuzah and tefillin check, shatnez check, information on making a home kosher, "toivelling" dishes, opportunities for zedakah, etc.

Religion on the job. A *Teshuvah* campaign for the High Holidays emphasizing how people can grow religiously in their own professions — law, medicine, business, etc.

Teshuvah campaign. A series of inspiring lectures preparing one for the High Holiday mood.

Ne'ilah appeal. Torah, Avodah, Gemilut Chasadim, asking all members to increase the hours of study for Torah, their involvement in daily prayer, social action, and tzedakah.

Other important synagogue-based activities. Events for singles, social events, shadchan committee. Hospitality committees for Shabbat, sleeping and/or meals, social action for homeless, clothing drives, toy drives, working with the Jewish elderly. New meaning can be given to synagogue membership by making Torah study and social service a part of the membership obligations. Getting the frum-from-birth membership involved in outreach can be a tremendous opportunity for internal growth on the part of the community.

RESOURCES

Many wonderful resources are available to synagogues for programming ideas.

1. The Max Stern Division of Communal Services, Yeshiva University, 500 West 185th Street, New York, NY 10033; (212) 960-5265.
2. Synagogue Services Commission of the Union of Orthodox Jewish Congregations of America, 70 West 36th Street, New York, NY 10018; (212) 244-2011.
3. Lincoln Square Synagogue, 200 Amsterdam Avenue, New York, NY 10023; (212) 874-6105.
4. Aish HaTorah, 1220 Broadway, Suite 610, New York, NY 10001; (212) 643-8800.
5. National Jewish Outreach Program, 485 Fifth Avenue, Suite 212, New York, NY 10017; (212) 986-7450, or 1-800-44-HEBREW.
6. Association for Jewish Outreach Professionals, 500 5th Ave., #3104, New York, NY 10010; (212) 221-AJOP.

4

The Rabbi as Proponent of the New Torah Life-style

Rabbi David Stavsky

Many are the rabbis who come into communities where Orthodoxy has few adherents, where Orthodox rabbis and synagogues
must fight against the odds to establish themselves as credible
alternatives to less traditional, even secular, leaders and role models, even while working within existing communal structures. It is
always a daunting task, requiring skill and sensitivity. Rabbi
David Stavsky shares some of his tried and proven methods.

Psychologists have reaffirmed what many of us have understood
instinctively—namely that people are influenced by their peers and
environment. There may be attitude changes, values may be internalized, and individual judgments are often made or changed as a result
of group or peer influences.

In attempting to impact the Torah way of life on people, I have
felt that it is crucial to create environments for individuals where
Torah values would be looked upon as emotional and intellectual
norms. These include environments where it is "normal" to observe
Shabbat, or Kashrut, or to wear a kippah, not only to do so because it
is the religious thing to do, but because there are others in the group
who are doing it as well. I came to Columbus, Ohio, in 1957 following
my work as an army chaplain. I was faced with a community nearly
totally void of Orthodox practices and observances. Literally a *midbar*.
The shul was without a mechitzah, the mikvah was in horrible condition in a dilapidated building in the old section of the town, and the

community did not have a yeshivah or day school. There were however, three kosher butcher shops and a local shechitah. There were fewer than a dozen Shomrei Shabbat in my congregation (which was the largest Orthodox shul). I felt the thrusts of my energies had to be directed to the young children, the teens and preteens, as well as to adults (ages 30–40). I felt that I had to create "environments" where members of a group would reinforce one another for attitudinal change.

To create the environment and "new attitude" for attitude change, I created innovative (at least they were in 1957) programs that became the new environment. For instance, in 1959 we introduced R.E.W., "Religious Emphasis Week," as a series of high-powered lectures and workshops on Torah Judaism, on a daily basis, held between Rosh Hashanah and Yom Kippur. Today they would be called Yemei Iyyun, or a Teshuvah Kinus. Outstanding lecturers, authors, rabbis, academicians, the very best spokesmen for the Orthodox viewpoint, were invited to Columbus to present the Torah perspective on life itself, and on synagogue life. From such topics as "Teshuvah, Tefillah, Tzedakah," to "Kiddush, Kaddish, Kedushah," to "Mechitzah, Muktzah, Mikvah," to "Kisso, Kosso, Ka'asso," to "Giyur, Geulah, Gittin," to the "New Morality" or "Identity," and so forth—all were discussed and analyzed by leading spokesmen. The concept was simple—packaging Torah values, Orthodox teachings, in dignified, modern settings, which would feed into the intellectual and emotional curiosities of the nonobserving person. In short, in order to expose the congregation to authentic Torah teachings, one has to create the environment to effect an attitudinal change.

In reaching out to the teenagers and preteens, and in conjunction with Yeshiva University's Communal Service Division (now known as MSDCS), I pioneered the concept of Shabbatonim (1957) by sponsoring two or three Shabbatonim a year in the synagogue. By bringing the resource people from Yeshiva University, we created an environment where the teenager would feel that he or she was not alone in his new discoveries about Judaism. We fostered excitement and positive reinforcement for the kids by sending them from time to time to other nearby cities for similar Shabbatonim (including Dayton, Louisville, Indianapolis, and Cleveland). In so doing we provided a continuous reinforcement of what was being projected as a new Torah life-style. Not having the financial resources to have a full-time youth leader, I developed excellent volunteer youth advisors, but insisted on bringing to Columbus *ruach* people from Yeshiva University for nearly every Yom Tov. Another program with which we began the New Year was the "cola and shmoos" during Chol ha-Moed Sukkot. Every teenager received a personal invitation from the rabbi—it was a social night, heavy on the ruach, and as many as sixty kids from the community would crowd into the house. There was singing and dancing, and then going into the sukkah, more singing, and so on. As the kids started to go on to yeshivot, this was the farewell social; it was also a time for them to describe life in New York or at a Stern College dorm in a light and jovial manner. It was—and still is—fun night at the rabbi's house. In the last decade, however, the more advanced students (today some of whom are rabbanim) would remain and have Tikkun Hoshanah Rabbah Learn-In sessions. Another benefit of this learning program was to evaluate which teen was a potential for a Torah life-style, and to be mekarev that kid during the year.

The Shabbat with the Rabbi Shabbaton, now in its twenty-ninth consecutive year, continues to be an exciting event for the Columbus teenager, as does Torah Day in the park held annually in August before school begins.

The programs must be designed to appeal to the social needs of the contemporary teen, yet must have enough intellectual challenge for Torah life. The keys to the success of the programs are twofold. Excellent dedicated staff (no deadwood) and enough teens from other cities (a minimum of fifty) who would reinforce the Torah attitudes and values, and create the reference groups and environments.

In 1969, to strengthen the positive reinforcement groups, we founded the Central Eastern Region of N.C.S.Y. Within a year, over 3,000 teenagers were affiliated with one another, and lovingly anticipated each upcoming Shabbaton. Countless young women of Central East N.C.S.Y. went on to Stern College for Women, and many young men went on to Yeshiva University and other yeshivot.

A relatively new program for adults (only six or seven years old) is the Rebbe's Tish Program. Held every sixth Shabbat after davenning, we all sit down to a Shabbat meal. The cholent is prepared by my wife and her committee. The tables are set as spokes from a wheel, with the Rebbe's Tish in the center.

When the chazzan leads in the opening zemirot, a lively Shabbat ruach atmosphere begins to prevail. The zemirot are followed by an

active Ask the Rabbi session that lasts about twenty minutes. The
questions come fast and heavy and give the rabbi an opportunity to
display both his Torah scholarship and (at times) wit. This segment is
followed by a five-minute dvar Torah, very seriously prepared and
presented by a member of the congregation. The chazzan then continues with a few nigunim (no words, just melodies). This is followed
by a short *Hasidishe Rebbe's Ma'aseh*, then Shir ha-Ma'alot and Birkat
ha-Mazon. What happens at the Rebbe's Tish is that people leisurely
enjoy both the emotional and intellectual challenge of being a
Shabbat observing Jew. Often I open new vistas and horizons for
many to try to conduct their own Rebbe's Tish at home, which has
worked out very well. The intellectual curiosity created during Ask
the Rabbi segment of Devar Torah is definitely internalized as there is
real Jewish learning and growth. The Ask the Rabbi portion is fun,
and they see a completely different aspect of the rabbi.

Another very successful program at our shul is the Sunday
morning Talmud class. Now in its fourteenth year, the class meets
every Sunday from October to June. Anywhere between twenty-five
and thirty men and women show up for this class. I am the instructor.
We have completed *Makot*, *Berakhot*, and *Kiddushin*, and we will soon
be completing *Beiyah*. I read the text in Hebrew, translate, and then
ask "Jack, why do you think Rebbe Yochanan is saying this?" or some
other leading question. For many young professionals who make up
the class (both men and women), this experience is an eye-opener that
demonstrates to them just how relevant modern Orthodox Judaism
can be. The give and take during the discussions is incredible. Their
minds suddenly open up to what the roots of Judaism are all about.
Again, the class is lively, fun—yet serious. Most important, the
students' minds are challenged. At times, I may introduce the *sugyah*
by quoting various commentaries as well as modern responsa (e.g.,
Reb Moshe Feinstein) on the issue to be discussed in the *sugyah*.

What takes place is a reinforcing of Torah attitudes and values.
The student gains a new insight as well as an appreciation of what
halakhah is all about. The student soon realizes that rabbinical,
halakhic decisions are not arbitrary but are the result of tested
discussions throughout the centuries. What is important is to get
down to the student's level and raise him or her up to yours.

Now in its third year, is our program titled Lunch and Learn
Chumash. The group meets every Wednesday at noon in three six-

week semesters from October to mid-April. The students are mainly young women, a number of whom are joined by their husbands for the class. The women prepare a light lunch, and the study period is from 12:15 to 1:00 P.M. We offer an in-depth analysis of Parshat ha-Shavua. The average attendance is fifteen to twenty people.

There are other excellent and innovative programs which we have created at Beth Jacob. Two examples will suffice:

1. The Mitzvah Mobile—Visiting the sick, bringing Hanukkah candles, matzot, lulav-etrog, and the like to patients in local hospitals.
2. Torah Day—Yeshivah without walls in a local state park. From talit and tefillin to closing barbecue kumzits, we provide an action-packed day of sport events, Torah workshops, ruach, and other activities, held every year in the third week of August. Kids from other communities and cities are invited.

Looking back over the years since our arrival in Columbus, I can say that I have experienced tremendous satisfaction from the many innovative ideas and programs that we have instituted in our shul and community. I hope that this short description will serve as a model and catalyst to similar successful efforts on the part of other rabbis facing similar challenges, in a variety of locales and times.

5

The Rabbi as Administrator

Rabbi Mordecai E. Zeitz

The rabbinate demands that, to build and then preside over successful synagogue structures, the Rav demonstrate organizational skills that allow him to maximize his impact on his community. And thus in many ways the rabbi functions, inter alia, as a Chief Executive Officer, bearing responsibility for office productivity, personnel and clergy relations, membership services, catering and hashgachah supervision, the needs of youth and elderly—even while he carries out his more traditional role as *Mara De'Atra*. Rabbi Mordecai Zeitz delineates some of the methods that work so successfully for him, in a large synagogue/day school setting that is part of a highly organized Jewish community.

All synagogues, regardless of size and scope of activity, represent an important link between the individual and the organized Jewish community. Very often, the decision to identify with a specific denomination can be determined by the organizational image that the synagogue projects. A synagogue that responds to the needs of its members or endeavors to present new options which capture the attention of its members has a better chance of nurturing growth and development for the individual member as well as for the congregation as a whole.

The synagogue office is the first line of communication between the synagogue and the public. It is a place for information gathering, storage, and the appropriate dissemination of courteous information. This must be done with the highest level of integrity, courteousness, and patience. Office staffing must be carefully chosen for its professional ability in various designated capacities. Office personnel work in the public eye and must at all times display the highest level of discretion and confidentiality. Their dedication and devotion to the ideals of the institution which they serve is the most positive statement which will greet much of our membership.

The efficiency and range of services to be rendered to a congregation is dependent upon the family information that we have at our disposal and the services for which this information will eventually be used. In addition to information gathering, it is also important to place into the hands of the membership appropriate and usable information as to what the synagogue offers and expects. Through effective synagogue administration, every family can be made to feel important and appreciated as part of the congregational family.

INFORMATION GATHERING

The Synagogue Membership Form is the basic tool for information gathering. This basic information should be solicited one time only with the synagogue office updating changes as they occur. Since the synagogue office is normally the last to know of these changes or additions to the family, it is important that at every High Holiday seating time, an update form accompany seating arrangement forms. Telephone follow-ups will update the remainder. When information gets outdated, the effectiveness of the synagogue office is severely hampered.

The synagogue application should be designed so that it is not intimidating in size, but detailed enough to provide the office with the necessary information to service the family. It should include

Family name
First names of husband and wife and their Hebrew names
Hebrew names of parents
Kohen/Levi/Yisrael
Home address including zip or postal codes
Telephone number
Dates of birth—Hebrew and English

Date and place of marriage and officiating rabbi
Hebrew and English names of children
Hebrew and English date of birth (children)
Types and number of years of Jewish education (children)
Yahrzeit information with English names, Hebrew names of the
    deceased and their fathers' names, English and Hebrew dates
    of death and if death was after sundown, and the relationship
    to member
Occupation of both husband and wife
Business addresses and telephone numbers

Many different forms can be designed, but the information stated
above allows the synagogue to service its families and project their
needs in the coming years. (See membership forms in Appendix 1.)
Synagogues vary in the types of memberships offered, and must
recognize

Standard family memberships, where both spouses are Jewish
Single parent memberships, where there is only one parent in the
    home
A senior citizen category
A young singles category
Newlyweds (first year – no charge)

Each congregation must assess its constituency and set up categories appropriate for its needs with fees set accordingly.
There is differing opinion as to offering synagogue affiliation to
families where one spouse is not Jewish. Some argue that the Jewish
family members should not be denied access to the synagogue. The
problem with that approach is that we are conferring a *hekhsher* on the
relationship. Of greater concern, in cases where the mother is not
Jewish, is that by association we are conferring upon the children
unofficial Jewish status, which has serious future ramifications.
The other approach is to set up standards of affiliation that
require both partners to be Jewish according to halakhic standards. A
separate form can combine the necessary information as to marriage,
Jewish by birth, and conversion information, if applicable, which
should include rabbi and/or Bet Din who officiated. The best time to
sort out Jewish status problems is when the family is contemplating

synagogue affiliation. In most cases, they are unaware that a problem exists and by setting halakhic standards at the outset of synagogue affiliation, there are no surprises down the road to disturb occasions of brit, bar or bat mitzvah, weddings, or funerals. Where possible, the rabbi can effectively deal with the family within an acceptable halakhic framework to attempt to alleviate the problem. During this time, some alternate means of synagogue affiliation and participation can be worked out under the guidance and supervision of the rabbi. All the while the family can participate, where appropriate, in all synagogue activities while avoiding formal obligations and commitments. We must recognize that there will be situations beyond our ability to correct. It does not mean that we should not exhaust every avenue to attempt to bring the family into the totality of *Klal Yisrael*.

PUTTING INFORMATION TO USE

Information facilitates synagogue programming and servicing. Up-to-date membership lists including names of parents and children, mailing addresses, and telephone numbers facilitate active communication. It must be clearly understood that all these lists must be treated as private and confidential. The "synagogue" must learn to say no. Certain guidelines have to be set up as to which officer or committee should have access to these lists. The membership should feel secure that their private information does not become public for every cause, institution, or outside interest.

Yahrzeit information must be organized to enable proper notification by the synagogue office at least two weeks prior to the observance of the yahrzeit and of the recitation of the memorial prayer (see Appendix 1). In addition to the normal card or letter, a phone call from a member of the religious committee advising the person of their yahrzeit observance and the time of synagogue services, with no strings or finances attached, is one of the most gracious gestures that can be extended.

The use of birthday and marriage information allows the synagogue to recognize special milestones in the lives of its member families. Names and birth dates of children allow the synagogue to monitor the Jewish educational needs of its member families. When children reach nursery and kindergarten age, a telephone call or letter from the rabbi suggesting various options available for Jewish education might make the difference in a child receiving a Jewish education. Children already advanced in age who are receiving no Jewish education can be identified. Proper planning for bar mizvah or bat mizvah observance could be made by keeping an updated list of birth dates. A listing of bar mizvah anniversaries can be used to rekindle the bar mizvah experience. The proper planning for youth activities, as well as informal and formal supplementary school activities, can be developed through a pool of names and birth dates available through membership rosters.

COMPUTERS TO THE RESCUE

While all of the above information is always available, its organization and updating, to say the least, is intimidating. With the age of the personal computer, all the information is at our very fingertips. Once the initial input is finished, the computer can respond to almost any need. For example, membership lists can be maintained and readily updated; mailing labels for the entire membership, Board of Directors, or select groups such as youth or senior citizens, and yahrzeit information and mailing can be automated; projections for upcoming bar mitzvahs and any other function can be programmed very efficiently and effectively (see Appendix 1: *Membership Work-Up Sheet*).

The full scope of accounting including records, billing, accounts receivable, can all be prepared with a simple PC (personal computer). Having updated budgets and statements readily available takes the guesswork out of synagogue finances. These functions are similar to those in a business environment and can be performed in the same manner.

The type of computer and the extent of the software/computer programs which are needed will vary from synagogue to synagogue. A committee of knowledgeable people must assess the needs of the shul. They must relate their needs to the range of hardware and software which is available. Each computer has its positive and negative features. No matter what is chosen, someone else will have a better idea. Cost, projected needs, and growth potential of the hardware as well as the software are all factors to be considered.

While the initial discussions of computerization of a synagogue office can be done by lay people, it is strongly urged that a professional be paid to help in the final selection of the system and its installation. Any computer installation will have bugs and flaws, and if it is done on a voluntary basis, there is always the problem of delay and "I did it as a favor, so now leave me alone." By paying a professional, you will have access to professional guidance and expertise for both the training and the initial start-up of the system.

Most of today's computer hardware operates efficiently. Software evaluation remains one of the most important criteria in selecting a system. Generally, financial requirements can be met by purchased (canned) programs that are operating in numerous companies and are sold commercially.

As a synagogue we should be wary of pirated or borrowed software. We must respect copyright laws, and not ignore both moral and legal ramifications. Therefore, the only custom programs that need be written are specific programs unique to the synagogue requirements, for example, yahrzeit.

We should be mindful that in our communities we have many high school and college students who are whizzes at computer programming. Having outlined the needs of what you would want the computer to do for you, these very talented individuals will amaze you as to what they could develop in special software. The programs can be written from scratch or existing software can be modified to meet your specific needs. Under the supervision of your professional, the available talent can be activated. Not only do you get excellent computer programming, but as well you activate young people within the synagogue family.

The following basic programs are readily available: dbase III Plus, Work Juggler, Apple Works, WordPerfect, and Word. All office staff should become computer-literate. Most machines are user friendly and it is very hard to make an error or lose a program. Once a system is decided upon, secretaries, bookkeepers, the executive director, and other professionals including rabbis should know how to use the basic machine. However, except for those authorized personnel, the synagogue computer should be off limits to anyone else. Again, the synagogue office and its staff must learn to say no. It is expensive machinery with a lot of information and must be treated accordingly.

Strict codes must be introduced to guarantee the security of the stored information.

The computer opens up the new world of word processing. The setup of letters, articles, sermons, flyers, and other forms of correspondence becomes more easily manageable through the world of word processing. The rabbi no longer has to be afraid of asking for revisions of changes of text, as the word processor makes it so much easier to accomplish.

Add a versatile printer to the PC and a whole new world of personalized letters and publications for all occasions becomes possible. Donation acknowledgments, membership letters, meeting notices, special program announcements, and so on can all have that personal touch through the use of the PC and the printer. In addition, imaginative flyers, announcements, posters, banners, and the like are at your fingertips. Once introduced, you will wonder how you ever got by without one.

GETTING THE MESSAGE TO THE MEMBERSHIP

With the exception of the small core of synagogue members actively involved in ongoing activities, most of our membership is uninformed. The synagogue bulletin is the basic tool by which we get the message across. While it is easy to rationalize that "nobody reads it anyway," the preparation of the bulletin is predicated upon the premise that people will read something which is interesting, short, and to the point.

A good bulletin will be professional in appearance, contain highlights of upcoming events, summarize religious information and the times for services, contain limited information on events within the synagogue family, and present the Rabbi's Message—short, sharp, and timely. To be avoided in the synagogue bulletin are stale information, an abundance of personal messages, too wordy and too many outside quotes, and sloppy layout.

Some other helpful hints for the synagogue bulletin include

1. Acknowledgment of donations to various funds, to give kavod and to generate additional donations.

2. Inclusion of advertising. While advertising helps make the bulletin self-sustaining, the drawback is that it tends to become commercial and one must be careful of who the advertisers are.

3. A bulletin can be professionally printed, but it is expensive. With word processing and modern-day graphics on the computer, the synagogue office can generate a beautiful layout for the synagogue bulletin. A photo offset print job with good paper can produce a very professional and impressive bulletin.

4. A budget must be established to determine the method of production. It is important that synagogue bulletins be published on a regular basis, albeit monthly according to the English or Hebrew calendars or according to whatever time interval is deemed necessary. A haphazard time schedule or a bulletin arriving after the fact detracts from the effectiveness of this crucial PR piece.

5. The major goal of the synagogue bulletin is to make the member who receives it proud that he is a member of a congregation whose activities and accomplishments are reflected on those pages. Anything less than that falls short of a synagogue bulletin.

In addition to a synagogue bulletin, other effective or planned pieces of publicity should project the ideals, activities, and special programs of the congregation. Each of these pieces should be attractive while getting the message across in a concise and precise way. Within every congregation there are very talented men and women who have the gift of words, art, and layout ability. (See Appendix 1: *Membership Interests and Experience.*)

THE RABBI AND OTHER SYNAGOGUE PROFESSIONALS

All those who professionally dedicate their time on behalf of the synagogue are appropriately referred to as Klei Kodesh. Through their actions, efforts, and behavior they reflect the sanctity and dignity of the very institution they represent. Above and beyond their individual professional expertise, they each serve as living examples of the highest values and principles of the synagogue. The interaction of these professionals may very well set the tone for the entire institution. No one professional, rabbi included, is an island unto himself. As in a family, each member makes a unique contribution and each is strengthened by the presence of the other members.

One minimizes frustration and confrontation when job descriptions are clearly defined. This eliminates misunderstandings and jealousy, which have a tendency to crop up. The rabbi does not sing while the cantor does not preach sermons. The only exception is by mutual consent. The rabbi should clarify right at the outset his expectations of the cantor who is serving with him. Is it merely to officiate at services? Is it to teach? Is it to deal with youth? Is it to participate in Adult Education? Is it all of the above or even more? These two top synagogue professionals must always support each other in public, resolving any differences that might arise on any aspect of synagogue life in the privacy of their offices. Neither should be put on the spot publicly so as to win a point. Both parties and the synagogue invariably end up the losers.

The nature of the services, its content and duration, must be discussed by the rabbi and the cantor. Some accommodation between cantorial renditions and length of sermon and other special parts of the service all must be blended together so as not to impose hardship or ego trips upon a congregation. *Tircha de'tzibura* is a primary concern whether it be Shabbat, Yom Tov, Rosh Hashanah, or Yom Kippur. Frequent dialogue and direct communication are the best preventive medicine.

DIRECTING BUT NOT DICTATING

In order to give direction to the synagogue, the rabbi must, in fact, play the role of the Chief Executive Officer. This in no way conflicts with the role of the elected officials of the congregation, including the President. As in industry, the Chief Executive Officer influences, but also carries out and directs the policies of its directors. If they are constantly at odds, one must question the basic relationship.

This does not mean that the rabbi makes all the decisions, or that he must be personally involved in all aspects of the synagogue. His influence and insight should be felt, but his presence should not be physically required. To do otherwise would indicate poor management and administration. By sharing your goals and ideals with your fellow professionals they in turn become part of your team who work together towards achieving the same goals.

The other professionals, be they Executive Director, Administrator, Educational Director, Youth Director, Shammes, Second Cantor, or office personnel, all must be given breathing room to do their jobs. The more secure they feel in the performance of their tasks, the more effective will be each of their individual contributions. The stronger the individual contributions, the stronger shall be the final collective result of everyone's efforts, including the rabbi's. The rabbi's major task is to share ideas and goals with his team. In certain areas, he must be prepared to roll up his sleeves to help the others be successful in their areas of endeavor. He must be prudent to sometimes let the others do their own thing and take the full credit and glory. The rabbi should *shep nachas* from the successes of his colleagues.

This approach enables the rabbi to discharge his own professional duties more effectively, while simultaneously remaining involved in all the other major areas of synagogue life. He also will reciprocally gain the support of his colleagues for his own programs and goals. Regular meetings and ongoing accessibility to colleagues keep the rabbi informed and allow for the mutual exchange of ideas.

It must be recognized that you cannot effectively coerce people to do things they just do not want to do. After a while, it just will not happen. You can't expect other professionals to always take a back seat. Everyone wants to be recognized for the job he is doing. This does not mean that you cannot influence others to your point of view. The rabbi can influence by example, by dialogue, and by engendering excitement and commitment.

The basic dictum, "Who is respected? He who respects others," is the golden rule for effective and productive internal synagogue relations. The rabbi must set the tone for the administration, in allowing each professional to play out his appointed role. It is a team effort, but the rabbi must generate this feeling of *achdut* and mutual *achrayut*.

HASHGACHAH – RESPONSIBILITY FOR KASHRUT WITHIN THE SYNAGOGUE

The rabbi is and must remain the *Rav ha-Makhshir* in his synagogue. No outside agency or other individual should usurp that responsibility. Depending upon the size of the congregation, there might very well be a Mashgiach who carries out the actual tasks of kashrut supervision within the synagogue. This at times can be the Shammes or any other appointed person. These individuals must receive their guidance and standards directly from the rabbi. The setting of all standards and the final decision making on many matters of kashrut must remain in the hands of the rabbi. *Hashgachah* in a synagogue includes

1. The initial physical arrangements in the kitchen that must deal with matters of meat and/or dairy and their separation, dishwashers, and stoves; Shabbat procedures that include blech, Shabbay clocks, locks on heating mechanisms and heating urns, and secure food storage.

2. Standards for preparation of food on premises dealing with the source of meat and all other products and ingredients being brought in. Also, the standard of supervision during period of internal food preparation.

3. Transfer and supervision of food prepared off the premises, which must include proper listing by the Mashgiach of the outside supplier of all foods and quantities shipped and a system of check-in by synagogue Mashgiach.

4. Establishment of a Shabbat menu of both hot and cold foods as opposed to a non-Shabbat menu; a standard of Shabbat warming procedures with provisions for pre-Shabbat and Shabbat procedures.

5. Guidelines for all internal use of the kitchen by various synagogue groups, including Sisterhood, Men's Club, and Youth Groups.

6. Establishment of guidelines to supervise all food products coming into the synagogue, which include bar products and mixes, candy in floral arrangements, specialties such as ice cream bars, doughnut machines, and cotton candy. These items are very often supplied by party coordinators and not necessarily the caterer. These products generally arrive separately and at times even unnoticed.

7. Establishment of a clear policy concerning food from private homes. The suggested procedure is not to allow any home-prepared food into the synagogue even from the rabbi's house. This approach avoids insulting anyone in making a decision as to the perceived standard of their kashrut observance. By insisting that everything

must be prepared in the synagogue and using his own home as an example, the rabbi will not hurt anyone's feelings. People can be invited to cook and prepare in the synagogue in conformity with the standardized kashrut regulations of the institution.

Very clear guidelines drawn up by the rabbi must be backed by the synagogue governing board. Thus, the implementation of these rules becomes synagogue policy and not merely the rabbi's policy. The rules must be clear and consistently applied. Any and all exceptions inevitably weaken the entire program.

We have the good fortune in Montreal to have one communal *Vaad ha-Kashrut*, namely the Vaad Hoir (MK). So as to strengthen the kashrut standards of the individual synagogues, all Orthodox synagogues in the city opted for Vaad Hoir-MK supervision in their kitchens. The rabbi of each congregation remained the *Rav ha-Makhshir* while all active synagogue Mashgichim had to be certified by the Vaad Hoir. A common set of procedures were worked out, which included standards for every synagogue kitchen, Shabbat and non-Shabbat menus, standardized shipping slips to be used by Mashgichim of caterers so as to transfer food to the synagogue, a check-in system for receiving food, and an agreement to permit only Vaad Hoir caterers into the individual synagogues.

A second Mashgiach is required for Shabbat morning to relieve the regular Mashgiach, who invariably has other duties in the synagogue, such as keriyat ha-Torah or as the shaliach tzibbur. This second Mashgiach is a *Yotzei Ve'nikhnas* into the kitchen and social hall throughout this period of time. This person could be a male or female who is approved by the rabbi, and trained by the Mashgiach and made aware of all of the procedures and problems.

Situations that cannot be routinely solved by the Mashgiach are always referred to the rabbi for final decision. A joint kashrut committee of the Vaad Hoir and the pulpit rabbis reviews all problems and new situations that arise. All new proposals and changes emanate from that committee. Periodic inspection of synagogue kitchens and meetings with the Mashgichim are conducted by the Joint Committee.

This system strengthens the standard of kashrut and its supervision in the individual synagogue since the very same procedures are followed in each and every institution. The united strength of the Jewish community assures the integrity of the standards that are established. Variations of the above scheme can work in larger and smaller communities if approached with the proper tact. Changes in established systems must be handled carefully so as not to disparage the past and thereby create misunderstandings with the intended modifications. Any system of kashrut within the synagogue must be rabbi initiated, rabbi supervised, and synagogue endorsed. (See Appendix 1: *Kashrut.*)

THE NEW *CHUT HA-MESHULASH* – RABBI, SYNAGOGUE, AND JEWISH EDUCATION

It is of primary importance that the synagogue be involved and committed to Jewish education. This essential service more often than not serves as the conduit for families to either join or become more actively involved in the synagogue. Since the child is going to school, there is a renewed sense of identity with the community, which is established through the child and filtered to the entire family. The more involved the synagogue is in those systems of education, the more apparent will be the ripple effect touching on the synagogue and the intensity of Jewish identity.

While most synagogues do not operate their own day schools, it is important that the rabbi's influence be felt in the community day school which services the children of his congregation. This requires him to serve on the Board of Education in which capacity he can foster positive personal contacts with the professional and lay leaders of the day school.

While more and more of the families of Orthodox synagogues enroll their children in the day school, we dare not close our eyes to the vast numbers within our own membership who remain outside the day school system and to the nonaffiliated who have no direction. The afternoon or supplementary school therefore remains the other source from which future Jewish commitment will develop. Wherever feasible, this educational institution should be part of the synagogue and not community based. This allows the rabbi and his educational associates to develop a program most conducive to the ideals and goals of the synagogue and brings a child, and indirectly, his family, into the synagogue and into contact with what the synagogue represents.

Since a supplementary educational system requires time, space, energy, and finances, it is one of the first things to be eliminated when the budget gets tight. There are many arguments raised to support the elimination of an afternoon school program. They range from declining student population, spiraling costs, and the greater possibilities of a more comprehensive Jewish education within a community Hebrew School. It is incumbent upon the rabbi to demonstrate by effort and energy the need and the desirability of retaining all or some of the program within the confines of the synagogue building. The school and its educational program must feel the direct input of the rabbi in its program. This is not to say that he should necessarily teach or administer the school himself—his time and priorities may well preclude such involvement—but his influence should be felt nonetheless.

GETTING THE STUDENTS

By using the birth date found on the membership forms, you know who should be starting kindergarten or grade one. Phone calls or letters from the office or committee, advising parents that their child is eligible to enter the school program, get the maximum potential number of children to enroll. There is no substitute for personal contact or follow-up. The Hebrew School must reach out to parents and not wait for parents to bring their children.

Setting a synagogue standard requiring a minimum of four years of Jewish education for a Shabbat morning bar mitzvah makes a strong statement about Jewish education to the membership. Such an approach declares Jewish education to be a structured and very professional endeavor. It is an experience unto itself and not just another name for bar mitzvah training. Since Shabbat morning is a very special congregational time, the bar mitzvah boy must exemplify certain basic educational and Jewish skills. This does not exclude any young man from being called to the Torah so as to satisfy the Jewish requirements of bar mitzvah. This requirement can be fulfilled at a Shabbat Minchah service or on Monday or Thursday or Rosh Chodesh mornings. We must educate our membership to the significance of formal Jewish education. (See Appendix 1: *Bar Mitzvah*.)

CURRICULUM AND STRUCTURE

The Hebrew School must present the same educational challenge that the child encounters in the secular school. A spiral curriculum so as to avoid repetition, challenging educational approaches, good text- books, and appropriate audiovisual material make effective teachers even more successful.

A departmentalized school structure allows for the grouping of children by interest and gets away from the traditional grade system. This approach overcomes the numbers game by affording the flexibility of mixing certain compatible age groups for different subjects.

The school must have defined goals, a structure, and effective management. There must be a sense of accomplishment felt by the child every single session. Above all, it must be enjoyable. Most major cities have excellent Jewish Educational Resource Centers as part of the community Boards of Jewish Education. Cities such as Montreal, New York, and Chicago have earned excellent reputations for both collecting and developing creative Jewish educational materials. Every advantage should be taken of these existing facilities.

High School Programs

The development of Jewish educational programs for high school students remains one of the most challenging endeavors. The rabbi's participation in the high school program immediately gives it a high profile. Under his guidance or through his participation various minicourses on relevant issues and topics can be developed.

Further ideas include high school credits redeemed with a partial scholarship for a trip to Israel, or community action programs effectively involving high school students in meaningful Jewish programs. Many communities, including Quebec, have worked out official government high school credits for courses taken in synagogue high school programs. This is one of the best incentives to involve high school students in Jewish educational programs. (See Appendix 1: *High School Students*.)

Informal Educational Programs

The Bar Mitzvah–Chaver Program

To broaden the bar mitzvah experience both for the child and the entire family, a group of committed and knowledgeable men and women of the congregation volunteer as chaverim. They contact the bar mitzvah family four to six months before the bar mitzvah date and invite them to join him or her at services on Shabbat morning. They become the synagogue liaison for the period before the bar mitzvah. The bar mitzvah boy and his family now have a familiar face to sit with during services. The chaver, in turn, points out the various aspects of the davenning to both the bar mitzvah boy and to the family. (Women are important to make the mother and sisters part of the bar mitzvah experience.) When the parent cannot participate with the child, the chaver becomes the surrogate parent, making sure the child participates and learns through the experience. Many incidental questions that the family would feel embarrassed to raise to the rabbi are handled by the chaver. The bar mitzvah period becomes a true learning experience for the entire family in a most friendly and informative way. (See Appendix 1: *Bar Mitzvah–Chaver Program*.)

This idea can be used for new members as a basic introduction of any family to synagogue services or activities.

At the Rabbi's Tish

Shabbat dinners or kiddush with the rabbi afford many families an opportunity to experience Shabbat and Yom Tov in a truly traditional manner. Discussions as well as sessions can be integrated with a dinner or kiddush.

Sukkah Hopping

Organized walking tours to visit existing sukkot of various families who volunteer to host the group along the route. This affords the opportunity to many individuals who normally would not have the opportunity, to be invited to a sukkah.

There is no limit to the ingenuity and creativity that the rabbi can apply to involve people in ongoing Jewish experiences.

THE RABBI AS YOUTH RESOURCE

While the rabbi must be involved with the youth of his community, his involvement should not be confused with that of a professional youth director. Where possible, a full and diverse youth activities program should exist within the synagogue building. Fun groups, specialty groups, sports programs, as well as drama and music, should be provided by the synagogue. Children should enjoy coming into the synagogue for no other reason but enjoyment. These programs can serve as a base to develop Jewish programming and Jewish sensitivity. The rabbi's role is to guide and to lend expertise in the development of these programs.

National organizations such as the National Council of Synagogue Youth (NCSY), Yeshiva University Seminars, as well as Bnei Akiva and other such organizational programs can supplement basic youth activities. These programs must be conducted by well-trained individuals who enjoy children and who possess the skills to make the programs effective. There is nothing worse than a bad or ineffective youth program to discredit the synagogue in the eyes of both child and family. Better less general programming if budget or personnel is limited, while giving greater emphasis to specialty youth programming that can only be housed within the synagogue.

SPECIALTY SYNAGOGUE PROGRAMMING

Sukkaton/Shavu'oton Programs

Special sessions including drama, story telling, prayer, and games and refreshments organized for children of various ages on Yom Tov morning. The children can visit the main sanctuary to participate in the closing of services and to see and hear the special Yom Tov symbols, that is, etrog, lulav, hoshanot. This is followed by kiddush or lunch. Parents, teenagers, collegiates, and a host of other people can assist in such a program. Being only once or twice a year, cooperation is normally forthcoming. The rabbi must help develop and implement such programming to assure its success. (See Appendix 1: *Special Programs.*)

Shabbaton Programs

Special Friday Night or Shabbat Experiential Programs can involve many different age groups or special age groups with or without their families. Many variations on this approach to program ming are available through Yeshiva University's Youth Bureau and NCSY. Materials are readily available as well as expert help from their respective bureaus.

Shabbat Afternoon Fun Groups

For children of observant families or for families moving in that direction, the organizing of fun and study groups on Shabbat afternoon conducted by teenagers or young collegiates is a most welcome program. It allows the family as a whole to deal with the Shabbat concept and gives an outlet to both children and young adults to get together on Shabbat afternoon. Once again, an abundance of material exists as to effective content for such programs. Sometimes it takes the initiative of the rabbi with a select group of individuals to recognize the importance of this program and to implement it.

SEMINARS AND JOINT SYNAGOGUE PROGRAMMING

It is important to put Jewish youth of different communities together. It reinforces their own ideology and allows for proper socialization. Yeshiva University and NCSY afford opportunities to attend periodic regional Shabbatonim. The rabbi, working with his colleagues, can help plan various events which will see greater contact amongst the youth of our communities.

TZEDAKAH AND GEMILUT CHESED PROGRAMS

The rabbi, by defining various social action causes, can activate groups of young people to take on the challenge. The application of the concepts of charity and good deeds into concrete terms is one of the most rewarding activities that can be experienced. Projects involving Soviet Jewry, Ethiopian Jews, hospital visitation, service to senior citizens, Shabbat and Yom Tov food preparation and visitation, Big Brother or Big Sister Programs are only a few practical applications of basic Jewish concepts.

The rabbi, after assessing the available youth activities in his community, can prioritize for his congregation the areas of unique Jewish and synagogue youth participation. By underlining its importance, the rabbi assures its support and continuity.

SYNAGOGUE AUXILIARY ORGANIZATIONS

It is common practice that the Sisterhood and Men's Club have distinct identities within the synagogue organization. While the programs might appear to be superfluous, these two organizations are most effective in the initial involvement of new people in synagogue life and in serving as a training ground for future synagogue leadership. With the rabbi's guidance, each of these organizations can pick up part of the overall synagogue program. Speakers, programs, fundraising, and community action can all be integrated as part of the total synagogue package. A Men's Club Breakfast can be integrated with a Sunday morning service, and Sisterhood can spearhead a Friday Evening Dinner with the rabbi. This only strengthens the support of the long-term goals of the synagogue. Organized lines for clearing dates and the planning of programs can avoid duplication and conflict.

There is also a need within the synagogue organization for fun or social programming to involve the masses. This can effectively be covered by these two auxiliary organizations. These organizations are excellent sources of manpower for overall synagogue projects that the rabbi can see are properly coordinated and organized. There sometimes arises a need, because of the age factor, to create a younger and older Sisterhood, as well as an older or younger Men's Club or Brotherhood. These creative approaches can keep everyone actively involved on many different levels.

PUTTING THE PIECES TOGETHER – THE SYNAGOGUE CALENDAR

There is a definite need for the rabbi to view the overall calendar of the synagogue to make sure that all of the pieces fit into the right places. Various programs should be responsive to various times of the year, that is, educational programming prior to the High Holy Days and Passover, with social programming in the lulls of the winter. Programming should not conflict with the sensitivity of the time of the year, such as a synagogue social program during *Yamim Nora'im*, etc. As Chief Executive Officer of the synagogue, the rabbi must be involved in not only individual programs, but in looking at the organization in its entirety, that not only the timing be proper but that the activities are aimed at the broader congregation. Program priorities as well as the variety of activities can be readily influenced with the rabbi's active participation within the organizational structure of the congregation.

A FINAL WORD – PERSONAL-TIME MANAGEMENT

The effective administrator will also effectively administer his own time. The tasks which confront us appear to be, for the most part, overwhelming and time consuming. In a people-oriented profession, we cannot always pick and choose our hours. This is all the more reason why personal-time management is of prime importance.

Days and hours should be structured so as to assure time for established priorities. The rabbi must effectively organize his professional and personal hours so as to anticipate the unique and special demands of his congregation. If involved in a Hebrew School, he knows which afternoons are already occupied. If there are many evening meetings, he must free some time during the day. Some adjustments can be made even during the peak periods of the High Holidays or the heavy bar mizvah and wedding seasons. The key to time management is to organize the routines so as to leave time for the unexpected.

Since the rabbi is expected to be visible and available, guidelines must be established to allow for some time that the rabbi is in but not available. Possible time structures to be considered include

1. Specific hours for consultation. Some to be designated as open, and the remainder by appointment only.
2. Designated "do not disturb time" periods, known as rabbis' professional prep time.
3. While office staff or secretary should be screening all calls and disseminating appropriate routine information, there can be a

designated time during the day for "messages only," with the rabbi returning the necessary calls later at his convenience.
4. Predetermined nonsynagogue time—day and/or night—barring emergency.
5. Designated conference time with professional associates on a regular basis.
6. Priorities established in other chapters in this volume must be incorporated into one's time structure.

It is so easy to lose track of time and mastery over the use of one's time unless one sees the larger calendar by week, by month, and by season. A professional's time is a most sacred commodity, and a rabbi must consider his time professional and sacred, and proportion it accordingly. Scheduling, tempered with compassion and common sense, will maximize the effective use of our professional time and skills.

6

The Rabbi as Caregiver

Rabbi Israel Kestenbaum

Concerned as the rabbi must be with the larger needs of his synagogue and community, not to speak of those of *Klal Yisrael*, he never loses sight of the personal requirements of the individual man or woman in the daily exigencies of life. It is here that he finds some of his greatest challenges—as well as satisfactions—in ways that often go unnoticed but hardly unappreciated. Often such pastoral skills are learned on the job, or by instinct, yet it is surely preferable to learn, both formally and informally, from the experiences and training of others. Rabbi Israel Kestenbaum provides a touching example of both.

Some years ago, Rabbi Baruch Silverstein presented a paper, "The Rabbi's Dilemma,"[1] at a rabbinic conference, in which he analyzed the predicament of the modern American rabbi. He noted that with the restoration of the rabbi to the "classic role as the all-knowing answer man", has come the awesome responsibility to explain the tragic episodes of modern Jewish history from the Holocaust to Kiryat Shemonah.[2] He argued that so much of the pain of the rabbinic experience today is in being called upon to provide answers to questions for which we have none.

While I do not discount the "dilemma" as presented by Silverstein, it pales before a more common and ongoing challenge to the rabbinic role as answer man, that of the everyday tragedy in the life of the congregation and its member families. Indeed, the urgency of a meaningful response to people in crises weighs heavily on the head of a rabbi. More immediate than the need to explain the evils of Jewish history, he feels it his duty and his call to be a caregiver to those he has come to care for in their time of need.

I have a feeling of dread time and time again when I am called upon to help. Sitting with parents in the bedroom of their 21-year-old daughter who lay dead in the bed after a long battle with cancer, intervening with a family whose daughter suddenly came home from college and admitted to a drug problem, offering support to a mother who gave birth to a stillborn infant—the situations are legion. In some way they arise every time someone dies, every time some new diagnosis is pronounced, every time life's circumstances change for people for whom I feel a responsibility. A part of me wants to run away. A part of me wants to escape into a functional role, simply performing the duties, with care, but not getting too close. And yet, there is a greater part of me that wants to make a difference, that wants to be a spiritual leader and healer, if only I could get beyond the fear, if only I knew what to do.

There is little doubt that people sense the discomfort of the rabbi. They understand his good intentions, yet his difficulty in being significant beyond the sympathetic word. They read his insecurities and his doubts, and often they simply look elsewhere for the spiritual and emotional help they require, or bury their problems within. I remember Jan, a young married woman of an assimilated family background who married the doctor son of a Holocaust survivor in my community. Two years after her wedding she confided to me with pain that her in-laws had coached her for three hours prior to her premarital visit with me so that she would say the "right things."

I suspect that "dressing up" for the rabbi is done as much to protect the rabbi as to safeguard the family secrets. The family in question, while discussing with me in some detail the qualms they had about their future daughter-in-law, could not allow me real entry into the ongoing struggle or give me the chance to intervene in a helping way. Perhaps they went to a social worker or consulted a family therapist. But people no doubt regularly see the problem as overwhelming for a rabbi and decide to leave him alone. It is one thing to share the problems with someone who can make a difference; while one may be compromised and made vulnerable in the process, the help received would make it worthwhile. But it is still another to lose face with no gain. Often the rabbi and congregant are happy to "talk around" a difficult situation rather than share the emotional suffering and stress that each is experiencing.

In a real way there is a dance being enacted between the rabbi and his congregant, as much amusing as sad. The rabbi enters a hospital room. He asks Jack how he is doing. Jack answers appropriately. The rabbi spends some time with Jack discussing the business of the shul, matters of family and the like. Both Jack and the rabbi compliment each other, a funny story is told, and with good wishes for Jack, the rabbi departs. No doubt a fairly typical pastoral visit.

But take a second look at that visit. Jack has real concerns about the implications of his illness. He is often afraid of the future. He feels vulnerable. He is worried. He cannot tell his wife or family lest he cause additional upset for ones he loves. He feels the need to be strong for their sakes, but he also needs to let go of the emotional suffering and stress he is carrying. Yet to whom? Suddenly the rabbi enters and asks Jack how he is doing. Jack has a decision to make. "How should I respond?" he thinks. "What is the rabbi prepared to hear? What can I trust him with? How invested in me is he willing to be? Will he understand?" Jack answers, "Okay," and goes on to describe the situation in a rather detached and clinical manner. The die has been cast. The rabbi then makes the next move, to persist or not to persist, to probe or not to probe. He suspects that there is more to Jack's story than he is letting on; he senses the strain. But more often than not, the rabbi takes Jack's cue and leaves well enough alone. The visit proceeds along the path a mile wide but an inch deep. Jack and the rabbi protect each other as they protect themselves. At one level nothing much has happened; at another a great coverup has been executed.

What would it mean for a rabbi to become an effective caregiver? Would he need a masters degree in social work or a doctorate in clinical psychology? The answer to both these questions is clearly in the negative. Not only is the M.S.W. or PH.D. unnecessary, to some extent it is unhelpful. For the rabbi to be a caregiver he needs to act out of his role as rabbi and to bring along the spiritual and theological insights that are unique to his area of expertise. Edwin Friedman has already pointed to the special position of clergy inasmuch as we become part of the family of our congregations.[3] Paul Pruyser, in his book *The Minister as Diagnostician*, decries the clergy's surrender of terminology and approach unique to the faith community in favor of the psychological model.[4] We do not have to go elsewhere, to other disciplines, to find a model for caregiving. It is very much within our own traditions that the words, the method, and the authority can be found.

What are the ingredients necessary for being an effective caregiver within the role of rabbi? For me this question had led to several years of training in clinical pastoral education. I have read a small but eye-opening portion of the vast literature on pastoral care, and have participated in didactics on method and content of clerical intervention. I have worked under the careful eye of a supervisor who regularly critiqued my efforts in congregant–patient/rabbi interactions. Having come through the process, I can now affirm the important and unparalleled place of the rabbi as part of the healing team. Moreover, I am keenly aware of the model for caregiving into which the rabbi needs to fit for the congregant–patient/rabbi interaction to be successful. It is a model very different from the one out of which the rabbi normally operates.

Ask a rabbi to define his role in one word and most will use the word "teacher." After all, "teacher, mentor, master" are all at the core of the Hebrew word rav or rebbe. As teachers we are forever guiding and leading others. It is important to note that in a teacher–student relationship there exists an implicit distance and polarity. For effective learning to happen, the two cannot be one. There needs to be a dialogue. While it is necessary to understand the student and his needs in the modality of teacher, the rabbi must project an otherness and a separation. This is not so in the rabbi's capacity as caregiver. Here, both the role as teacher and its concomitant calling for distance are inoperative.

Imitatio Dei, a universal ethic of Judaism, has added consequence for the rabbi. After all, he is the person charged with reflecting God's teaching and God's way to his community. Our Sages understood the prophet's challenge, "For the priest's lips should preserve knowledge and they should seek the law at his mouth; for he is the messenger of the Lord of hosts" (Malachi 2:7), as requiring spiritual excellence of the rabbi worthy of instructing others (*Hagigah* 15b). With regard to the teaching of Torah, the Talmud tells us that rabbis must do so without seeking compensation. Employing the lesson of the Divine, the requirement is, "Just as I taught for nothing, so shall you teach for nothing" (*Nedarim* 37a).

What does *Imitatio Dei* have to say to the rabbi as caregiver?

God is healer, savior, redeemer, protector, and more. To attempt to play the role of God for our families in crises and rescue them from their predicaments might be tempting, but it would most often be unsuccessful. How do you save someone from a malignant brain tumor? How do you resurrect a dead spouse? While surely a rabbi is called upon to emulate the way of God, its expression cannot be understood as a charge to bring about God-like changes in the circumstances of life. We are not asked to play God but to follow His ways.

Sometimes in response to crises we feel responsible to answer for God, to explain the reasons why. Harold Kushner, in his *When Bad Things Happen to Good People*, challenges the universal need to come to God's defense.[5] While I do not accept the thesis of Kushner's work, I do find his criticism of the common attitude appropriate. God does not require our interpretation. One justification for the whys of life is that they are for the benefit of the sufferer, as a move toward healing and reclaimed wholeness. *Imitatio Dei*, the model of the call to chesed, is in no way achieved through apologetics, no matter how profound or even how true.

If God's ways are not to be imitated by saving a life and if excuse-making is not called for, what, then, is a rabbi's obligation? The answer is found in the Ninety-first Psalm, where God is envisioned as protector and redeemer, provider and savior, listener and empathizer. While the first expressions of providence are impressive, it is not from the first pairings but from the last that our work of caregiving takes its cue. "When he calls upon me, I will answer him: I will be with him in trouble" (Psalm 91:15). God listens to those struggling with the hurt of life. The affirmation of this Divine blessing is found throughout scriptural literature. "The Lord is near to all who call upon him" is at the core of our commitment to prayer. It is not that God always protects but that He is always present. "Yea, though I walk through the valley of the shadow of death, I fear no evil for Thou are with me" (Psalm 23:4). Death may be imminent, but it loses its terrifying dimension because God is present.

What is the nature of God's presence as evidenced in our tradition? "I am with him," says God in Psalm 91. "You stand with me," says the psalmist in Psalm 23. God's presence is clearly evidenced as an empathic one, feeling, as it were, our pain and suffering. The rabbinic tradition speaks often of the mystical theme that when Israel sustains periods of affliction God's own Shekhinah experiences similar sensations of hurt. God is not apart from us; He is near and close and identified with us in our time of trouble. In that presence, independent of relief of our symptoms, we feel secure and uplifted. We call this empathy, that is, being with someone in his or her predicament. Empathy is the most important single component of effective caregiving. It is at the core of *Imitatio Dei*.

Empathy is at the center of the loving act; I suspect it is the real meaning of "And thou shalt love thy neighbor as thyself" (Leviticus 19:18). Moreover, as an imperative, it challenges us to chesed in the form of *Imitatio Dei*, its purest expression.

The empathic response is more than the depth of caring as expressed from one person to another. When present, it reflects the presence of God as well. I remember leaving a hospital room after a visit. The private-duty nurse whom I had known from other cases followed me out. Stopping me before I got far from the room, she said she needed to tell me something. "I just want you to know that whenever you enter a room you don't go in alone," she said. Sometime later, I rather proudly shared her statement with a skeptical M.S.W. friend of mine. "God had nothing to do with it," he said. "It's just your listening presence she is sensing." In truth, both the nurse and my M.S.W. friend were right. The empathic response allows for an interaction in which a spiritual aura is present. When the rabbi as a caregiver gives of himself in order to be there for the other person, he allows the other to feel loved not only by the rabbi but by the Divine.

Empathy is the work of the rabbinic caregiver, and work and discipline are necessary to become empathic. For the work to be accomplished, the rabbi must surrender the role of teacher with the implicit distance between himself and the student as discussed above. Instead, he must be willing to become a partner with the person requiring the care. He must be prepared to make himself available to the person's conditions and circumstances. There is no room to be judgmental. The rabbi and the congregant–patient are one, sharing in the congregant–patient's process.

As many of us have come to learn in our own spiritual quest, nullification is a difficult business. While hitbattelut is the way to God, it requires enormous discipline. Getting oneself out of the way is a painful struggle; it requires a thorough knowledge of oneself and an understanding of one's own needs and issues. The same kind of hitbattelut is necessary for the empathic encounter in caregiving. For it to occur, the rabbi needs to be knowing of himself. He needs to work at getting himself out of the way so as to be fully open to the other; he needs to be of the sort for whom people do not need to dress up. Indeed, they expect him to be naked for them.

When responding empathetically, one does not come in with answers. The fear of not knowing what to say dissolves. Whatever preparation is appropriate is connected to an inner readiness to receive rather than to formulate ready-made solutions. The person being cared for and the caregiver will find a way. No agenda is predetermined. That, too, takes courage. And yet, the rabbi is freed in the awareness that he need only be present. He need not supply anything but a listening ear and a knowing heart.

Being empathic is not an all-or-nothing proposition. It is expressed in degrees according to the skills of the caregiver and his frame of mind. To the extent that empathy exists in the encounter, the rabbi will experience a concomitant openness in the congregant-patient. The degree of empathy will also affect the capacity of the encounter to facilitate change in the congregant-patient.[6] Most important, the more empathic the response the more the love and presence of God will be felt, with all the healing of the spirit associated with it.

Having outlined the model for the rabbi as caregiver, the remaining issue is how to bring the model to life. The importance of addressing the practical side of the topic is more than simply to meet the frustration phenomena commonly experienced by the rabbi and described earlier in this paper.

People of faith need the response of faith to their life's predicament. It is not enough for Scott Peck, Rollo May, and Erich Fromm to address their problem; they need to know what their rabbi has to say. Nor is it enough for the rabbi to theologize on guilt, anger, God's love, evil, life, death, or sin. Theology is good from the pulpit, not at the bedside.

Jewish family service organizations simply cannot do it all. Men and women with a sensitivity to religion have the right to expect a religious response, if not a religious answer, to their life's circumstances. The rabbi must be the respondent of faith even as the doctor is the respondent of science and the social worker or psychologist is the respondent of mental health to the life issues which confront us.

In the remaining section of this chapter I will flesh out briefly a number of proposals.

1. Any effort intended to affect quality caregiving requires education. We should take note of the policy at major non-Jewish seminaries that require their divinity students to take an internship in pastoral care. Students work in a hospital or nursing home setting, functioning as chaplains, while being supervised and while receiving instruction in the art of religious caregiving. The action-reflection model is used to foster the student's understanding of both his work and his self in caring for others. The centers designated for training are established under the auspices of the Association for Clinical Pastoral Education, which sets both the standards and the guidelines for the program.

I feel it of enormous importance that our own rabbinical students experience a similar internship as part of the requirements for semik-hah. After all, the precedent for shimush is well established. No one argues the benefit of a hands-on experience for the rabbi-to-be in hilkhot Gittin, Nidah, and Treifot. Text learning, even for the most imaginative students, is simply not sufficient to meet the call to practical decision-making in these areas. Human problems are no different. Good intentions and theoretical knowledge alone will not do; supervised clinical training is necessary. The model for such a program is already in place. Its implementation requires adaptation and resolve.

2. This clinical experience should not be limited to students preparing for the rabbinate. While an internship for a summer might be too much to ask for a pulpit rabbi already in the field, possibilities exist for establishing programs which include clinical training and which allow for a more limited investment of time. The purpose of the proposed experience is not to train rabbis for chaplaincy, but rather to give them greater skills at doing the chaplaincy work which they are already called upon to do in their own congregations. Through the process of skill-building and self-reflection, the rabbi's confidence in caregiving is enhanced and the congregation benefits in the quality of its spiritual care.

3. However, a clinical training experience as described above cannot do it all. How do we as rabbis respond to marital discord,

homosexuality, parent–child conflict, alcoholism, and other problems, when they occur in our congregations? More than crisis intervention is asked of us. The problems mentioned have long-term implications. Empathy is fine as far as it goes; but these situations, if they are to be remedied, require more. They require a counseling relationship. And such a relationship often requires different professional intervention.

Therefore, it is very important that the rabbi know how to make a referral and to whom to refer. No one should minimize the significance of this role; it can make all the difference in the world between healing and lingering dysfunction. In order to perform his responsibilities well, the rabbi will have to know how to diagnose. To expect every rabbi to be skilled in this area is as naive as to expect every rabbi to be so skilled in medical ethics or gittin. Rabbis have always relied on other rabbis with greater expertise in areas in which they are less knowledgeable. Not surprisingly, then, resource rabbis must be available for each cluster of Jewish communities to serve as specialists for consultation and guidance in making diagnoses and referrals. The combined effort of the sensitivity gained through the clinical training of the rabbi, and the presence nearby of rabbinic experts in pastoral care and counseling as support, will guarantee, as closely as possible, that religious caregiving will be offered in a responsible and effective manner, even in the most complex of circumstances.

If I write with a passion it is because these matters are extremely important to me. To the extent that I have known religious experiences at all, many have come in the intimacy shared with a congregant-patient in the empathic encounter. Each visit with a hospital patient or home-bound congregant, each counseling session, presents an opportunity for the rabbi to sense the holy. Intuitively we know that. Our communities, our congregations, our very selves would be best served if we trusted our intuitions and began to take caregiving more seriously. While the call to clinical training may emerge out of the need of both the rabbi and his congregation, the blessings of pursuing the process in education and practice extend beyond meeting the need. Meaningful and empathic caregiving will further bring God's presence into the fabric of our life. It will help make us truly a *Kehillah Kedoshah*.

NOTES

[1]Baruch Silverstein, "The Rabbi's Dilemma," in *Papers Presented at the Annual Rabbi Harold Gordon Conference 1979–1980* (unpaginated pamphlet) (New York: New York Board of Rabbis, 1980).

[2]*Ibid.*, p.6.

[3]Edwin H. Friedman, *Generation to Generation: Family Process in Church and Synagogue* (New York: Guilford Press, 1985).

[4]Paul Pruyser, *The Minister as Diagnostician: Personal Problems in Pastoral Perspective* (Philadelphia: Westminster Press, 1976).

[5]Harold S. Kushner, *When Bad Things Happen to Good People* (New York: Schocken Books, 1981).

[6]Rollo May, *The Art of Counseling* (Nashville, TN: Abingdon Press, 1967), p. 150.

7

The Rabbi as Counselor

Rabbi Joel Tessler

As with the previous chapter, this one addresses the pastoral dimension of the rabbi's daily docket. Rabbi Joel Tessler focuses on counseling aspects of the rabbinate, be they in the context of the emotionally needy, the socially distressed, those facing death, members of troubled families, and the like. Part of counseling is to know when and how to refer, or defer, to others more qualified in given situations. In addressing these questions, Rabbi Tessler touches on what is surely a fundamental concern of the contemporary rabbi.

On the Yamim Nora'im we refer to God as shepherd and pastor, tending to the needs of his flock. The outstanding character trait of Abraham is *chesed*, kindness to others. The greatest person to have walked this earth, Moshe, is given one title after his name—Rabbeinu, our teacher and leader. But, what do we know about Moshe's personality or talents that would give us insight into God's selection of this man? Does the Torah talk about his intellectual or analytical genius? No. Only three stories are selected to glean insight into Moshe, the man. In each case, he witnesses injustice and feels for others in pain. "And it came to pass in those days when Moshe was grown up, that he went out unto his brethren" (Exodus 2:11). He saw an Egyptian smiting a fellow Jew, and later witnessed two Jews striving against each other, and still later he protected the daughters of Yitro against the neighborhood shepherds.

77

The Midrash illuminates even further what ultimately made Moshe Rabbeinu our leader. Moshe the shepherd, we are told, counts his flock and discovers that one sheep had wandered away. This very young sheep is too weak, lame, and scared to return unaided to the herd. As tired as Moshe is, he nevertheless carries the animal all the way back. These images of our leader's concern and empathy for every member of his flock rest firmly in the minds of all in reflecting upon Jewish leadership and being a Rav be'Yisrael.

Intellectual prowess and mastery of sources is crucial for the rabbi/teacher. But the elements of empathy and chesed have also served as the hallmark of the rabbi/pastor. Indeed, the success of every congregational rabbi depends upon the degree to which he is able to synthesize the skills of educator and pastor.

A national survey has found that nearly one in four adult Americans have felt sufficiently troubled to need counseling at some time, that one in seven has sought help, and that forty-two percent of those seeking professional help have approached a clergyman. It could be estimated rather crudely that the two hundred and thirty-five thousand parish clergyman in the United States counsel approximately six million five hundred thousand persons per year.[1]

In spite of these extraordinarily high statistics, most rabbis have deep feelings of frustration, uncertainty, and even a sense of personal inadequacy when called upon to help. People can sense these feelings in their rabbis and therefore have difficulty in presenting their psychological and emotional needs to them. Yet, by the nature of their role in the community, rabbis are the people who can and must be able to meet these demands.

When a person comes to see a rabbi, there are definite expectations, both conscious and unconscious, on either side. The individual understands that the rabbi represents a religious point of view and value base. The rabbi assumes that the congregant is looking for help from a religious perspective. People bring many concerns to the rabbi. Often they seek a rabbi's help with interpersonal or intrapsychic problems. Sometimes the person comes seeking immediate relief, what is termed crisis intervention. "The intent of parish pastoral counseling is to consider the issues brought by the individual in light of his/her own resources and to cope in dialogue with the faith tradition. It is a triadic relationship: the seeker, the minister, and the faith tradition."[2]

Rabbis can use their own religious methodology. Richard Mollica encourages the pastoral counselor to "develop the specific skills generic to his own unique religious world view that can actively be tested out and evaluated by him in his 'priestly function.'"[3]

But what are these skills? I enrolled in the M.S.W. program at Wurzweiler School of Social Work to facilitate my future career as a rabbi. I had been studying at Yeshivat Har Etzion in Israel and the Rosh Ha-Yeshivah, Rav Aaron Lichtenstein, had suggested that if I was planning a career in the rabbinate, the best secular degree I could receive to expand the scope and refine the skills of a modern rabbi would be the M.S.W. He felt that social work training would complement the rabbi's role and enhance the counseling work which is so vital for today's clergy.

I listened to Rav Lichtenstein's advice and have benefited from the Wurzweiler experience. I have seen how the body of knowledge we call social work can create a better professional rabbi and pastor.

Judaism believes that man is made up of diverse entities and natures which conflict and are mutually antagonistic.[4] We all have certain innate tendencies, but Judaism believes that a person can change his or her innate characteristics, actions, or behavior patterns. One is still able to choose freely between good and evil because every human being has the power of free will and free choice.[5]

The Jewish values guiding the rabbi and the professional values guiding the social worker seem to be in harmony. In the book of Genesis, the Bible gives dignity and great worth to all individuals when it proclaims that man was created "in the image of God."

Pumphrey states that the importance of every human being is a basic premise to social work. Pumphrey identifies what she sees as ultimate social work values: that each human being should be regarded by all others as an object of infinite worth, to be protected wherever possible from suffering; that human beings have large and unknown capacities for developing inner harmony and yet contribute to the development of others; in order to realize potentialities, every person must engage in interpersonal relationships; human betterment is possible; change may be aided by purposive assistance from others; most effective change cannot be imposed; a person has the capacity to discern and direct his or her own destiny, and this must be respected.[6]

Both Judaism and social work recognize and value the uniqueness of all people and believe that change is possible. But the initial area of difference between the rabbi and the social worker is in the definition and obligation of the two roles. Charles Levy states:

> Jewish educators and Rabbis are obliged directly to communicate to, nay, perhaps even to urge upon—agency clients the beliefs and behaviors represented by the institutions through which they function. Social workers, on the other hand, guided by a knowledge and understanding of Jewish clients, Jewish agency and the Jewish community, help agency clients in the way they need to be helped—whether that be through increased self understanding, environmental change, application of various resources and so on.
>
> The Jewish educator and the Rabbi necessarily have a predetermined end. The social worker does not.[7]

How does a rabbi implement the Jewish value system in working with a congregant?

CRISIS INTERVENTION

Very few rabbis have the time or skill to engage in a long-term counseling relationship. Therefore, the majority of pastoral work done by a rabbi is crisis intervention. Whether it is a 2 A.M. phone call of anguish because a loved one has just died, or a frantic message that someone has just been seriously injured in a car accident, or parents shuddering because their teenager's drug habit has just been uncovered, or a wife's pain—fearful that her marriage is about to crumble; all of these call for the rabbi's immediate response. He must be prepared to interact with a fragile or explosive situation in a matter of minutes or hours.

Once the crisis arises, there is not much time to prepare oneself for the meeting. It happens often when we seem least able to find the "time" for what we know is an all encompassing emotional involvement. Yet, to be involved, we must.

The rabbi can gain important insight into himself and thereby improve his ability to counsel others by developing his "conscious use of self." Conscious use of self requires the rabbi to be totally "tuned in" and all of his resources available to the other person's circumstances. His concern and empathy must be professionally directed. "The reflective awareness of self or aspects of self makes it possible to discern patterns of one's participation and engagement, to hold self itself, up as an 'object.' "[8] This process helps to frame and direct one's intervention. Self-awareness and conscious use of self can help a rabbi be more effective as a counselor.

REFERRAL

The skills needed to counsel individuals are vital to the rabbinate, yet just as important is the skill of referral. The rabbi needs to be taught the tactics of entering a new community and rapidly introducing himself to the existing helping resources such as psychiatric facilities, social service and welfare agencies, and health facilities. The man to whom forty-two percent of troubled people turn for help should know intimately the helping resources of his own community.

Though the rabbi is limited with his time, the congregant's problems persist. As an example, a woman who loses her husband is often closely involved with the rabbi from the beginning of the illness through the shiva, but afterwards, the rabbi goes on with other congregational needs. The widow is now left, lonely, confused, and disoriented, needing support from a skilled professional to meet emotional and other needs. A referral to someone in the helping professions could prove very useful for this woman. Support groups for certain specific needs, that is, widows, couples, and bereaved parents, either run by outside agencies or the synagogue, could be an invaluable resource to those in need. Groups develop a life of their own. Friendships are created, relationships established, and a network of shared pain develops. The rabbi's follow-up months and even years later are most appreciated. But ongoing groups in the synagogue fill part of the endless void created by the rabbi's lack of time.

SINGLES, SHIDDUKHIM, AND INTERFAITH MARRIAGE

Singles are a population often overlooked. Today's singles are usually financially successful and independent. Being single may span a time period of twenty-five years or more in the life cycle. Many Jews desperately want to meet other Jews. They also seek spiritual fulfillment from the synagogue. Unfortunately, most synagogue programming focuses on families and intergenerational clusters in the community, that is, youth groups, couples clubs, and family shabbatonim. Programming specifically geared for singles is often nonexistent. Singles will come out of the woodwork and travel forty miles or more for a singles program. Participants are very loyal and attend regularly. A conservative synagogue in Washington had a rabbi who specialized in singles programming. A monthly Friday night service had attracted over a thousand Jewish singles regularly. The hit and miss of the rabbi/matchmaker must be replaced by a central referral bank in each community. The rabbi is pivotal in the accumulation and referral of this information.

Single parents are another group overlooked by the synagogue. They do not really fit in anywhere. It is crucial to be sensitive to programmatic terminology. Father/son breakfasts or mother/daughter luncheons are seen as insensitive and cold rejections of a single mother and her son, or a single father and his daughter. Such a caring, popular event if titled incorrectly can shut out and disenfranchise single parents and their children. The mechitzah sometimes serves as a barrier for a mother or father with children of the opposite sex, especially new members or unaffiliated Jews. Care must be taken to look out for their special needs. They do not know anyone and cannot even sit with their relation. For a newcomer this can be a lonely and frightening experience. All the boys have a father to run over to except the son of a single mother or the daughter of a single father. We cannot eliminate the mechitzah for these individuals but must be sensitive to this inherent dilemma. Often a child is dropped off by parents at the synagogue and is all alone yet surrounded by hundreds of other Jews. I cannot forget the sight of a woman who had lost her husband and had subsequently started coming to shul on Shabbat. How difficult it was for her and her son to disengage physically when they desperately needed each other.

The rabbi must be aware of this issue and teach the community to be sensitive and caring of such circumstances, which are now very common. Rabbis and congregants must be on the lookout for these families. The Torah reminds us over and over to deal gently and kindly with the widow and the orphan. In a sense the single parent family suffers from similar problems facing the widow and the orphan. The Torah tells us that this is everyone's responsibility.

When one refers to the less fortunate, the poor and homeless are important segments of our communities. Even in affluent areas, rabbis would be amazed at the numbers of Jews in need of financial aid. I remember how Mayor Ed Koch of New York decried the fact that many synagogues and churches had not opened up their doors or resources to the homeless. Judaism was founded on the great institution of zedakah, yet many synagogues have lost this concept as it pertains to *local* residents. We are very generous and give great sums to institutions or to the people of Israel, but to real people in our own backyard we have been remiss. The prophets admonish us for turning our back to *our local* needy. In theory we agree to be involved but in practice very few rabbis or their synagogues work with indigent Jews. It is not glamorous work, but it is our responsibility nonetheless. For example, there is much waste in the food business so some synagogues and caterers have given their unused foodstuffs to shelters and soup kitchens. My father is a butcher in New Jersey. He puts aside all the meats and chickens not sold by the end of the week and gives them to the local Jewish Social Service agencies and shelters free of charge. A rabbi can serve as a role model to all by his involvement with those who are overlooked by most of the community.

A rabbi must also realize that the best of intentions are often futile. There is a homeless Jewish woman who is driven to motels and shelters by congregants of my shul. Her case is well known by our local Jewish social service agency. She has been given an apartment and a stipend. Yet, her psychological problems do not allow for our long-term help. She has abandoned the apartment, and in spite of numerous attempts to mobilize various parts of the helping community, she has preferred the streets. She goes from city to city, returning when the weather is favorable. A competent rabbi knows when he can no longer help and must move on to other situations. Unfortunately, some clergy suffer from the illusion that they are "omni-competent" in meeting human needs.

CARING FOR THE CHRONIC SICK IN
NURSING HOMES

There are various levels of functioning within a nursing home setting. There are skilled nursing facilities and health related facilities. They serve different levels of need. Nevertheless, the nursing home population is an extension of the congregation. Some residents of the nursing home can participate in a wide range of shul programs. Some are less active and can only participate minimally. The nursing home population for the most part has difficulty coming to the synagogue. We therefore have to come to this population or we have to bring these residents to the synagogue. This relative lack of mobility isolates or removes this segment of the Jewish community from the synagogue. How sad it is for a long-time member of a synagogue to be institutionalized in a nursing home. Being out of sight often means being out of mind. Our elderly deserve our visits and involvement in improving their quality of life. The rabbi brings a great deal with his visits, especially for an older population. His visits are greatly appreciated by the staff and the residents. Many residents appreciate the religious services and traditions a rabbi can bring to them. In addition, a visit by the rabbi reinforces the residents' feeling of self-worth.

Institutions in general can rob a person of many individual freedoms, such as privacy. Residents of institutions are dependent on others. Yet, when the rabbi takes time from his "busy" schedule to visit a nursing home he provides an important spiritual dimension to an often sterile setting. The nursing home is the final residence for some of our elderly. Jews tend to use nursing homes in disproportionate numbers for our aged population. At one time many of these people actively participated and lived near the shul. Today they are removed from us. The rabbi has an opportunity to bring Judaism and the shul back to them.

HOSPICE

Hospice is truly a mizvah of *chesed shel emet*. Some hospices have live-in settings similar to hospitals, while others work totally out of the patient's home. Many hospice groups will only serve a person diagnosed as having six months to live or less. Yet, as we all know, a patient often lives for two years or more in spite of these predictions.

Hospice is so successful because of the team approach: doctor, nurse, social worker, volunteer, and rabbi. The rabbi is at different times the most critical member of the support team. Hospice serves the entire family during illness and follows up for months after death. The dying patient often finds the rabbi, through his presence, his or her comfort, and his spiritual contribution crucial to the ability to deal with reality and meeting his Creator. The rabbi offers comfort and support to an entire family at a time when most other professions have given up in futility.

Quality of life and basic philosophical and ideological issues are present constantly. The meaning of life is questioned. Who should be better equipped to handle these unknown mysteries than the rabbi? Elizabeth Kubler-Ross taught that one need not have the "answers." There really are no answers. That is where faith comes in. This is God's domain. But the rabbi's involvement, his concern, his love, his empathy, are what hospice and the families desperately need and appreciate.

JEWS IN PRISON

There are Jewish prisoners in almost every penal institution in the United States. They are small in number but they require a rabbi's presence. Sometimes rabbis are needed to locate kosher meals or help with job placement. Other times a rabbi can provide a word of encouragement and guidance to help in his rehabilitation. Rabbis can provide some semblance of Shabbat and Yom Tov by distributing seasonal goodies or sharing religious objects such as a siddur, lulav, and etrog, and so forth.

Of all segments of our population, it is the Jewish prison inmate who is most neglected. He needs spiritual guidance and comfort. The rabbi in the prison can provide a religious well from which to drink. We ought to remember that when Yosef was thrown into jail, he begged for kindness and to be remembered. It is the rabbi who can provide such an answer to Yosef's prayers. It is very lonely to be a Jewish inmate in prison. Often one suffers for his Jewishness. If a rabbi does not service these needs, who will?

HOSPITALITY

We all know that hospitality to strangers, or a newcomer, is even greater than entertaining the Shekhinah. Rabbis are gracious to a fault in opening up their homes to all for meals, sleeping, and study.

People in the community, rightfully or not, often consider the rabbi's home as their second home. Rabbis teach by example. Yet, there are many souls that slip through the cracks and are not approached.

All studies on cults suggest that their greatest allure is their initial kindness and concern. There is a great attraction when someone welcomes a perfect stranger and offers help and hospitality. The greatest outreach tool a rabbi and community have is their genuine hospitality and concern for each and every individual.

Hospitality committees must be established to open many homes for strangers or newcomers. Another function of the committee would be to look out for new faces and offer assistance in making them feel at home. We are implored "to love the stranger because we were strangers in the land of Egypt." We are all strangers during certain times in our lives. There is nothing more memorable than a kindness offered to a stranger.

PREVENTIVE COUNSELING

The rabbi has a genuine and unique opportunity to perform preventive counseling at many of the key points in an individual's life: before selection of a career, before marriage, before the arrival of a first child, before retirement and the onset of old marriage, and other normal, critical life adjustments. The rabbi as teacher and counselor for normal and productive living could find a role that is missing in society and one which is eminently consistent with the highest aims of religion.[9]

Throughout most of Jewish history, the Jewish community has been a self-contained kehillah. We have taken care of our needs and have serviced our people. Today many see the synagogue only as a Bet Tefillah, a place for prayer. The synagogue must once again become the center of the Jewish community, a true Bet Knesset. The synagogue should be an all-purpose agency. The rabbi is the one and only individual who can organize and direct such a return to the primacy of the synagogue. This is not a turf battle, rather an attempt to meet the challenges and needs of our people, which are multidimensional. The rabbi must be the conduit from which activity and need funnel throughout the community. To do less abrogates our raison d'etre: to teach others how to realize the mitzvah of chesed and to provide with pastoral care, concern, and comfort. As rabbis we are called upon to be the shepherds of God's holy people and to view them as our flock.

NOTES

[1]Gerald Gurin, Joseph Veroff, and Sheila Feld, *Americans View Their Mental Health* (Report of the Joint Commission on Mental Illness and Health, vol. 4, 1960).

[2]Frederick Streets, "Clergy as Counselor: A Question of Identity and Effectiveness," *The Jewish Social Work Forum* (New York: Alumni Association of Wurzweiler School of Social Work 18, 1982), p. 26.

[3]Richard Mollica, "On the Technology of Pastoral Counseling," *Pastoral Psychology* 28 (1975), p. 108.

[4]Bachya ben Joseph Ibn Paquda, *Duties of the Heart*, vol. 1, trans. Moses Hyamson (Boys Town, Israel: Jerusalem Publishers, 1965), p. 195.

[5]Maimonides, Eight Chapters, in *Commentary to the Mishnah* in *A Maimonides Reader*, ed. I. Twersky (New York: Behrman House), pp. 379–386.

[6]M. Pumphrey, *The Teaching of Values and Ethics in Social Work Education* (New York: Council on Social Work Education, 1959), pp. 43–44.

[7]Charles Levy, "Jewish Communal Services: Health, Welfare, Recreational and Social," *The American Jew: A Reappraisal*, ed. Oscar I. Janowsky (Philadelphia: Jewish Publication Society, 1965), p. 275.

[8]William Rosenthal, "The Emergence of the Professional Self" (New York: Wurzweiler School of Social Work, Yeshiva University, 1979), p. 3.

[9]Richard N. Robertson et al., "The Parish Minister as Counselor: A Dilemma and Challenge," *Pastoral Psychology* (1969), p. 30.

8

The Rabbi as Guide—At the Chuppah and Graveside

Rabbi Haskel Lookstein

To many congregants, the most direct and memorable contact with the rabbi—or for that matter, with religious life—comes at moments that mark so-called "rites of passage" from the cradle to the grave. At such times, the rabbi bears special responsibilities and roles that can serve to extend genuine caring, and also can reach and touch people in profound and lasting ways. Two such moments occur under the chuppah and at the graveside. Rabbi Haskel Lookstein provides valuable insights and suggestions that serve to heighten the effectiveness of the rabbi's role. In these situations, the rabbi's style and personality will effect how he handles them. Rabbi Lookstein's style is readily seen as more formal and structured.

PREPARING FOR THE WEDDING

In preparation for a wedding, the rabbi should have a premarital interview of at least an hour to an hour and a half with each couple at whose wedding he officiates. During the premarital interview, the rabbi ought to discuss the marriage registry form, become acquainted with the couple, review the details of the wedding, discuss the couple's religious life, and review the prenuptial agreement.

Filling Out the Rabbinical Council of America Form

The marriage registration form of the Rabbinical Council of America (RCA) (see Appendix 2) ought to be filled out and sent in to the RCA with a copy provided to the couple themselves after the wedding. This will provide a central registry for all marriages which Orthodox rabbis conduct. This information may be useful to the couple in the future. In addition, the rabbi should keep a file of all weddings which he conducts, including the RCA form and any necessary documents connected with it, a photocopy of the marriage license, and a copy of a prenuptial agreement if one is executed. That should be filed in the congregational files by the name of the groom or by the date of the wedding (if possible, file them in both ways).

The RCA form is also useful at the premarital conference for a number of other reasons: It provides information which is important for the rabbi and the couple; it enables the couple to record the Hebrew names of their family so that they will have them for the future; and it elicits background information about the couple and their families—where they were born, where their parents come from, etc. In addition, the RCA form requires the critical information which must be available in order to conduct the ceremony. For example, it asks the question, "Are both parents Jewish by birth?" This kind of question is absolutely essential and may necessitate more meetings with the couple. A final advantage to discussing the registry form at the premarital interview is that it is a good opening for the rabbi as he begins to discuss the wedding with the couple. It is an easy way to start to get to know them.

Getting to Know the Bride and Groom

It is important for the rabbi to know both partners to the wedding as well as he can, so that he can speak personally to them under the chuppah and guide them as best as possible in their preparations for the wedding and for marriage. One should elicit from the couple information on family background. Are parents and grandparents living? Where do they come from? What activities are they engaged in? What education has the couple received? What professional or business activities are the bride and groom involved in? What is the religious background of the bride and groom?

When talking about this kind of information, the rabbi might throw a question at the couple such as: "What do you want to do with your lives?" That kind of open-ended question may startle a couple about to be married, but it is one they ought to be considering and it may provoke discussion of vital subjects.

Discussing the Wedding Details

The wedding should then be reviewed in detail, covering the areas discussed below.

Location, date, and time. It is very important for the rabbi to write down in his diary, as well as to keep careful notes on paper, the specifics about the location, date, and time of the wedding—the time of the invitation *and the time of the chuppah*. There is nothing more embarrassing or disturbing for the rabbi and for the couple and their families than for the rabbi to go to the wrong place for the wedding, or to show up late. A careful record will help to avoid this. In general, careful notes should be taken on all the items in the premarital interview.

Tena'im. Determine whether the couple wants to have *tena'im* signed before the wedding or not (and make a note to bring *tena'im* if they will be needed).

The veiling. Determine whether the veiling of the bride will be done in public or in private (not everybody wants a public veiling).

Officiants. Determine the number and identity of officiants. It is important to have a good idea of who else will be officiating. Will there be other rabbis and what will their role be? Will there be cantors and what will their role be? Will members of the family divide the berakhot? All this information should be recorded so that it can be reviewed on the day of the wedding and the rabbi will have this knowledge at his fingertips.

The role of the chatan. Does the chatan want to say *"Hurrei at"* with help or without help? Must it be translated or not? Does the bride want to say something? These days even in very Orthodox weddings some women want to say something at a wedding. I usually suggest that they say "thank you," or "I accept."

The bride's walk. Will the bride walk around the groom seven times or three times or no times? Do not assume that it is going to be done the way it was done at your wedding.

Double-ring ceremony. Sometimes the couple will request a so-called double-ring ceremony. One ought to be sensitive to such requests without necessarily encouraging them. Most probably there will be more of this in the future rather than less. It is our job to find a way to do this without in any way doing violence to the fundamental laws of kiddushin. That is why any such ceremony should be entirely separate from the giving of the ring by the groom to the bride. One of the ways to do it is to have the kallah give the chatan the ring in the *yichud* room. Another way would be to wait until after the reading of the ketubah or even the chanting of the seven blessings and then for the kallah to give the chatan a ring and either say nothing or say something like: "*Ani le'dodi ve'dodi li*" with or without translation.

The ketubah. The rabbi ought to inquire as to whether the couple will have a ketubah handwritten or would like him to bring a ketubah to the ceremony. If they want one handwritten I would suggest that the rabbi fill out a form for the calligrapher to follow, simply leaving out all or part of the word *ve-kanina*. (See Appendix 2 for a copy of the RCA ketubah for a woman who has never before been married. This is a good form to follow.)

If there is a need for a special ketubah for either a divorcee, a widow, or a convert, the RCA has another form for that. It is advisable for every rabbi to have a copy of *Kitzur Nachalat Shivah*, which is an excellent source for the necessary forms and which also has a section on the spelling of names for both men and women, an indispensable tool when filling out a ketubah.

Discussing Religious Life

Choosing a community. Talk about where the couple is going to live and that they should determine where they are going to live based upon what kind of religious institutions are there to help them in their family life. They should, if possible, visit a community before deciding to live there and making an investment in housing. They must consider the shul to which they will go and the school to which they will send their children.

Kashrut. In some cases one ought to talk about kashrut, including caveats about the choice of butcher and the kashering of meat. For example, many young brides do not know that with some kosher butchers they have to specify that they want their meat kashered. It is not automatically done by some butchers, even very reputable and highly kosher butchers. Such a caveat, therefore, should be mentioned in the premarital interview if the atmosphere seems correct.

Shabbat. Discuss Shabbat with the couple, how to make their home an open home on Shabbat, why Shabbat enhances their family life (if they need encouragement in the observance of Shabbat), etc. The degree to which one will discuss something like Shabbat will depend of course upon the nature of the couple to be married.

Taharat ha-Mishpachah. It may be that the couple needs absolutely no instruction in this matter, or it may be that any mentioning of the matter may prove counterproductive. A rabbi has to use his best judgment as to how much to say and how to say it. If information is desired by both the chatan and the kallah, or by either, I would strongly recommend Rabbi Moshe Tendler's *Pardes Rimonim* (New York: Judaica Press, 1979) as an excellent guide. If a couple wants more instruction, there are of course classes that are given for this. The rabbi might offer to give such instruction himself, depending upon his relationship with the bride and groom.

Discussing a Prenuptial Agreement

Finally, I strongly urge the rabbi to recommend to the couple that prior to the wedding they sign a prenuptial agreement that will provide that in the event of the civil dissolution of this marriage, God forbid, each agrees to cooperate in the giving and receiving of a get. Such a prenuptial agreement is a necessity in our day and, in my opinion, an obligation upon every rabbi to suggest to each couple. If every Orthodox rabbi were to do this we could wipe out in one action the entire problem of *agunot*, at least as far as weddings conducted by Orthodox rabbis are concerned.

It is not difficult to explain this to a couple. One simply says that this is a standard form which the rabbi requests that each couple sign in order to eliminate this problem in the Jewish world. He can say with confidence that such an agreement is being executed these days by hundreds of other couples and that if it were to be standard we could solve an extremely pressing religious problem. It is an act of love and respect on the part of the chatan and the kallah to agree to sign this for the protection of each other. My own daughter was the first one to sign such an agreement in my experience in the rabbinate and I have no difficulty in presenting this suggestion to any couple. We discuss much more touchy subjects than this one during the course of premarital interviews and other counseling sessions.

Several versions of such a prenuptial agreement, one of which I use, are presented in Appendix 3. Before I started using it seven years ago I brought it to the highest halakhic authority that any of us modern Orthodox rabbis can go to and his response was unequivocal. He said, "Some people will say that a get issued because of such an agreement is a *get me'useh* [a get given under duress]; but the woman will be divorced and that's the important thing. You may use it." That was enough for me and I think it should be enough for other rabbis to act responsibly in this most critical matter.

Closing the Discussion

One ought to ask the couple if they have any questions about the ceremony or anything else that was discussed. One ought to encourage them to be open and frank about those questions. Depending upon the rabbi's inclination, he might offer them a suggestion or two about how to care for each other in developing a happy married life. The rabbi should also offer to be available to them at any time between this interview and the wedding for further questions or discussion and, of course, to be available to them after the wedding if any further questions or issues arise.

THE MARRIAGE CEREMONY

I would suggest the following organization of a marriage ceremony, and have included some of the things I usually say at a wedding. These are, for the most part, formulae which I learned from my father, Rabbi Joseph H. Lookstein, of blessed memory.

Mi adir. After the singing by the cantor or somebody else, when the chatan and the kallah are standing before you, it might be appropriate for you to say the *mi adir* once again in Hebrew and, at the very least, to translate it into English in the following way: "Eternal God, thou who art mighty over all; thou who art exalted above all; thou who art supreme beyond all; do thou bless the bride and the groom."

The wedding address. At that point one should give a brief wedding address. The content of that address might be structured as follows: a brief word of Torah, based upon the Portion of the Week, the time of the year, or some other subject appropriate for this particular chatan and kallah. Stay away from canned wedding talks. This should be followed by applying the dvar Torah to the couple themselves. One ought to address the chatan and the kallah personally and talk about *them* rather than dwell too much on the specifics in the lives of their parents. It is very important to balance the talk between the chatan and the kallah and their respective families. Try to avoid saying such things as "I really do not know the bride's family very well but I know the groom's family very well" and then go into a long discussion of the outstanding qualities of the groom's family. The goal should be personal words, direct and to the point, and balanced.

The first cup of wine. The first cup of wine is raised and the two *birkhot erusin* are recited. If you would like to do this, you might say to the chatan that you are saying these berakhot for him and that he is fulfilling his obligation through you. Following the berakhot you (or the mothers) give a drink to the chatan and to the kallah.

Witnesses. At that point you ask for the witnesses and for his ring. You tell him that these two witnesses will be the exclusive witnesses for this part of the ceremony. Then you ask the kallah to stretch out her right index finger, while the chatan, before placing the ring on her finger, says to the kallah: *hurrei at.* . . . (Help him with the words if necessary and help him with the translation if necessary. Do not be afraid to say *"li."* She doesn't think that you are *"li."* She does not think that you are marrying her. If she does, she may not be of sufficiently sound mind to participate in this kinyan.)

The ketubah. Read the ketubah in its entirety. Learn how to read the ketubah correctly. There is nothing more embarrassing than to hear a rabbi read the ketubah with mistakes. It should be read clearly, with feeling and with precision. After you have finished reading the ketubah, you might say something like this:

> This ketubah is the Jewish document of marriage. In it are set forth explicitly (in the case of the chatan) and implicitly (in the case of the kallah) your mutual obligations to love, honor, cherish, and care for each other as it befits a Jewish husband and wife. A similar document was read at the weddings of your parents and theirs, going back two thousand years. In accordance with a tradition that is as old as this ketubah, the ketubah is

placed by the chatan in the hands of the kallah to be retained by her for as long as God grants you life. And may He grant you both a very long and a very happy life together.

You then give it to the chatan and tell him to give it to the kallah. (You can then tell the kallah to give it to her mother or one of the attendants to hold for her.)

The seven blessings. The seven blessings are recited over the second cup of wine. Make sure that, if the blessings are divided among a group of people, the first two berakhot are recited by one person. After the completion of the seven blessings give the cup first to the groom for a drink and then to the bride for a drink.

The benediction. Following all of this you might say to the couple:

> And now, by virtue of the authority vested in me as a rabbi in Israel and because of the formula of marriage which you as chatan pronounced while placing your ring on the kallah's finger in the presence of accredited witnesses, I now pronounce you husband and wife in accordance with the Law of Moses and Israel and in keeping with the statutes of the State of _____ . I send you forth on the happiest journey of your lives by pronouncing over you both the ancient priestly benediction.

The *birkat kohanim* should then be recited without, of course, raising one's hands and by introducing before it the words *bakhem yekuyam ha-katuv*. It can then be recited in Hebrew and translated into English. (All of this is optional, of course. My father, of blessed memory, used to do it and I continue. Other rabbis have other biblical blessings which they use. This is simply my way, presented for your own information.)

The breaking of the glass. Before the breaking of the glass you might say something as follows:

> This is the happiest moment in your lives. And it is precisely at this happiest of moments that Jewish tradition requires us to remember the destruction of the Temple in Jerusalem almost two thousand years ago. Although the State of Israel has been restored to us, our Temple and much of Jerusalem still lies in ruins. To symbolize this continuing deficiency in our national character, we complete the wedding by breaking this glass.

Then make sure that a covered glass is put under the chatan's right foot and get out of the way.

Yichud. The rabbi should make sure that immediately after the recessional the chatan and kallah go into a room together which has only one door, outside of which two witnesses should stand and make sure that the couple is alone for a period of at least eight minutes.

SERVING A FAMILY AT A TIME OF MOURNING

When a death occurs in a community which the rabbi serves, it is the rabbi's responsibility to go to wherever that death occurred and help the family immediately. In addition to arranging for the removal of the remains in a proper fashion, the rabbi should sit with the family, commiserate as best he can, and together plan the funeral.

Making the arrangements. Arrange for the time and place of the funeral. Discuss with them where shivah will be held and plan a minyan, morning and evening, if possible and if necessary. Plan in advance for people to come to the minyan and to help with the *seudat havra'ah* and the other meals during the week. There is an opportunity here to involve many people from the congregation in these acts of chesed.

Talking with the family about the deceased. Ask a lot of questions. Write down as much as you can on a pad, indicating to the family that you want to use their information in preparing your eulogy. Do not be embarrassed about using paper and pen for this. You are arranging to comfort the family and honor the deceased. Your seriousness will be greatly appreciated. The important thing is the immediacy of your response. Congregants will remember or forget sermons and lectures. They will never forget the service that you render to them at a time like this and they will also never forget if you do not render the service at a time like this. So be very careful to do everything you possibly can to help a family at the time of their bereavement.

At the chapel (or synagogue). Noted below is the order of a service that I follow for a funeral:

1. The rending of a garment (this can also be done at the cemetery).
2. Procession of the family, followed by the rabbi, into the chapel or synagogue.

3. Reading a chapter from Psalms (in Hebrew and in English). Some of the best chapters are Psalm 23, Psalm 15, Psalm 121, *Tefillah le'Moshe*, and, of course, *Eishet Hayil* (which should be used only when it is truly appropriate). If a psalm or a passage is long, it is not necessary to read the entire passage. Read selections.

The eulogy. The eulogy ought to be composed of a dvar Torah related to the Portion of the Week, the time of the year, or in some very direct way connected with the life of the deceased (avoid canned eulogies or divrei Torah. The congregation has probably heard them already and they are rarely as effective as your own creative work). The dvar Torah ought to be short and uncomplicated. It ought to lead naturally into an analysis of the life of the deceased, preferably in three parts. One of those parts should be a discussion of the deceased as a family member. Remember that whatever else the deceased did, he or she was first and foremost a child of parents, a spouse (if applicable), a father or mother (if applicable), and a sister or brother (if applicable). Then one may take two other aspects of the person's life such as: piety, communal leadership, acts of chesed, generosity, scholarship in Torah, etc.

Following the eulogy the rabbi should recite (or the cantor should sing) a *kel malei rachamim*. Following that, the rabbi ought to announce where shivah will be held, when it will end, and the times of services. He then follows the coffin in the recessional, reciting *yoshev be'seter, aloud,* clearly, grammatically and—preferably—by heart. One ought not to be chained to a prayer book at such a time.

At the cemetery. The following procedures should be observed at the cemetery.

1. Remove the coffin from the hearse onto a carrier, or onto the shoulders of the pall-bearers.

2. During the processional, recite *yoshev be'seter* seven times if the distance will allow it, or stop every couple of sentences if the distance from the hearse to the grave is short.

3. Observe the seven stops (except on a day when *Tachanun* is not said).

4. Lowering the coffin into the grave. It may be advisable for this to be done by the professional gravediggers themselves, except in cases where the family is insistent that it be done by people who are

attending the funeral. The professionals know what they are doing. Well-meaning people do not. If an accident occurs and the coffin is dropped it is a terrible *chillul ha-met*. One has to use discretion in this regard.

5. Filling in the grave. Let the mourners fill in the first few shovels and then say: "All those who would like to deposit some earth in the grave are invited to do so. Besides being a mitzvah, it is the greatest act of kindness that we can do for a person and the last act of kindness that we can do for _____."

6. Perform the berakhah at the cemetery if one has not been on the cemetery for thirty days.

7. After the grave has been completely filled in (or if weather conditions are extremely severe, then at least after most of the grave has been filled in), recite out loud, clearly, and with feeling, the *tzidduk ha-din*.

8. Recite *Mikhtam le'David* (or some other psalm).

9. Ask the mourner(s) to recite (and if necessary recite it with them) the special kaddish (or a regular kaddish if it is a day on which *Tachanun* is not said. On such a day, of course, *tzidduk ha-din* is also omitted and a simple psalm, like Psalm 121, is recited, followed by a regular kaddish. Where there are no *yetomim*, the regular mourner's kaddish should be recited).

10. Chant or recite a *Kel Malei*.

11. Then face the mourners and the assemblage and say the *bila ha-mavet* (continue with the rest in Hebrew) and then say:

> May death vanish into life eternal and may the Lord, God, wipe away the tears from all faces and bring relief and strength to all who mourn and sorrow. May He grant that the gatherings of this family and those of all its friends and loved ones be held henceforth for a long time to come only in health, happiness and peace. Amen.

12. Arrange a *shurah* by saying: "Will all of those present, except for the immediate mourners, please form two parallel lines, leading away from the grave, so that the mourners can pass through and we can address them properly."

At the home. If at all possible, the rabbi should return to the home with the family and make sure that everything is set up properly.

He should encourage women from the congregation to help arrange for the first meal and also for the washing of the hands outside the door of the house. He will want to check to make sure that the necessary siddurim and other items for the daily minyanim are present and, if not, he will make sure that they are brought over immediately. He can spend some time with the family and then go about his business.

The rabbi ought to try to be at as many minyanim as possible during the course of the week. It is advisable to learn a mishnah at the end of each service, or between Minchah and Ma'ariv, arranging to spell out the letters of the name of the deceased. When learning the mishnah one ought to try in some way to apply the mishnah to the deceased or to the family which is mourning, or to the general subject of mourning. The extent to which a rabbi will give attention and thought to the family during shivah will determine many things: how well they recover from this loss; how good they feel about their association with Judaism; how close they feel to the rabbi personally and to the congregation generally. It is important that the rabbi take a leading role in bringing people to the minyan. Don't leave it to chance. Have a sign-in sheet available at the house of mourning so that at the first service you can plan out who will come for the other minyanim. The more attention you give to this the more it will be appreciated and the more help you will be giving to a family that needs it particularly at this time in their lives.

9

The Rabbi as Preacher and Public Speaker

Rabbi Abner Weiss

There are few areas in which the rabbi can communicate as directly and with as many of his congregants as when he speaks publicly from the pulpit, week after week. When properly prepared and effectively delivered, the sermon can make the key difference between images of a rabbi that are either dynamic or lethargic, creative or commonplace, insightful or platitudinous. Effective public speaking is a key to the public perception of the rabbi. Rabbi Abner Weiss summarizes some of the essential skills that he has honed, sefarim he has utilized, and methodologies that are particularly helpful.

EFFECTIVE PUBLIC SPEAKING

The classical definition of man, *the* social being par excellence, was *chai medabber*—a living being capable of speech. Our most important social skill is communication. Communication is not only vital in establishing *any* kind of interpersonal contact, but is also essential in persuading others about the validity of our special point of view. Accordingly, successful communication is a primary tool of the salesman, the teacher, and the politician. It goes without saying that the effectiveness of the contemporary rabbi as leader, teacher, and spokesman is largely a function of his skills as a public speaker.

More often than not, effective public speaking is a learned skill.

If one wishes to develop these skills, one should keep a number of important factors in mind.

The Written and the Spoken Word

There is a profound difference between the written and the spoken word. The reader of a lengthy piece of writing may lose the trend of thought of the writer. Should this happen, he simply goes back over what he has missed, and nothing is lost. If a listener loses the train of thought of the speaker, on the other hand, he cannot go back, and is likely to "switch off." An effective speaker should constantly be aware of this problem and structure his address accordingly. When a reader is confronted by a particularly difficult passage or a subtle argument, he simply pauses, analyzes the problem, contemplates the possible meaning, and, when the difficulty is cleared up, proceeds with his reading. In the same situation, a listener cannot take a contemplation break. If he does so, he will miss what comes next. An effective public speaker will not overlook this problem. A tired or bored reader can put the book or article aside and take it up again later, when his mood or condition changes. The bored listener will simply let his mind wander elsewhere. Speakers who are not actively aware of differences such as these between the spoken and written word greatly impair their effectiveness as public communicators.

Simplicity of Content

The primary component of effective public speaking is *what* one says. An effective speaker will respect his audience and never speak without preparation. Bearing in mind the differences between written and oral communication, he will take great pains to keep his presentation clear. He will keep the content of his address as simple as possible, never confusing simplicity with vulgarity and simple-mindedness. The most profound thinkers are capable of presenting their thoughts simply and directly. An effective public speaker will know exactly what his message is, and will prepare to communicate it with clarity and simplicity.

Structure

Clarity of presentation is a direct function of structure. First and foremost, there must be a rational progression of ideas from the introduction through the development of the theme and its application, to the conclusion of the address. The logical flow of ideas must be rigorous. Because the listener cannot go over a missed point, the speaker must consciously make explicitly smooth transitions between the various stages of the presentation. These transitions are the keys to a comprehensible and effective address.

No tangential discussions should be introduced. It will only distract the listener, interrupt the flow, and obscure the main theme. Inexperienced speakers are too often guilty of introducing extraneous detail, unable to resist the temptation of showing off their knowledge, and thus hanging ideas together by loose association rather than by tightly structured logic.

Style

Second only to *what* one says is *how* one says it. Style is only a little less important than structure.

Style has two components: expression and delivery. To be effective, a message should be expressed elegantly. The *language* of communication should be accurate and rich. Syntax should be correct, words and phrases carefully chosen, and sentences skillfully crafted. Adjectives enrich images. Similes, metaphors, and other figures of speech enhance the understanding of ideas. Speakers who debase their language of communication impair their effectiveness. There is nothing cute about the use, for example, of "yinglish" in a rabbinic address. It may be "yeshivish," but will cost the speaker the respect of his educated listeners.

Great speakers take advantage of the mesmerizing effects of powerful oratorical devices. Of these, one of the most striking is the repetition of a phrase or a recurring refrain and motif. Martin Luther King's "I Have a Dream" and "Let Freedom Ring" are among the best-known examples of this technique. In a sermon, a phrase from a biblical or rabbinic text serves the same oratorical purpose. Alliteration, too, is a riveting oratorical device.

Elegant language and striking oratorical devices make up the *written* components of the spoken words. They are central concerns during the writing and preparation of the address. But, in the actual spoken presentation, style has entirely different connotations. The success of the spoken word is largely a function of the speaker's style or delivery.

The entire focus of the listener should be upon the speaker. To maintain this focus, the presentation should not become monotonous and boring. Since the purpose of the address is communication, every mode of communication should be employed. The *voice* is of primary importance. One's tone should vary. One's voice can be raised and lowered. A whisper at the appropriate time can command more attention than a shout. Even a sing-song tone can sometimes be effective.

But the voice alone is insufficient. Meaningful hand gestures enhance communication, as do facial expression and other body language. Indeed, in effective public speaking, *kol atzmotai tomarna* — the entire person becomes a medium for communication — providing always that gestures are appropriate and not exaggerated. Inappropriate and exaggerated gestures distract rather than enhance communication. As in most cases, less is more in this regard also.

Clearly, an effective address is far more than a mere vocalization of a written passage. An effective speaker *speaks* to his audience. He does not simply *read* aloud a written text in their presence. An unanimated reading of a prepared text is a sure turn-off. Very few readers have the gift of holding an audience's attention. With training and practice — and hard work — a speaker can do precisely that.

THE SERMON

The rabbi will be called upon to deliver different types of public address — sermons, sermonettes, lectures, speeches, and shiurim. The techniques of preparation and delivery vary in each case, and are conditioned by their purpose.

The Modern Pulpit

The modern pulpit offers enormous opportunities. In many cases the rabbi speaks to more people during synagogue services than at the best publicized lectures and classes. He should utilize these communication opportunities by making the weekly sermon a centerpiece of the services. He should not abuse his captive audience; his members legitimately resent being put upon, shouted at, spoken down to, and addressed interminably. A great preacher of the last generation, Rabbi Joseph B. Lookstein, once proclaimed that if one has drilled for fifteen minutes without striking oil, one should stop boring. The late Chief Rabbi of South Africa, Louis I. Rabinowitz—a master preacher—never preached more than twenty minutes. Ultimately, the congregants will vote with their feet.

A rabbi must respect his audience and be sure to include something for everyone in his address. It should enlighten and entertain. It should impart a Torah teaching and touch upon an important topic. To be authentically Jewish, a sermon should expound upon a scriptural passage and draw upon rabbinic literature. If it provokes positive comment and stimulates conversation at the Shabbat table, it has usually succeeded.

The KIS Rule

Jewish preaching is a form of teaching. But preaching is not *pure* teaching. It is *applied* teaching. Its purpose is to communicate a relevant message which is based upon the text to which we have referred. Its structure is determined by the need to communicate that message most effectively. Ultimately it is judged by a single criterion: was the message clearly conveyed?

Rabbi Louis I. Rabinowitz was fond of reminding his students that a successful sermon has a single message. Once, in criticizing a local preacher's presentation, he told him pointedly that he had given three sermons in a single address. In this regard there is a simple rule of thumb for a successful sermon. If, upon its conclusion, most members of the congregation can correctly guess its unadvertised title, it has succeeded in making its point clearly. It has also complied with the foremost rule of public speaking—KIS: Keep It Simple.

Types of Sermons

The type of sermon the rabbi delivers is a function of its particular message. Although there are numerous types of sermon, most fall into one of five categories.

Guidance on Contemporary Events

The primary purpose of this type of sermon is to apply the world view of the Torah to such contemporary problems as attacks on the

State of Israel, the harvesting of human body parts for later transplantation, economic corruption, mixed marriage, and so on. This type of sermon offers the opportunity of communicating an authentically Jewish position on a burning issue. Its purpose may be to persuade the congregation, to convince one's members, or merely to articulate the unarticulated views of the members. The dangers to be avoided in this type of sermon are the mere regurgitation of news items (for which congregants do not require a rabbi), the repetition of editorial comment (for which a reputable paper is quite adequate), and specialized pontification and theorizing (for which most rabbis, untrained in political science, are totally inadequate). The unique perspective of the authentic Jewish sermon is the application of scriptural and rabbinic insights to the situation under review—as we shall demonstrate in a sermon outline below.

Remonstration

The primary purpose of this type of sermon is the castigation of the community for a perceived lapse either in religious observance or moral attitude—such as proliferation of mixed dating in the community, increasing patronizing of non-kosher restaurants by the purportedly observant, neglect of the laws of family purity, disrespect for the elders by children of the community, insensitivity to the evils of gossip, and so on. The purpose of the contemporary mussar sermon is to modify attitudes and behavior, to move the listeners, and to touch them. This purpose will be frustrated if the criticism is unduly harsh, the expectations of the preacher totally unrealistic, and if the speaker appears to exclude himself arrogantly from the castigation. Also, too many preachers address those who are not present to hear their remonstrations.

Fundraising

The purpose of this mode of address is self-evident. Its effectiveness depends on the creation of a sense of need and the establishment of a mood of participation and involvement. Its medium is passion rather than pensiveness, emotion rather than cogitation. Its purpose will have been realized to the extent that the listeners will be persuaded that participation is a privilege as well as a challenge, an opportunity as well as a burden. The limited announcement of contributions is a good technique, provided always that it does not embarrass any listener. The rabbi need not be apologetic about motivating his members to respond to the moral imperative of charity.

Inspiration

This type of sermon is woefully neglected by contemporary speakers. It responds to the perennial personal needs of members of the congregation, recognizing their fears, vulnerabilities, hopes, dreams, and aspirations. It offers hope, courage, support, understanding, and sympathy. It touches more souls than do the other types of address because it discloses and reacts to the essential humanness of the listeners. And it shows how the Torah remains our guide, and God our protector in all of life's crises.

Instructional

A sermon need not always relate to something outside of the text. It can be announced as a lesson from the weekly Torah portion, and used as a mini-lecture on a text. The rabbi will not always find an uplifting message to deliver or an urgent problem to which to relate. The imparting of a Jewish value based upon the Torah reading is always valid and welcome.

The Sermon Structure

The common elements of the Jewish sermon are the introduction, the text, the commentary on that text, the application of the text to the situation which the rabbi has chosen to address, illustration of the point, and the conclusion.

There are two basic structural models. One introduces the subject under discussion at once. It may be a news item on which the rabbi wishes to comment or a problem to which he wishes to relate. By coming to the point at once, he grabs the attention of the audience.

When he has elaborated his subject, he relates it to the weekly Torah reading, whose interpretation, in turn, throws light upon the subject and constitutes the message of the sermon.

The *classic* structural model introduces the text, develops that text, applies it to the sermon's purpose, illustrates the emergent message with examples and/or stories, and ends with the concluding comment.

Elements of the Sermon Outline

The introduction. The importance of the introduction lies in its role as attention-getter. As such, it should be carefully crafted. If the sermon is of the first type, the introduction should come to the point at once. In the second type of sermon, the introduction relates to the text itself—rather than to the problem to be discussed—the background, context, and so on. If this is the preferred structure, it is sometimes wise to omit the outlining of the introduction until the rest of the outline has been completed.

The text. The verse should be read carefully and translated. A problem should be raised in the text which requires rabbinic elucidation.

The development. The Midrash or classical commentary that serves as the elucidation of the text should be read, translated, and analyzed. Lengthy midrashim should not be read in their entire Hebrew original. A phrase may be selected by the preacher as the potential oratorical refrain.

The application of text. The lesson of the rabbinic text or commentary should be spelled out. It should then be applied to the situation which the rabbi is discussing. (Three-part midrashim offer great opportunities for application of text.)

The illustrations. The lesson at hand should be illustrated with appropriate examples from life or with a good story. A powerful story will be remembered, and has universal impact.

The conclusion. The concluding comment usually conveys the message in succinct and uplifting form. Experienced speakers transform the conclusion into a peroration. All their rhetorical experience will go into the delivery of this peroration, for it is with this that the congregation is ultimately left.

Sermon Outline Model

Title: Finding Fault from Afar—Parshat Shemini (*Leviticus* 11:13–14)

Introduction. One of the topics of the Torah reading is a listing of birds that are not kosher. These forbidden birds are listed in Leviticus 11:13–14. Provide full text in Hebrew and English and place this text in a box as follows:

> *ve'et elu teshaktzu min ha-of; lo yay-akhlu sheketz hem. Et ha-nesher . . . ve'et ha-da'ah ve'et ha-ayah leminah.*

Development of Text. Interestingly, this list is more or less reproduced elsewhere in the Torah—but with a strange variation (Deuteronomy 14:12).

> *ha-ra'ah ve'et ha-ayah ve'ha-dayah leminah*

Problem: Why is the *da'ah* of Leviticus called a *ra'ah* in Deuteronomy? The Talmud addresses itself to this problem (*Chullin* 63b).

> *De'amar R. Abahu: Ra'ah zu da'ah. ve'Lamah nikra shmah ra'ah? She-roah be'yoter. ve'Khen hu omer.*

Application of text. Rabbi Avahu's insight is striking on a metaphorical level. The *ra'ah* bird is by no means an endangered species. There is no shortage of *neveilah* in Bavel = Iraq. Seven years of bitter war—huge casualty figures. Corruption/dictatorship/persecution of the Kurds/disabling of non-military shipping, yet overlook their own *neveilah*.

> *Omedet be'Bavel ve'roah neveilah be'Eretz Yisrael.*

Describe what they say about Israel: Arab criticism of human rights violations in Israel while no non-Muslim can vote in Saudi Arabia.

Refrain . . . *omedet* . . .

U.S. castigation of Israel's treatment of PLO rioters as contrasted to the reaction to events in China, Vietnam, El Salvador, Cuba, Panama. Those were not unjustified, but where Israel is concerned, there is nothing but condemnation.

Refrain . . . *omedet.* . . .

In Russia they arrest an Ida Nudel for hanging a poster from her windows, and exile her from her home. Only in Israel is expulsion of terrorists abhorrent.

Refrain . . . *omedet* . . .

Conclusion. Why is the double standard applied to Israel alone? Why is it that?

Refrain . . . *omedet.* . . .

Our sages tell us that Shinar and Bavel are identical. So why is Bavel called Shinar? Because (*Berachot* 4:1).

Ha-amdu soneh ve'ar lashem

Why the double standard? Because of *soneh ve'ar* the enmity and hatred of those who stand in Bavel and see the ugliness of Israel.

Refrain . . . *omedet.* . . .

We cannot reverse the enmity and hatred of our enemies, but at least *we* should not swallow their lies and imitate their false perceptions; at least *we* should not be of those who (refrain). At least *we* should not have unreasonable expectations of Israel. At least *we* should not be embarrassed and apologetic. If *they* see the *neveilah* of Eretz Yisrael, let us see its beauty and salute its achievements—*u-re'eh betuv Yerushalayim.*

Let us see it personally—by visiting Israel. Let us contribute to it personally by giving to Israel. Let us not surrender to the views of fault finders from afar.

Same Theme: Alternative Structure

Introduction

- Daily barrage of TV pictures of Israeli cruelty to Arabs in "occupied territories."
- Response of English Minister of State.
- Universal criticism—even by U.S., Israel's only friend.
- Embarrassment of Jewish community in U.S.
- Self-hating response of some Jews and many Jewish leaders.
- What is *our* response to be?

Text. Remarkably, this situation is not new. It is presaged in an unlikely rabbinic comment upon a most unlikely text in this week's Torah reading. Text in question is a list of forbidden birds—assumed not kosher. Continue as in previous model outline.

Resources for Sermon Preparation

The Parshah with classical commentaries. The most important resource for the weekly sermon is the weekly Torah reading—and the most important source of material is the standard *Mikraot Gedolot.* The preacher is advised to read the daily parshah each day with Rashi and one other commentary. Every year he should select a different commentary. He should jot down homiletic ideas on a card system, attempting to envision sermons immanent in the commentaries. This practice will help to develop the "homiletical eye."

The Parshah with Talmud and Midrash. The anthology of rabbinic sources provided by the *Torah Temimah* is an invaluable source. The notes will explain the peshat. The inventive preacher can suggest another, deeper homiletic meaning of the same dictum, thus giving both a lesson in Torah and applying it sermonically. The *Torah Shelemah* is an invaluable source for midrash and aggadah. *Sefer ha-Aggadah* by Bialik and Ravnitzky is a rich resource. The *Midrash Rabbah* itself should not be overlooked. For quick reference, *The Midrash Says* (ed. Moshe Weissman) is a useful tool.

Anthologies. These are two kinds. The most useful provides sermon *ideas* rather than fully developed sermons. Of these, Benzion Zaks's *Menachem Zion* is easily the best available. Ya'akov Duschinsky's *Be'Ikvei Parashiyot* is also rich in material. *Ma'ayanah shel Torah* and *Itturei Torah* are very useful.

The second type represents anthologies of completed sermons. Best among these is Sidney Greenberg's High Holiday sermon anthology, *High Holy Day Bible Themes*. The sermon manual publications are usually of an uneven quality, but are useful as sources for ideas. Of these, the Rabbinical Council of America's Sermon Manual series and the *Best Sermon* series of Saul Teplitz are the best. The anthology published by the New York Board of Rabbis, *The Rabbis Speak* (ed. Saul Teplitz), is excellent.

Master preachers. A reading of the collected sermons of master preachers is a self-contained course in homiletics. Their styles are worthy of imitation. However, there is a danger that the developing preacher will become overly dependent upon the masters and not develop his own style. Indeed, Louis Rabinowitz forbade his students even to *read* his published sermons during their first two years in the pulpit. His *Out of the Depths*, *Sparks from the Anvil*, *Sabbath Light*, and *Light and Salvation* are outstanding examples of the genre. His notes to preachers remain as valid today as they were when they were printed. The published sermons of Avigdor Amiel, Israel Leventhal, Joseph Lookstein, Sidney Greenberg, Norman Lamm, and Joseph Herman Hertz are classics and should be acquired by every aspiring preacher.

Illustrative materials. Sidney Greenberg's *Treasury of the Art of Living* and *Treasury of Comfort* are rich resources, carefully indexed and easily retrievable. Morris Mandel's *Story Anthology for Speakers* and *A Complete Treasury of Stories for Public Speakers* are useful, as are Jacob Braude's *Treasury of Wit and Humor* and *Complete Speakers and Toastmasters Library*.

How to Actually Prepare a Sermon

The first step is to note down materials and ideas throughout the week. The great Louis I. Rabinowitz was actually never without a clipboard. No good idea slipped away.

By Thursday morning, at latest, the sermon should be *fully* outlined. The outline will probably be redone several times to assure the logical flow of ideas and clarity of transition between points. Key phrases will be [blocked in] for special attention. The sermon will be as good as the outline, *or as weak*.

When the outline is completed, the entire sermon should be written out or typed. This alone will assure its literary quality, elegance, and flow. It alone will allow for the inclusion of alliterative phrases, rich adjectives, choice words, resonant refrains, and other oratorical devices. It will also limit the length of the actual presentation, since it is easy to time a fully prepared text and to prune away the extraneous minutes. *Remember:* a sermon of ten minutes is not too short; a sermon of twenty-five minutes is too long.

It is most useful to *recite* the sermon in front of a mirror, to discover the most effective body language. A tape recorder with a built-in microphone should record the practice sessions. Speakers are often quite unaware of how they actually sound. The feedback from the tape is extremely valuable.

Recitation should be repeated until the sermon is learned by heart. This exercise should not be considered a drudge. It serves several purposes. It allows the preacher to speak rather than to read the sermon. It trains him to get his own material by heart increasingly quickly. It establishes a treasury of his own language in his personal memory bank. This, in turn, will allow him to "think on his feet" when he is obliged to speak extemporaneously in debates, discussions, and at meetings. It may be time consuming initially, but it is invaluable in terms of one's development as an effective, fluent, and articulate public speaker. Indeed, after two or three years of this process, it may be possible to omit writing out a full text. The outline will automatically trigger the memory bank of words and phrases.

When one has the sermon by heart, it should be filed away. One's outline is all one needs to take into the synagogue. In this way, one will be compelled to deliver a sermon rather than to read a paper.

One's recollection of one's materials, body gestures, and tonal intonations will enable one to speak with authority, fluency, and conviction.

OTHER RABBINIC MODES OF ADDRESS

The Sermonette

This form of rabbinic public address differs from the sermon primarily in one respect alone—time. A sermonette should never exceed five minutes. It is presented at *shalom zakhor, brit milah,* and *pidyon haben* celebrations, bar/bat mitzvah parties, engagement parties, weddings, marriage celebrations, eulogies, and so on. In these cases, the application of the developed text is to the occasion and to the celebrants. Apart from the weekly parshah, the halakhah or ritual that governs the occasion can be used as the peg upon which to hang the message.

The Lecture

Whereas a good sermon has only a single message, a good lecture is crowded with information. The abundance of information can lead both to a loss of flow and forgetfulness on the part of the listener. To avert these problems, the lecture outline should

1. Introduce the subject in general, indicating its importance/relevance.
2. In a second introductory passage, summarize what will be covered. This summary will form the main subdivisions of the outline. The subdivision and sub-subdivisions will flow logically from one another as in the sermon outline.
3. Explicitly note the completion of each subdivision and summarize the contents of the subdivision in a sentence or two (to compensate for lapsed attention).
4. Make explicit transition to the next major subdivision as per the second introductory paragraph.
5. Conclude with a summary of the entire presentation.
6. End with a general concluding comment or message.

Since a lecture is usually longer than a sermon, a good lecturer will use as many aids as possible to focus the attention of the audience—blackboard, slides, and so forth. In the last analysis, however, the lecturer himself is the central focal point, and must maintain this focus with all the communication devices described earlier in this chapter.

Speech

In a sense, a speech mediates between a sermon and lecture outline. Its purposes, generally, are to persuade, praise, or criticize. The latter type is usefully introduced with a joke, story, or wise dictum. This material is then applied to the individual about whom one is speaking.

If a speech is to persuade, its thesis should be stated clearly in the introduction. The outline of the speech will be a rigorous development of the argument in favor of the thesis (and, if applicable, in rebuttal of the antithesis). The flow between the sections, subsections, and sub-subsections must be logical and clear, with the transitions explicitly made. The conclusion should be a restatement of the thesis and a summary of the arguments proving that thesis, and, if applicable, rebutting the opposing view. The presentation should end with a peroration—an oratorically elegant and appealing statement explaining the advantages in accepting the stated thesis and in supporting the stated position. A good story which makes the point is a particularly useful tool for this stage of the presentation.

Again, it should be recalled that both speech and *speaker* persuade (or fail to persuade). Accordingly, the best prepared text will be an effective instrument only if it is delivered dynamically, and with all the oratorical devices referred to above—as well as (where appropriate) a dash of humor, sarcasm, irony, and so on.

Shiur

Sermons, lectures, and speeches are essentially *instructive*. The speaker literally communicates his ideas *to* the listener. A shiur, on the other hand, is essentially *educative*—the speaker draws the materials *from* the listeners. A shiur is a *participatory* experience. As such, the method of giving a shiur is dialogical, and its structure consists of a series of questions and sub-questions.

In planning the shiur, the material should be outlined in lecture form. When the instructor is satisfied with the flow and clarity of transitions, the outline points should be rewritten as questions. By sticking to this outline, the instructor will prevent the shiur from dissolving into endlessly distracting tangents.

Typically, a text shiur will begin by having someone read a text and by asking leading questions about the text. After the participants have made their suggestions, the instructor will direct them to another text, which relates to the questions. This text, in turn, will be introduced with a question: "How does this text deal with our problem?" and so on. Finally, after all the texts have been analyzed in this fashion, the instructor will summarize the shiur and, if appropriate, reach a conclusion.

The works of Nechamah Leibowitz are the illustrations par excellence of this method of presentation. She is without peer as a master teacher.

What has been presented above represents the result of almost thirty years' experience as a public speaker. It reflects the techniques of Louis I. Rabinowitz, whose voice still echoes in the mind of this writer every time he speaks, and other master orators and teachers. It is only the barest outline for a course in public speaking for rabbis, but is, hopefully, suggestive, and will be helpful despite its brevity. While some speakers are born, most are made—and *all* can benefit from training. There are no short cuts. Preparation is hard work. It is justified to the extent that, fairly or unfairly, a rabbi is judged by how he speaks, and is usually engaged on the same basis. More importantly, the rabbi's effectiveness as a public speaker is, in the final analysis, a visible measure of his leadership and the medium for his attainment of success as a teacher.

BIBLIOGRAPHY

Bailik, C. N., and Rawnitzsky, Y. H. (1956). *Sefer Ha-Aggadah*. Tel Aviv.

Braude, J., ed. (1964). *Treasury of Wit and Humor*. Englewood Cliffs, NJ: Prentice Hall.

_____ (1965). *Complete Speakers and Toastmasters Library*. Englewood Cliffs, NJ: Prentice Hall.

Duschinsky, Y. (1977). *Be'Ikvei Parashiyot*. Tel Aviv.

Freedman, H., and Simon, M., eds. (1961). *The Midrash*. London: Soncino Press.

Friedman, A. Z., ed. (1956). *Ma'ayanah Shel Torah*. Tel Aviv.

Greenberg, A. Y., ed. (1967). *Itturei Torah*. Tel Aviv.

Greenberg, S., ed. (1954). *Treasury of Comfort*. North Hollywood, CA: Wilshire Book Co.

––––––– (1967). *Treasury of the Art of Living*. North Hollywood, CA: Wilshire Book Co.

––––––– (1973). *High Holy Day Bible Themes*. North Hollywood CA: Wilshire Book Co.

Kasher, M. M., ed. (1949–1982). *Torah Shelemah*. Jerusalem: Koren Publishers.

Mandel, M., ed. (1972). *Story Anthology for Speakers*. New York: Jonathan David.

––––––– (1974). *A Complete Treasury of Stories for Public Speakers*. New York: Jonathan David.

Midrash Rabbah (1960). Jerusalem: Lewin-Epstein.

Rabinowitz, L. I. (1951). *Out of the Depths*. New York: Bloch.

––––––– (1955). *Sparks from the Anvil*. New York: Bloch.

––––––– (1958). *Sabbath Light*. Johannesburg, S.A.: Fieldhill.

––––––– (1965). *Light and Salvation*. New York: Bloch.

Teplitz, S., ed. (1986). *The Rabbis Speak*. New York: New York Board of Rabbis.

Weissman, M., ed. (1983). *The Midrash Says*. New York: Benei Yakov.

Zaks, B. (1976). *Menachem Zion*. Jerusalem: Makhon ha-Rav Frank.

10

The Rabbi as Leader of Prayer Services

Rabbi Charles D. Lipshitz

Tefillah represents a special challenge to the rabbi: while he davens with all his heart, he also has to officiate and lead, sensitive to the needs of the tzibbur, maintaining a delicate balance between spontaneity and decorum, listening to the shaliach tzibbur and involvement in tefillah itself. Leading tefillah properly cannot be achieved casually, and while each congregation is unique, certain common approaches have been found effective. Rabbi Charles Lipshitz carefully delineates a number of key considerations that he has utilized to good effect in a smaller congregational setting.

DESIGNING APPROPRIATE MODES OF TEFILLAH

It is essential for the Rav to evaluate the composition of his congregation, and to do so honestly, in order to determine the mode of tefillah best suited for the worshipers. Just as a derashah delivered in Yiddish would be out of place in a synagogue where most *mitpallelim* are Yiddish "illiterate," so too would English readings or constant page announcements be inappropriate in a minyan frequented primarily by yeshivah graduates.

Today, many congregations are comprised of a small core of Shomrei Shabbat worshipers, some with strong Judaic backgrounds, with a much larger group consisting of traditionally minded but less

observant and much less knowledgeable Jews. On the High Holy
Days, this group is further diluted by many whose entire annual
tefillah experience is limited to a few hours spread out over two or
three days.

Taking these factors into account, and adding to them the Rav's
personal preference, biases, background, and experience, the Rav
must attempt to instruct and assist his chazzan and/or *ba'alei tefillah*,
lay or professional, in developing a style of tefillah for Shabbat,
Chagim, Yamim Noraim, and weekdays that will involve and inspire
the *mitpallelim*. I am a firm believer in the value of participatory
tefillah. This is not, however, as simple as it might seem. Many
worshipers in many of today's Orthodox congregations have come
from non-Orthodox backgrounds. In many of their former congregations, participation was minimal and whatever participation there
was, usually consisted of English readings, in unison or responsively.
Even today in many non-Orthodox congregations, the worshipers are
primarily spectators, there to listen to the sermon, enjoy the performance of the cantor and choir, and for the most part to sit back and
enjoy the show. "Davening" doesn't really take place—certainly not as
we know it. It is therefore not as easy as it might seem to encourage
people to daven, to become involved in one's tefillah, and to sing out
loud. I have found that the more an individual becomes involved in
tefillah, the more often one tends to participate in other synagogue
activities and in other areas of Jewish life. To bring someone to this
point is, I believe, the greatest challenge for the Rav and his co-offi-
ciants in the area of tefillah. The more singing, the more ruach, the
more "leibidik" the davening is, the greater the chance is that even a
spectator will eventually be drawn in and become an active partici-
pant. As for those who are already daveners, a little more ruach will
not hurt. The source of this ruach cannot be left to anyone else—not
even the chazzan. It must emanate from the Rav.

PROJECTING RABBINIC PRESENCE THROUGHOUT
THE SERVICE

While many rabbis assume what can be best be described as a
passive role during tefillah (sitting in their place of honor and quietly
davening while the respective *ba'alei tefillah* perform their tasks) and

ascend the bimah only to address the congregation, I have always taken a much more active role in tefillah. In all areas, I feel that the Rav must be an activist and tefillah is no exception. It is very unusual to find me sitting in my chair. With the exception of *birkhot keriat shma*, when I do sit, and *keriat ha-Torah*, when I stand in observance of a personal minhag, I can almost always be found behind my lectern. The reason is simple. A rabbi's enthusiasm is contagious, not only when he speaks but also when he davens. *Hitlahavut* need not be restricted to a yeshivah minyan, nor to a hasidic shtible. *Hitlahavut* is quite appropriate in every synagogue, and it is the *hitlahavut* of the Rav, together with that of the other *klei kodesh* that sets the tone. The more enthusiastic singing that comes from the bimah, the more likely that even reticent worshipers will ultimately be moved to participate. Even when someone cannot read Hebrew, a melody can always be picked up and enjoyed. While the chazzan's choice of tunes does, of course, play a major role (it's so hard to join in with an operatic aria), so does the participation of the Rav, good voice or not.

This same principle applies to occasions of public simchah, such as Simchat Torah and Purim. The Rav may deliver dozens of derashot concerning simchah, but as long as he remains aloof from the celebrations, his congregants will remain confused as to their own involvement. The Rav is a leader, and he must always lead, thereby reaching out in an attempt to draw in even those on the periphery.

The rabbi's role during a service is, of course, much more than that of a cheerleader. He is primarily a teacher, and that role must never be overlooked. Certainly on Shabbat and Chagim, and if possible on weekdays as well, no worship service should be without some element of learning. While some occasions call for a sermon or derashah, other occasions call for a dvar torah or dvar halakhah or be'ur tefillah. What is taught is not nearly as important as the fact that something is being taught, not only to reinforce the role of the Rav as teacher, but also to reinforce the primacy that Talmud Torah holds in the life of the Jew. There is no congregation where limud Torah, in whatever form that takes, would not be appropriate.

DECORUM VERSUS SPONTANEITY

It is vitally important for the synagogue worship service to be conducted in a decorous manner, not only to be able to compete with the decorum of a non-Orthodox house of worship and not only to try to erase the publicly held stereotyped image (which is all too often quite accurate) of the noisy Orthodox shul, but because the halakhah demands it and because our philosophy of tefillah requires it. The principle of *da lifnei Mi atah omed* must never be compromised, nor must the negative principle of *ish kol ha-yashar be'einav ya'aseh* ever be deemed acceptable.

I am not, however, recommending that the "strict" decorum commonly found in non-Orthodox houses of worship be imposed in our own congregations. A "happy medium" must be found, not an easy but quite an essential task. We want our *mitpallelim* to "feel at home," but we also want them to remember that while sitting in our sanctuaries, they are also sitting in God's presence, and they need to feel that as well. We want children to feel welcome, but just as running up and down the aisles is not acceptable in any public place, it is equally unacceptable in the synagogue. (Baby-sitting or junior congregation can help alleviate this problem.)

The rabbi must not allow himself to be put in the position of a policeman. While an occasional (not weekly) reminder of the halakhic and philosophical requirements of proper conduct during tefillah is appropriate, any further reminder should be the responsibility of the synagogue's ushers and/or officers. In my congregation, the service stops whenever there is any type of significant disturbance, a very rare occurrence.

One or more ushers should always be on duty at every "major" service. While the function of an usher in the sanctuary is, primarily, to maintain decorum, and while such a position might be unnecessary in some congregations, an usher stationed at the entrance to the sanctuary is always appropriate. The tasks of this usher are many: to greet both regular worshipers and guests with a friendly "Shabbat Shalom" and to let them know that they are welcome, to direct people who need such direction to their seats (a first-timer in an Orthodox congregation can easily become disoriented, confused, and embarrassed) as well as to where they might find a kipah, siddur, chumash, or talit, and to cover the door so that no one enters the sanctuary at an inappropriate time (to be decided by the Rav). This usher can also find himself in the position of having to answer important questions that cannot wait, such as "Someone in my family just died. How, or when, can I let the rabbi know?" or "I need a *Mi Shebeirakh* made. Can you tell the gabbai?"

The distribution of honors must also be handled in a decorous manner, without needless disruption of the service. The Rav must insist that the gabbai distribute the honors in advance, and after forethought, and that each honoree should position himself near the bimah, so that the service may continue without interruption.

DAILY MINYAN

It is a given, or at least it should be a given, that uniform siddurim with English translation be made available to all worshipers, and that these siddurim not be in a state of disrepair. The image that we want to present of both our congregations and the important place that tefillah plays in the congregation must be constant; the daily minyan is just as important as the Shabbat or holiday service. The room (Bet Midrash, chapel, classroom) that is used for the daily minyan, just as the main sanctuary, must be clean and neat, properly lighted, ventilated, heated, and air conditioned, with ample seating for even a larger than usual crowd. Although it is unusual for women to attend the daily minyan in most congregations, a women's section should be present in the minyan room just in case, and also to send a message that woman are, in fact, welcome. The mechitzah and ezrat nashim should be just as attractive in this room as they are in the main sanctuary and arranged in such a manner as to make women worshipers feel that they too are part of the tefillah experience.

Many congregations face difficulties in maintaining a twice daily minyan, and some have opted to schedule only morning minyanim, or only evening minyanim, or only twice-a-week minyanim, etc. The rabbi, together with his lay leadership, must decide what is realistic, with the ultimate goal being to expand the schedule of minyanim. Whatever the frequency, every effort must be made, in advance, to guarantee that a minyan is present at every scheduled service. Starting a minyan late, or having to wait in the middle for the "tenth man" to arrive in response to a phone call, is simply not fair to those who arrived on time and need to leave on time. I am not suggesting that the burden of making phone calls, and it is a burden, be counted amongst the rabbi's responsibilities. Yet in many congregations minyan phone calls are the rabbi's responsibility; that is something that needs to be worked out between the rabbi and his lay leadership. Whoever is charged with that responsibility, however, must take it seriously. I have seen committed "minyanaires" become so frustrated at having to wait for a minyan, sometimes in vain, that they either stopped coming or shifted their allegiance elsewhere. That must never be allowed to occur.

Refreshments of some sort should be provided, especially following the morning minyan. Coffee and cake, juice and crackers, or a more elaborate menu are all good choices, as is a sit-down breakfast on a daily, weekly, or monthly basis. Of course, it is local factors (time of minyan, age of participants, etc.) that will determine what food will be served. The synagogue itself need not be the source of funds for the post-minyan refreshments; special funds, or preferably the contributions of the participants themselves, is the way to go. It goes without saying that the rabbi should not be the caterer.

Great care should be exercised in determining the starting time of the daily minyanim. While the time of shkiah and pelag ha-minchah will be the major factors to be considered for the evening minyan, the decision of when to begin in the morning must take into account many other factors, such as the average age of participants, where most people work and when they have to be at work, car pool arrangements, traffic conditions, and the like. Even after the decision has been made and the minyan functioning, it is not a bad idea to periodically reevaluate and to make changes, if necessary. The selection of a proper starting time might also open up the possibility of a pre- or post-minyan shiur or class, even if only a very brief one. An important problem to be avoided is that of the "race car minyan," where the starting gun is sounded, the shaliach tzibbur races out of the starting gate and finally reaches the final flag, having left the other mitpallelim hopelessly behind, frustrated, and out of breath. While it is necessary to have ten men to form a minyan, it is also important that the minyan become a tzibbur of *mitpallelim* and that the worship experience be a positive one. Choosing the right starting time is important, and so is choosing the proper shaliach tzibbur. The Rav should give guidance to the gabbai for establishing the proper qualifications for a shaliach tzibbur, taking into account, of course, chiyuvim. "Speedy Gonzales" is not a proper shaliach tzibbur, and neither is someone whose pace is excruciatingly slow. One other comment about timing: punctuality is important. Start on time, and help destroy once and for all the concept of "Jewish Standard Time" in all areas of Jewish life.

While worshipers should be encouraged to don their own kipah, talit, and tefillin, the synagogue should have kipot, talitot, and a few pair of tefillin for those who arrive empty-handed. As with the siddurim and chumashim referred to earlier, all *tashmishei kedushah* should be clean and fit for use, and stored or displayed in a dignified manner. Once again, the message that is sent by providing dirty talitot and torn kipot is not the message that we should want to send.

Someone, and what better person that the Rav, should always be available to help a newcomer don his tefillin. Someone who enters without tefillin should be offered a pair, and, if needed, assistance in using it. Care should be taken to avoid embarrassing or offending the person. We do, after all, want him to return. Even if he declines our offer today, he may well accept the next time. The Rav should find the time to talk to the worshiper (not necessarily then and there) and explain to him the significance of the tefillin and to offer a private lesson in their use, thereby avoiding any kind of public embarrassment. If the rabbi is not in a position to deal with this situation, he should certainly see to it that the person who does make this overture does so in a proper and respectful manner.

Page numbers should be announced as frequently as halakhah permits, or posted in an area clearly visible to all, unless, of course, the minyan is made up entirely of regular and knowledgeable *mitpallelim*. Even if only one person might benefit from page announcements, or an occasional "please rise" or "please be seated," then it should be done. An occasional be'ur tefillah is always appropriate, as is an explanation concerning the omission or addition of a certain tefillah, and time should be allowed for that.

While most weekday minyanim contain little if any singing, English readings, or Hebrew readings in unison, what is not needed in one synagogue might be absolutely necessary in another. As stated earlier, the Rav must try to balance the needs of his *mitpallelim* so that everyone feels comfortable and can become involved in the tefillah experience. The same format need not be used daily, and periodic evaluations are always advisable, as is taking into account the reactions, responses, comments, and requests of the worshipers. The davening should not just be allowed to happen, nor should the Rav relinquish his control over the proceedings.

Decorum at the daily minyan is just as important as it is on Shabbat and Chagim, but due to the smaller crowd, small room, and hour of the day, should be much easier to enforce.

The rabbi must make every effort to be at every minyan. While this statement should be a given, not only for professional reasons but because every Rav presumably understands the importance, and obligations, of *tefillah be'tzibbur*, it needs to be written. The rabbi's participation (and punctuality, or lack of same) sends a very clear message. The rabbi is, after all, a role model, and he must practice what he preaches. When circumstances prevent the rabbi from attending the minyan, the gabbai should be informed.

The daily minyan is often frequented by mourners, and if it is the only show in town, nonmembers will also attend. A mourner must be made to feel welcome, not only by perfunctory expressions of sympathy but by sincere expressions of concern. It is not at all unusual for a mourner who had previously never attended a daily minyan to become a regular worshiper even after his period of aveilut has concluded, nor is it unusual for a nonmember mourner to choose to affiliate. To obtain these positive results is certainly one of the challenges that faces the Rav.

SHABBAT, CHAGIM, AND YAMIM NORAIM

While much of what has been written concerning the daily minyan is also applicable to the major services of the year, some brief thoughts concerning these services are in order. For example, the Rav might want to consider shifting his derashah from before Musaf to after Musaf on occasion, thereby keeping the *mitpallelim* guessing, if not *whether* the rabbi will speak (I feel strongly the rabbi should always speak), at least *when* the rabbi will speak. Such factors as theme and attendance might be considered in determining exactly when to speak.

The format of the rabbi's derashah might also be varied to avoid the problem of monotony. An open forum, question-and-answer sessions, textual study (with everyone having a copy of the text), *bein gavra le'gavra* discussions, are all appropriate formats. (In any event, the Rav should also be sure to summarize both the Torah and Haftorah portions.) In terms of content, the Rav should remember that Torah is relevant to every issue but that he is not necessarily the best political analyst or book reviewer in the world. The essence of the Rav's remarks should always be based on an appropriate text.

The question of English readings, responsive or unison, might be dealt with differently depending on the occasion. While on Shabbat English readings might be limited to one or two, or none at all, the crowd that is present on Rosh Hashanah and Yom Kippur might benefit from, and be able to participate more fully with, a greater number of English readings. Explanations of special holiday prayers, why we stand, when we stand, why the *Aron Kodesh* is opened for certain tefillot, why we read two portions on one Shabbat, why we read from two Sifrei Torah are always in order.

SPECIAL PRAYERS AND CEREMONIES

One of the first changes that I instituted in both congregations I have had the honor of serving was the introduction of the Prayer for the Government of the United States and the Prayer for the Welfare of the State of Israel. While these additions met some opposition from people who did not understand the need for them or who were concerned about the service being prolonged, that opposition gradually disappeared and both tefillot have remained an integral part of every Shabbat morning service. Both are read in English by the entire congregation, and, with the exception of a bar mitzvah on Shabbat, constitute our only English readings, thereby providing our non-Hebrew readers with the opportunity of participating fully at least in this part of the service.

Yom Hashoah, Yom Hazikaron, Yom Ha-Atzmaut, and Yom Yerushalayim are observed on the proper day of the calendar with the appropriate tefillot added to the services. It is up to the Rav to determine what the nusach ha-tefillah should be on each of these special days, but certainly the days themselves must never be allowed to go unnoticed during tefillah. It would, of course, be better if one were to emphasize the significance of these days, rather than to downplay their importance, by holding special services in the sanctuary conducted by the Rav and chazzan, seudot, chagigot, and so forth.

Whenever the need arises (crises in Israel, Soviet Jewry, personal illness, etc.) extra tefillot (*tehilim*) are added, always with the appropriate explanation. These *tehilim* are recited in Hebrew and/or English, depending on the occasion.

My congregation was blessed recently with the donation of a Torah scroll which survived the Holocaust. While the Torah is pasul, I decided that it could and should be used in other ways. We use it during Kol Nidre, it is used during the *Hakafot* on Simchat Torah, and it is also removed from the *Aron Kodesh* and held by the chazzan while he recites the *Kel Malei Rachamim* in memory of the *Kedoshim* during Yizkor and on Yom Hashoah. This special Torah is then returned to the *Aron Kodesh* together with the other Sifrei Torah following Yizkor, thereby enabling the *mitpallelim* to kiss and touch it, and to be touched by it. The appropriate *Kel Malei Rachamim* in memory of the soldiers of *Zahal* is also recited during each Yizkor service.

For reasons of *tircha de'tzibura*, both the number of Mi Shebeirakhs and Hosafot should be severely limited and controlled, if they can not be avoided entirely.

When it comes to a Mi Shebeirakh for the sick, I suggest using a number of approaches, thereby encouraging everyone who needs to offer a prayer on behalf of a sick relative or friend to do so. If the gabbai is made aware of the need for someone to have a Mi Shebeirakh recited he will, if possible, offer an aliyah to the person making the request, and, of course, the Mi Shebeirakh itself will follow the aliyah. Additionally, before *hagbah* but while the congregation is already standing, I recite a collective Mi Shebeirakh for all the names on my list. This Mi Shebeirakh is recited in Hebrew and English and I use whatever names I happen to know (Hebrew or English). I also pause at the end of my list, but before concluding the Mi Shebeirakh, so that any worshiper at his/her seat may silently add the name of a loved one. In this way, even those who are reluctant to approach the rabbi or gabbai, either because they do not want to bother anybody or out of embarrassment at not knowing the proper name, may still have a Mi Shebeirakh recited in their behalf.

THE PROBLEMS AND OPPORTUNITIES OF THE BAR AND BAT MITZVAH

Every bar mitzvah boy should be given the opportunity to participate in the service up to the level of his capabilities, even if that means that the role of the chazzan is restricted to "*Ya'amod . . .*" and "*Mi Shebeirakh. . . .*" Of course, no bar mitzvah boy should be made to feel inferior because he is only reciting the berakhot for Maftir or some other short part of the service.

All of our Bnei and Bnot Mitzvah are encouraged to twin their simchah with another child who is unable, due to political or health reasons, to celebrate his/her own simchah. The twinning is incorporated into the service in a variety of ways (invitations, rabbi's derashah, child's derashah, special tefillah, etc.).

Following the *Mi Shebeirakh* recited in honor of the bar mitzvah boy, it is the custom of our congregation for all to join in the singing of *Siman Tov U-Mazal Tov* while showering the boy with candy (which was distributed during the last aliyah). The younger children look forward to the opportunity of retrieving the candy, as at an aufruf. This singing accompanies every simchah in our congregation (baby naming, special anniversary or birthday, etc.).

Every bar mitzvah boy delivers a derashah before I speak, and I respond to the boy in the course of my remarks, while making certain that my remarks are directed to the *mitpallelim* and not exclusively to the bar mitzvah boy. When I address the boy (or the girl at a bat mitzvah), I make it a point of not speaking about the parents or a sibling unless there is a special reason to do so. It is the young man or woman who is the focus of everyone's attention, and it is about him or her that I speak.

In the event that a simchah attracts a large crowd of non-participant guests, I will add some additional English reading, page announcements, *be'ur tefillah*, and the like.

My congregation averages five to eight bar mizvah celebrations per year, so I am not faced with the problem of congregants who are bored with the weekly bar mitzvah. In any event, it is always the regular Shabbat service that takes precedence, and our regular *mitpallelim* are always made to feel that they come first.

The bat mitzvah presents unique problems as well as opportunities. I have thoroughly enjoyed the challenge of developing appropriate bat mitzvah ceremonies for the young women of our congregations. I have even arranged for bat mitzvah ceremonies for adult women who felt that they wanted a ceremony that was denied them in their youth. While some ceremonies have been as simple as a dvar Torah at Seudah Shelishit or at a special seudah on Sunday, others have taken the form of ceremonies held in the sanctuary on Motzei

Shabbat or Sunday. The young lady, in addition to presenting a dvar Torah, leads the guests in appropriate readings, songs, etc. This form of ceremony sometimes includes chanted selections from Tanakh using the traditional trop, if the theme chosen for the ceremony (e.g., mitzvot, Soviet Jewry, Israel, Shabbat, women in Judaism) lends itself to that. If the parents wish to speak to their daughter during the ceremony (in addition to the Birkat ha-Bat), they are given the opportunity to do so. I have even been able to incorporate a girl's bat mitzvah ceremony into the Sunday morning Rosh Chodesh bar mitzvah of her one-year-older brother.

In each case, a special booklet is printed containing all the readings, songs, and other materials that will be needed for the ceremony. This booklet, prepared at the family's expense, is personalized and serves as a keepsake of the bat mitzvah, in addition to alleviating the problem of having to jump from place to place in the siddur for each reading or song.

With the exception of the Rosh Chodesh bat mitzvah referred to above, all our bat mitzvah ceremonies that take place in the sanctuary are clearly described as not constituting a religious service and, as such, we permit mixed seating during such ceremonies. Of course, the halakhic issues raised in the issue of bat mitzvah and the appropriateness of the different possibilities outlined above must be decided by the Rav. No matter what model is used, it is essential, in our day and age, that every girl be offered the possibility of having a meaningful bat mitzvah ceremony conducted in her synagogue and officiated at by her rabbi.

CHOOSING THE RIGHT SIDDUR AND CHUMASH

Most congregations have already chosen a siddur, chumash, and machzor long before the rabbi's arrival on the scene, and the most that the majority of rabbis can do is praise, or learn to live with the choice of their predecessors. If a rabbi, however, is in the enviable position of having to make such a choice, he must make such an important decision as carefully as possible. The selection process should not be limited to the rabbi but should instead involve a cross-section of congregants whose deliberations will be guided by the rabbi. While cost certainly is a factor that must be considered, there are other factors as well: good English translation and clear instructions, good print, paper and binding, durability, comments and explanations, and the like. What is best for one synagogue might only be second best, or not at all appropriate, for another synagogue. Consulting with rabbis of comparable congregations will certainly be beneficial.

DEALING CORRECTLY WITH CANTOR AND ASSISTANTS

The rabbi is the chief of staff and captain of the team. He is also the Rav. These facts must govern the rabbi in his relationships with all members of the synagogue staff, both lay and professional. He must always remember that all *klei kodesh* are the rabbi's partners in a joint effort *"le'hagdil Torah u-le'ha-adirah."* The Rav is the only authority in halakhic areas. The rabbi too should feel comfortable in offering suggestions or recommendations to the cantor or assistant rabbi, never forgetting that while every "buck" stops at his desk, they too are professionals and should be treated as such. The chazzan, for example, in most cases has musical expertise that the rabbi lacks. Just as the rabbi might properly resent the cantor suggesting how and about what the rabbi should speak, so too might the cantor properly resent the rabbi's suggestion of how and what to sing—unless mutually respectful relations have been created. Regular staff meetings, as well as frequent one-on-one discussions, will help keep open channels of communication, the most important factor in eliminating the possibility of bruised egos and hurt feelings. The rabbi must always remain publicly supportive of, and respectful toward, all members of the synagogue staff, with any and all problems involving personnel being dealt with out of the public view.

Vacation schedules are often a subject of dissension between rabbi and cantor. Again, early and honest discussions should be able to lead to agreement on this and other areas.

These are some of the means and methodologies that I have found practical in upgrading the quality of tefillah in full accordance with the halakhah as well as contemporary sensibilities. While every congregation and rabbi are unique, these experiences and perspectives can, I believe, go a long way toward maximum realization of the goal of inspired *tefillah be'tzibbur.*

11

The Rabbi as Community Relations Professional

Rabbi William Cohen

Beyond the confines of his synagogue, the rabbi is called upon to interact with the larger Jewish community, its leaders and existing structures. In many ways he must see to it that community-wide organizations maintain minimally acceptable halakhic standards, are sensitive to Orthodox concerns, and reflect the primacy of Torah in Jewish life. On the other hand, he is confronted with issues of pluralism and recognition toward the non-Orthodox, where Orthodoxy is often a small minority. These delicate issues require sensitivity, balance, and more than a little practical wisdom. Rabbi William Cohen shares his own successful approach to these concerns.

To understand the role of the rabbi vis-à-vis his community, we must first distinguish between communities of various sizes and Jewish populations. The Orthodox rabbi who serves in a community where his is the only Orthodox synagogue must assume the role of *Mara De'Atra*—which implies a responsibility not only for his own synagogue and its membership, but for the entire Jewish community. It will be his responsibility to supervise the local kosher butcher, the bakery, and to set kashrut standards for caterers who will be permitted to cater in his synagogue. If there is a mikveh in his community, it will be his responsibility to see to it that it is maintained according to halakhic standards.

Perhaps one of the most difficult tasks for the rabbi in such a community, where there may not even be a Jewish undertaker, is organizing and maintaining a Chevra Kadisha to provide *Taharah* and *Takhrikhim* and the most basic requirements for Jewish burial. The American culture in which we are immersed has, we might say, almost an aversion to contact with death in any form, and Jews are also affected by this phenomenon.

The Rav in such a community must also project himself as the representative and spokesman of authentic Judaism to the non-Jewish community. He should not, indeed must not, abdicate this role to the Conservative and Reform spiritual leaders.

The rabbi whose pulpit is in a major metropolitan area with a large Jewish population, areas such as New York, Los Angeles, Chicago, and the like, faces an entirely different situation. For one thing, he may be totally unknown outside of the immediate area of his synagogue. The problems of kashrut standards and supervision in such large areas are often too complex and wide-spread for the individual rabbi to handle. Here the rabbi would do best to join and become active in already established Orthodox rabbinic bodies. These exist in most of the larger cities. There is strength in numbers. The organized group can set and enforce standards which the individual rabbi often cannot do. An organized rabbinate can do more for the support of day schools and yeshivot, for building mikvaot where needed, for establishing funeral standards, than can any rabbi acting by himself. Moreover, such an organized rabbinic group becomes the spokesman for the rabbinate vis-à-vis the Jewish lay community and the non-Jewish community at large.

The third type of Jewish community might be described as the middle-sized Jewish community with a Jewish population of anywhere from 5,000 to 25,000 Jews. This type of Jewish community is today located largely in the suburbs of the core city from which the Jews moved in the 'fifties and 'sixties. This was the period of the *drang nach suburbia* that left the central city largely denuded of its Jewish population. Such was the case in my own community where the last remaining synagogue in Hartford, Connecticut, closed its doors some three years ago, and the Jewish population is now concentrated west and north of the city.

Such communities will usually have from two to five Orthodox synagogues plus Conservative and Reform temples. Greater Hartford, for example, has four Orthodox synagogues, two Young Israel synagogues, and a Chabad House. All of the synagogues and one of the Young Israel's have rabbis. There is an Orthodox day school and a Conservative Solomon Schechter day school. There is a very strong Federation that raises close to eight million dollars annually for Israel, and for national and local agencies. Among the local agencies, the Community Center is the largest recipient of funds. Jewish education is also generously supported through the funding of a Commission on Jewish Education with a paid professional staff, a community high school, and generous scholarship support to the two-day schools on a student per-capita basis.

The first question that faces an Orthodox rabbi who accepts a pulpit in such a community is Competition or cooperation? Should he try to protect his own turf, run his own small Talmud Torah, conduct his own youth and adult education programs, or should he join with his colleagues of the other Orthodox synagogues to run joint programs wherever possible?

Obviously, if the rabbi chooses the first option, the Orthodox community will be divided and subdivided into competing and contending groups and institutions with the resultant weakening of Orthodox power and prestige in the community. This is true of so many areas of Jewish life, whether it be adult education, kashrut standards, community services and the like.

My plea is for coordinated activity and cooperation among the Orthodox synagogues of a given area, for the pooling of resources and efforts for the common good instead of dissipating them in competitive undertakings.

To use two examples from my own community, the Orthodox rabbis and synagogues organized a joint Institute for Jewish Studies in the area of adult Jewish education many years ago. All the Orthodox rabbis as well as the principal of the Orthodox day school joined the faculty of this institute. This enabled us to give many more and varied courses than any individual rabbi or synagogue could give by itself. This institute lasted successfully for thirty years.

Hartford, like so many other communities, had older European-trained rabbis who controlled kashrut supervision of the kosher butchers and the chicken slaughterhouses with their *shochtim*. As these rabbis retired and a younger, American-trained Orthodox rabbinate took their place, a Vaad ha-Kashrut consisting of all the Orthodox rabbis was organized. The rabbis served without any remuneration, and thus were able to strengthen standards considerably. At the present time, through the joint efforts and cooperation of the entire Orthodox community, an eruv for our area has just been completed. We can point to many other areas where the motto "in unity there is strength" can be applied.

The strongest power in the organized Jewish community is the Jewish Federation. In addition to raising funds for U.J.A. and Israel, the Federation controls the allocation of funds to local and national organizations. As indicated earlier, substantial funds for Jewish education and for the local day schools are given out by Federation. Tremendous power goes with control of the purse-strings, and it is vital and urgent that the Orthodox community play an important role in Federation, not merely for the financial benefits to specific institutions, but more important, out of concern for the unity of the kehillah. Here, too, Orthodox rabbis cannot sit on the sidelines. They must become involved. In the Greater Hartford Federation, every rabbi holding a pulpit is a member of the Federation Board of Directors with full voting rights. But if the Orthodox rabbi stays home, he is not seen nor is his influence felt. On the other hand, by being active in Federation, I have served on Federation allocation committees, long-range planning committees, and others. The power center of the Jewish community and the major controller of its funds dare not be ignored by the Orthodox community.

What of relations with the Conservative and Reform rabbis? There are areas in communal affairs in which the cooperation of the entire rabbinate is required in order to accomplish desired ends. Thus it was pressure from the entire rabbinate, including Reform spiritual leaders who are indifferent to kashrut, that moved our Federations to have only kosher fundraising dinners.

In our community the entire rabbinate is organized in a loose Rabbinic Fellowship that meets about four times a year to tackle communal problems. The chairmanship of the Fellowship rotates every two years among the Orthodox, Conservative, and Reform à la the Synagogue Council. One major stipulation was made by the Orthodox rabbis when the Fellowship was formed, and that was that no clergyman who officiated at mixed marriages could ever become a member of the Fellowship.

One of the major accomplishments of united rabbinic action was our success in blocking the opening of the Jewish Community Center on Shabbat. With the exception of one Reform rabbi who favored the opening, the entire rabbinate joined hands in voicing its opposition to the opening with its attendant *Chillul Shabbat*, and we were prepared to take the fight into the Jewish community. Today the Greater Hartford Jewish Community Center is still one of the few throughout the United States that is closed on Shabbat.

Last, but perhaps not least, one should not underestimate the chizuk that one gets from working together with one's Orthodox colleagues and the sense of friendship and camaraderie that can develop, making rabbinic burdens somewhat easier to bear.

12

The Rabbi as Political Activist

Rabbi Louis Bernstein

The successful rabbi is ever mindful of the political needs of *Klal Yisrael*, within and beyond the confines of his congregation and immediate community. For this reason he often finds himself called upon to become involved with various political organizations, be they Jewish or otherwise. Israel, Soviet Jewry, community relations groups, political parties and leaders in local, state, and national capitals, and the like, often demand that the rabbi assume an ambassadorial function. Rabbi Louis Bernstein presents his own special perspective on the effectiveness of the rabbi as a *Shtadlan*.

When I was interviewed initially at the Young Israel of Windsor Park, I specifically stated that I wanted to be a rabbi whose activity extended beyond the community. I had already served as a chaplain in the United States Army and had been active in HaPoel HaMizrachi even while in college. Rabbi Abraham Avrech, who was then the executive director of HaPoel HaMizrachi in New York, knew that I had been editor of *The Commentator*, the Yeshiva College undergraduate newspaper, and asked me to edit *Kolenu*, the council's newspaper.

My favorite teachers at Yeshiva University and even some of the roshei yeshivah were active in Mizrachi and Jewish life. Yeshiva was a single family then, and older alumni volunteered to help Jews during the Holocaust years. I got to know the alumni leadership intimately when I joined the college alumni association while still in Yeshiva

University. Jewish issues and interests can be limited to the local community, but national issues can also have an impact on individual Jews.

There are synagogues in which the lay leaders severely reduce the scope of a rabbi's activity. They require that the rabbi keep office hours and be available to answer the phone. The community which I serve is of average size and I teach a full load at Yeshiva University. I am at services every morning and almost every day for Minchah, so the time I spend in the office is limited.

Over the years, some people would grumble. (Once, in the early years, I was able to demonstrate to officers who did not attend services during the week that I was in the synagogue by the large number of Mishnayot I had taught daily between Minchah and Ma'ariv).

Some of those same people subsequently availed themselves of the contacts and expertise that I acquired over the years. The synagogue itself has been enriched by guests who have visited the community during the same time.

Most communities today understand that the rabbi's involvement in local and national organizations is important to the community. The Rabbinical Council's Bet Din is a good example. I, as an officer of the Bet Din, have on occasion been called upon to solve difficult family situations in which the immediate relatives of my own *balebatim* were involved. Another time family tragedy over mamzerut was avoided because of my ongoing working relationship with Chief Rabbi Shapiro.

Rabbis should be active in their rabbinical groups. My activity in the Rabbinical Council commenced before there was a local rabbinical group. There is a limit to the time that even the most ubiquitous rabbi has at his disposal. Long ago, I decided to devote my volunteer efforts entirely to Orthodox organizations. While professional organizations and the Federation are important and I am delighted that some good friends are active in the Synagogue Council and the New York Federation, I just don't have the time to get involved with them. In those organizations in which I'm active, I try to limit my time to political issues and education which are my areas of interest and expertise. On the other hand, kashrut is an area which is of no special interest to me, other than becoming involved when it was a matter of massive fraud, or on another occasion when I felt it was a matter of principle. Certainly, rabbis should be involved in kashrut, but this is an issue which consumes much time and tends to be confounded by an unhealthy mixture of halakhic and personal priorities. It requires expertise and knowledge not to be found in the *Yoreh Deah* alone. Education is another area in which rabbis become involved on the questionable assumption that every rabbi is an educator.

Time and again, I have found it necessary to call on political figures to help a congregation. Knowing the government process and political officials is most helpful to congregants. I have turned to political leaders to have congregants admitted to hospitals, to help in educational, immigration, and employment problems. One of my congregants recently left his passport in a vault over a two-day holiday period and was due to depart for Israel before the banks would open. When I was asked to help, I recalled that years ago, in an immigration situation, I learned from my congressman that the State Department has an emergency deputy officer. A call at home to an Orthodox lay leader on Senator Daniel Patrick Moynihan's (D.-NY) staff, helped solve the problem.

There is a debate whether a rabbi should be actively involved in politics. From my perspective, there is no reason why he shouldn't when he is an American citizen and should provide moral leadership. Should he do so, however, the pulpit should not be used for that purpose. Colleagues who know of my commitment are surprised to hear that I never discuss politics during a sermon. There are no exceptions to that rule. I usually give a current event briefing on Shabbat afternoon, especially when I return from Israel. Since many of the people live a distance from the synagogue, I recently gave a report when I returned from a weekend visit with Orthodox leaders, after Musaf was completed, because of the specific request of the president of the synagogue.

There is quite a difference between backing a political party and being involved in politics in the clubhouse or as a candidate. I was a block captain in the Democratic Party long before I was a rabbi because of my proclivity for political liberalism. In my borough of New York, if one wants to be helpful to one's congregation, I believe that supporting any other party is equivalent to slamming the doors of the political machinery. From the district captain to the congressman and mayor and for that matter the foreman, all are Democrats. Even so, a rabbi can retain his independence by supporting candidates of any party in a general election.

There are times when the very existence of the community can depend on utilizing the system. Some sixteen years ago, when the Forest Hills community was endangered, Mayor John Lindsay worked to contract a very large, low-income housing project in the area. Rabbinic leadership in Queens was a major factor in preserving the community which is the linchpin for Jewish activity in that borough of more than 400,000 Jews. Even one of our most politically reserved and scholarly colleagues became involved in the fight.

Several years earlier, it was a Fair Sabbath Law that had to be pushed through legislation over the opposition of church groups. In more recent years, it was the "get" law. All political figures respond to their local rabbi. I once took a class from Yeshiva University to Washington. We ran into Congressman Charles Rangel in front of the House Office Building. He was in the middle of a conversation. I stopped to say hello and to state that we were from Yeshiva University. He stopped the conversation short and said to the individual with whom he had been speaking, "Excuse me, there are more important people in the world—my constituents."

To sum up, my experiences as a rabbi active in communal work have been extremely rewarding in many ways. These activities have enriched my life and are a constant source of new learning experiences. I hope they have enabled me to make significant and meaningful contributions to the Jewish people. These activities enable me to offer to the community, membership, friends, and colleagues resources that would ordinarily be unavailable to them.

13

The Rabbi as Resource for Youth

Rabbi Elan Adler

The rabbi is certainly more than a youth director. Yet he is never free of the obligation to be ultimately responsible for the positive involvement of young people in the affairs of the synagogue and community. Ideally he should cultivate a close and formative relationship with each of them, but this is not always possible. Thus he must rely upon other personnel, lay leaders, and committees to supplement his own efforts in youth affairs. The direction he gives, the priority he attaches, and the assistance he can offer are often crucial to the success of youth programs in his synagogue. Rabbi Elan Adler provides specific ideas and guidelines to make this important task easier—and more effective.

Every group within your synagogue is important. Whether it is the Sisterhood, Men's Club, Youth, Collegiates, Young Couples, Singles (older and younger), Leisure Adults, or other category, each must receive attention and direction from the rabbi. Perhaps the group most difficult to deal with, for various reasons, is the youth group. First, since the rabbi is an adult, he can relate better to people his own age within the congregation. Second, you need a lot more creativity and personal charisma to capture the attention of the youth. And third, the youth in the congregation always need a lot more time than you can give them. Almost always, no matter how much time one gives to them, it is not enough.

CONSTRUCTING A MEANINGFUL PROGRAM

As you approach working with the youth, know that the term "youth" may encompass anywhere from dealing with a nursery school program to establishing on-going Torah study for high school seniors. This section will deal with how to construct a program for elementary grades and up.

As you begin to tackle the major task of establishing a meaningful program for "your kids," there are some questions that need honest evaluation.

What Is Your Role with the Youth of the Synagogue?

Are you the senior rabbi or the assistant rabbi in the congregation? Were you hired specifically to work with the youth? If you are an assistant rabbi dealing primarily with youth, be prepared to be known as the youth director of the synagogue at the expense of being called upon for your wider talents and abilities. In such a case, it is important for you to make positive contributions in other areas of the synagogue as well, so as to avoid being "typecast" as the youth director. More thoughts about your role: Have *you* chosen youth as your primary group, or has the congregation chosen it for you? Are you naturally comfortable with youngsters, or is it forced? Are you confident with your ability to guide them and befriend them, or do you need some help?

What Are Your Resources?

What do any former synagogue personnel have to say about the youth or past programs? Who are the interested parents? Is the synagogue board of directors behind you fiscally? Which teens can you target for leadership? What about the local Jewish community center—how can you offer each other assistance? How many local day school and Hebrew School teachers can you interest in offering you a hand? How many of your youngsters are members of the National Council of Synagogue Youth (NCSY)? Of Bnei Akiva? How many have attended Torah leadership seminar of Yeshiva University, or have siblings who have attended? How are the other local youth groups doing, and *what* are they doing?

Perhaps the most important question you must ask yourself is the following one.

What Kind of Time Do You Have to Give the Youth?

Do you have evenings available for classes or trips? Do you have Sunday mornings for a Brunch and Rap with the Rabbi, or a Talit and Tefillin Club, or do you teach in the Hebrew School (which is also important but it locks you in)? Are Sunday afternoons free, or is that family, funeral, wedding, and "other" time? What about Shabbat and Yom Tov—will your wife and family enjoy the company of youth at your home?

Yes, there is a lot to think about, but then the youth of your synagogue are worth every minute of planning and involvement.

TRIED AND TESTED TIPS IN SETTING UP A SUCCESSFUL YOUTH GROUP

Get a chairperson of the youth committee. You and the chairman must now select a committee (parents, someone from the board of the synagogue, and one or two hard workers, no matter the age) and propose a budget. In general, ask for $100 for each child that you expect to participate per year. If the budget is more liberal, ask for more. It will never be enough.

Involve other organizations. Call the regional and national offices of the National Conference of Synagogue Youth, Bnei Akiva, and Yeshiva University's Department of Youth Services. Have them send you membership information, if applicable, and a list of dates of upcoming events, including regionals, conventions, and seminars. Mark these dates on your calendar. You will want to send your youth away to large programs, and these will form an important facet of your overall programming. Your synagogue can also be the host of a Reunion Shabbaton for NCSY, or a Torah Tour Shabbaton for Torah Leadership Seminar. Also, your youngsters will always return from these programs with the names of collegiate advisors whom they adore. Invite them for a Shabbat. These may be your future leaders in your synagogue, or your future chaperons for programs you cannot personally attend.

Create a calendar of events for each three-month period. The idea is to gather a small, representative group of youth (one or two from each grade), and invite them for a meal and a planning session. Don't go for big numbers at this meeting; you will defeat the purpose and nothing will get done. On your calendar, mark down this planning meeting for every three months.

Prepare for elections. Have you noticed that you have not yet held an election of officers? Good! Hold off. Do not kill the excitement before it has a chance to build.

Plan your programs. What kinds of programs do you plan? There are several types, but remember that there are *two major kinds of Jewish programming*. One is when Jewish children get together for an activity, and the other is when they get together for a *Jewish* activity. Being lopsided during the year on one or the other may fit your synagogue best. In general, a balance makes everyone happy, and makes the best of time and money spent.

Some categories of programming include Torah study or general Jewish discussions. In-synagogue activities such as a movie night, overnight, or CPR and karate demonstrations, out-of-synagogue activities in the neighborhood, sports activities, either participatory or viewing, tzedakah projects of fundraising or volunteering, and programs which directly relate to the personal growth of the youth. Lists upon lists of suggested activities are available from the Regional Offices of NCSY, Bnei Akiva, and Yeshiva University's Department of Youth Services.

Involve the kids in programming. How do you decide on programs? Ask your kids. Project your own interests and talents into the program. Expand your horizons. Take them to a concert if you can. Take them to a farbrengen. Read the papers and see what is in the area. Pick a theme for the month/year. Get together with other youth groups so the old faces are not the same. If *your* group is good, you will see them again.

Use publicity. Publicity is critical. Make your flyers and notices a piece of art. Mail things out well in advance. Send reminders. Get deadlines of local newspapers for the Community Calendar column. Create your own newsletter. Prepare a Youth Column for your bulletin. Order youth group stationery. Get all youth programs announced in shul on Shabbat. Tell where the youngsters have been and what's coming up next. Have members of the youth group do them. Report to the board on a regular basis on youth activities.

Get feedback from the kids. Ask your youth members how they have enjoyed the activities. Are they having fun? Are they learning anything? Do they feel like it's *their* program? Are *you* an important part of the success? Are you on a roll with the youth group? You are? Ah . . . *now* is the time to elect your officers!

Ask parents to help. They can chaperon, drive, set up in the synagogue, and make phone calls for housing when you host a Shabbaton. If you have their interest and confidence, they will look forward to having their children spend time with you.

Take pictures. Take as many pictures of your activities as possible. They are great for newspapers, for group morale, and terrific when budget time comes around. No board can deny you your requests when they see a scrapbook filled with happy children.

Giving of yourself to the youth is a lot of fun, while at the same time very taxing of your time. If you wish to be successful in your work, you may want to consider the other roles you play with the youth you guide.

THE RABBI AS TEACHER

You are, in the final analysis, a teacher of the collective wisdom and faith offered by Judaism. You are where you are in order to dispense Judaism, judiciously, whenever and wherever you can. You are there to be a fountain of knowledge, a source of strength, a bearer of a kind heart and gentle spirit. All the children in the youth group know that. Do not disappoint them, or shortchange them, by being one of them. Judge carefully when you can go down to their level, and when it is imperative that you pull them up to yours. It does not take much to have them lose their respect for their rabbi.

As a teacher, you teach both formally and informally. You may do so in a classroom, in your office, in someone's living room, and by the way you handle an anti-Semitic remark at a bowling alley. You teach in what you do, what you say, and how you say it. And in dealing with youth, you do all this with the most impressionable age group.

THE RABBI AS SPORTSMAN

You can gain the loyalty and respect of your youth group by not holding back on your talents and interests. Share as much of yourself with them as you can. Let them grow from what you do, and from your including them. Go to games, be at the Jewish Community Center when they choose up sides, play some hoop, pick up a glove, get some tickets and take your kids anywhere. Go hiking with them. Take them to a campsite. Go rafting. Play tennis.

THE RABBI AS COUNSELOR AND CONFIDANT

There is no dead time when you are with children. Even when you are on a bus, or in line, or find yourself next to someone, each time is a ripe opportunity to get know each other better. Questions about family, school, and hobbies inevitably lead to at least a superficial relationship. Say hello personally to everyone at every activity. Find a pet topic with each. Thank everyone for coming at the end. You will notice that before long, the young lady who asked you for a dime for a phone call, and whom you treated so nicely, will call upon you for something greater. And so will the sixth grader who fell on the skating rink and *you* carried to a seat. Don't miss opportunities to make a difference in their day, one day at a time.

As for being a confidant, there are books written about the confidentiality between professional and client. You have to decide how to handle your personal situation, but know that before long, children will tell you things about their parents, and parents will tell you things about their children. You will be sharing the confidences of many people, including the youngsters in your youth group. The bottom line is that if you are a caring and loving individual, and your synagogue knows it, and you have a measure of common sense about what to say to whom, you should be able to retain the trust that people have in you.

THE RABBI AS RABBI

It's hard to go from sweating with youth on a basketball field to pontificating before them in a sermon. Don't be afraid to be seen by them in a different light. They also feel awkward when you see them in *their* own setting, whether it be at school, in the mall, or with other friends somewhere. They also have to switch roles when you are invited by their parents to see them perform, or sing, or do magic. It's not easy for you . . . it's not easy for them. Congratulations! You *now* have something to talk about with them.

THE RABBI IN THE COMMUNITY OF YOUTH

Get around as much as you can to the other youth groups. Pop in on things. Become known to as many youngsters as possible. Teach in the Hebrew high school. Invite the other youth groups to special programs in your synagogue. Go to community marches. Go to graduations. Offer to bring greetings, or say the benediction, at youth programs. Go to the library during finals week. Going to where the kids are is the other half of youth involvement, the first half being having the kids come to you.

THE RABBI AS MINISTER

As a rabbi officiating at a wedding, funeral, or family celebration or commemoration, do not miss the opportunity to bring your kids in. If a youth group member loses his grandmother to a sickness, call him over during the keriyah and explain it to him. During shivah, spend time with the youngsters. Under the chuppah, give some part to the children. Say something nice about siblings at a family simchah. Have the children stand next to you at a bris; have them assist in the Priestly Blessing over the infant. Invite a youngster to join you on the bimah. Join the Bimah Brigade once in a while for Anim Zemirot. *Do not ignore the children! Watch for them, and bring them in.*

THE RABBI AS FRIEND

If you never have a religious discussion with a youngster, or even anything approaching Judaic content, don't feel as though you have failed with that young man or woman. If they like you, if they feel good when you give them attention, if they call you a friend of theirs, you have done a wonderful service to the profession of rabbi. And consider the rabbinate a calling, because, eventually, even these whom you suspect you haven't touched in a meaningful way will end up calling. Guaranteed.

II

THE RABBI'S PERSONAL AND PROFESSIONAL LIFE

14

The Rabbi as a Personality

Rabbi Reuven P. Bulka

It is crucial that the rabbi have the right attitude toward his congregation and its *balebatim*. All too often rabbis who are bright, energetic, creative, and talented run into problems because they fail to understand the needs of the congregation and the congregation's perceptions of the rabbi. Idealism must be tempered with a healthy realism as to what is or is not possible in a given congregational setting, and the rabbi must always be sensitive to the need to establish a balance between his private and public persona. Rabbi Reuven Bulka provides some pointed advice, which is sure to ameliorate, and possibly avoid, such problems.

THE POWER OF THE PULPIT

The pulpit is a most powerful instrument, both because of what the rabbi can do with it and because of what it can do to the rabbi. Insofar as what the pulpit can do to the rabbi is concerned, it is important that the rabbi not get an overexaggerated sense of self-importance because of the fact that he has an unassailable forum with which to deliver powerful and potent messages to his flock.

It is an illusion to think that just because the rabbi speaks, the congregation jumps. In the modern Orthodox congregation, it is likely that many members will feel that their opinions are just as valid as the rabbi's opinions, and that the rabbi has no direct conduit to claim for infinite wisdom any more so than members of the congregation. Just because the rabbi preaches, it does not necessarily mean that the congregation practices. The rabbi should therefore be wary of letting the pulpit be an all-consuming ego bastion.

It is best that the rabbi look upon the pulpit as a medium, as a forum from which the rabbi can convey messages to the congregation. Before the rabbi conveys the message, it is important for the rabbi to ask himself the following questions: (1) What message is it that I want to impart to my congregation? (2) Is the method and the content of my presentation likely to convey that message? (3) Is this the type of a message that the congregation can assimilate properly and digest effectively? (4) Will this message be helpful to them and accepted in a positive manner?

Many times a rabbi, legitimately and genuinely driven by pangs of conscience, gets up on the pulpit and lashes out, sometimes meaning the congregation, sometimes addressing the empty seats—the congregation that is not there. Very often, it is the spray gun approach which scatters out in all directions and the only one that is left satisfied afterwards is the rabbi who can say with a clear conscience, "I spoke out."

In every communication, there are two individuals, the one doing the communicating, and the one who is communicated with. It is senseless to use the pulpit as a place from which one ventilates, and therefore gets rid of whatever feelings, whether they be anxieties, angers, or concerns, while being oblivious to the congregation, which ostensibly is listening. It is more important to be conscious of the audience, to gauge who they are, where they are, and what it is that should be spoken to them.

Rabbis should avoid at all times speaking down to the congregants, and should at all times speak with an evident respect for the intelligence and the sensitivity of the congregation.

Bawling out the congregation, reading the riot act, haranguing them on any issue, is most likely a self-defeating approach. Anyone who is bawled out immediately gets the dander up and questions the right of the haranguer to engage in such conversation. This leads to rejection both of the message and the one who delivers the message.

Uplifting a congregation, speaking in a positive manner, reinforcing the good, and applauding capacity and capability, are much more preferable to lambasting and denigrating.

Oratory too has its place in rabbinical "pulpitations," but very often, in the oratorical flow, the eloquence becomes an end in itself. Many a rabbi is happy to hear how much his diction or his command of language is admired, even at the same time as a congregant would be hard pressed to state exactly what it was that the rabbi said. "I don't know what he said, but he said it nicely" is a remark that is often associated with oratory.

True enough, many congregants would like to be entertained, but it is unlikely that any rabbi, no matter how talented, can maintain the entertainment level on a continuous basis, over the course of many years. Rabbis should definitely avoid trying to be what they are not, and though it is always good to have a light remark or joke as part of a sermonic interchange, the basic sermon should be message-oriented or education-motivated.

While rabbis normally may gain their position through a superior sermon given on their trial Shabbat, it is very rare that a rabbi maintains his position merely by virtue of the effective sermons that are given on Shabbat. After the initial trial, the pulpit is nothing more than another avenue of communication between rabbi and congregation, and possibly not even the most important. Rabbis are certainly ill-advised to spend endless hours on perfecting speeches, at the same time as they neglect some of the more basic components of rabbi–congregation interaction, such as hospital visitation, shivah empathizing, and other person-to-person encounters that develop and cement long-lasting relationships. Over the long haul, congregants reaffirm their original choice of rabbi on the basis of personal experience rather than public performance.

Thus, it is important for the rabbi to place the pulpit, its allures and its pitfalls, into proper perspective when mapping out rabbinic priorities.

THE RABBINATE AS A PROFESSION

There are some who choose to become a rabbi as a career choice, much as they would choose to be a lawyer, a doctor, an architect, or an accountant. There are others who embrace the rabbinate because of a sense of mission. For them the rabbinate is a calling.

These are the individuals who are more likely to be very idealistic, and these are the types of individuals who would be most likely to be disappointed, if not immediately, then eventually. For, unfortunately, their idealism is very often not matched by that of their congregants. A sense of frustration sets in at the inability to do that which one sets out to do, whether it is to make the congregation more sensitive, more religious, more cohesive, or a combination of the three.

The individual who has placed all of his eggs in the rabbinical basket is the one most ripe for disappointment at the results of such an investment. The individual who is on fire when entering the rabbinate is one who is most in danger of eventual burnout. Burnout has a greater chance of occurring among those who have high ideals which are unfortunately not reciprocated.

It is obviously folly to tell an individual contemplating the rabbinate to forget about ideals and just approach the rabbinate as a profession. By so doing, the rabbinical candidate will be a much less effective rabbi. However, it is important to have some sense of balance, a perspective on the situation. One should have ideals, but one should make sure that the ideals do not have him.

There are expectations that one should have entering the rabbinate, but they should be realistic, and they should be long range. Instant change is a myth, and the great rabbis who have served their North American congregations have, with rare exception, achieved within their congregations only after having established solid and lasting relationships within the congregational family. So it is important to have high expectations, but it is also important to expect that it will take a while for these expectations to materialize.

Also, one should always contemplate the possibility that one will fail to achieve the ideals. In the end, one is merely obligated to do one's best, and to leave the rest to the unfolding of fate. It is a two-way street that the rabbi embarks upon, and for all that the rabbi works doggedly, determinedly, and devotedly to better the congregation, the congregation may simply not want to adopt the rabbi's agenda. This does not indicate rabbinic failing, it is more a failure of the rabbi–congregation dynamics.

However important the congregation may be in the rabbi's life, the rabbi should never put so much emotional and psychic energy into the congregation that nothing is left for family. The rabbi's wife and children often suffer from the neglect that comes from the rabbi placing too much emphasis on the congregation, and literally waking up and going to sleep with congregational matters on his mind. But every rabbi, at some point or another in rabbinic life, confronts a crisis situation or a disappointment, and there is usually no better confidant with whom to discuss congregational matters in a confidential and helpful manner than one's wife.

The rabbi who has neglected the wife and family in favor of the congregation runs the risk of not finding a receptive and understanding spouse when the need arises. Spouses may understandably build up a hefty reservoir of resentment against the congregation which has stolen their mate, and in a time of need may offer less than constructive advice, as their way — unconscious but real — of redressing a bad situation.

Additionally, there are so many occasions when the rabbi may be disappointed, upset, or even depressed, and if there is no home life, then that depression will only be more deeply entrenched. A happy home life helps to place things into balanced perspective, helps to neutralize budding depression, and in many instances helps to avoid it. The rabbi who knows that after a harrowing board confrontation he can go home to a happy family is much better off for it, and can deal with the unpleasant situations in a more confident and effective manner.

While being a rabbi is an imposing and often exhausting calling, rabbis are well-advised to have something aside from the rabbinate that deflects from the intensive involvement with life as a rabbi. A scholarly project, a book, further studies, are all things that the rabbi should contemplate, among other possibilities that will give an added dimension to life.

In tackling the all-encompassing tasks that are demanded of a rabbi, the question often arises of where should one place one's energies. While this obviously depends on the needs of the particular congregation, it can be generally stated that a rabbi is best advised to do a little bit less, but do it better, rather than do so many things but none of them well. Concentrating, for example, on solidifying the youth component of a congregation, even if it may be to the relative neglect of social events, may be a worthwhile investment, rather than doing them both in a half-baked manner.

Of course, depending on resources, the rabbi may be able to generate positive results in both dimensions, but generally it is worthwhile to gauge where the priorities should be, and then assure that what is undertaken is done with maximum impact and effectiveness. The rabbi should at all costs try to avoid the administrator/ fundraiser/benediction giver pattern that often afflicts the rabbinate. The rabbi is primarily an educator, and a catalyst for communal betterment, rather than merely an executive, or a pontificator, and should try to whatever extent possible to make sure that this is how the rabbinical endeavor expresses itself. The rabbinate as a profession is thus ultimately what the rabbi professes it to be.

PERSONAL MATTERS

The individual who decides upon the rabbinic way of life obviously cannot succeed if meek. A meek person is a very unlikely leader. Submitting oneself to the very process of selection demands a sense of confidence, even a slight tinge of aggressiveness.

However, the aggressive cum arrogant personality is likely to turn people off, and make too many enemies before even having a chance to make friends. It is therefore vital for the rabbi to behave in a humble manner, although in a realistically humble manner. The rabbi should not be self-effacing to the point of being a convenient target, instead quietly confident while not being cocky; self-assured with a good sense of self-esteem, but certainly not arrogant.

The rabbi who has his ego out front is much like the pugilist who has his nose out front. Both will get battered. There are certainly many opportunities for ego fulfillment within the rabbinate, but a rabbi is ill-advised to seek these out in the course of rabbinic expression. When and if they come, they should be appreciated, but if they are sought after, then they become an impediment to sober judgment and effective leadership.

In this regard, the rabbi should not be dependent on compliments, or depressed by criticism. The compliments are often ingratiating, and not seriously meant; the criticism may be well-intentioned advice that can really help the rabbi.

Rabbis particularly enjoy being told by their congregants how much a speech was enjoyed, and are particularly unhappy with negative reactions to speeches. As mentioned previously, one should in the first instance not put that much stock in speeches. Additionally, one should not place the ego out in the fore to the extent that it needs steady massage, and cannot tolerate a little bit of a puncture in the ego balloon. Either situation makes the rabbi a vulnerable, fragile personality who cannot lead.

It is true, as many claim, that the rabbi is human like anyone else, but the nature of the rabbinate as a profession demands that the rabbi be a little bit more mature than is required in other professions. As leader of a congregation, the rabbi cannot afford to have the host of character aberrations that will impact negatively on his ability to lead.

A leader must be above pettiness, above trivial concerns, and well adjusted personally. A true leader need not insult or put down, a true leader dare not sulk at the slightest insult or ill-advised remark hurled at him, a true leader should be mature and well developed personally, to be above being affected by insignificant and ultimately meaningless nonsense.

It is not often the case that rabbis fit this mode, but rabbis are well advised before becoming leaders of the congregations that without this quality, they will encounter difficulties that could have and should have been avoided.

The rabbi, in approaching his congregational obligations, should not be in a rush to change the world. People react quite negatively when they are told, either explicitly or implicitly, that what they have done until now has been wrong, and must be improved or changed.

The rabbi who starts off in this direction is immediately branded as an interferer, an upstart, and by being so labeled almost instantaneously loses the congregation's confidence. The rabbi is best off using the first year or two as a learning experience, to understand what makes the congregation tick, what is the nature of their way of doing things, and only afterwards seeing how he can make significant but not drastic and revolutionary adjustment for the better.

It is useful for the rabbi to adopt the following general rule without exception, even though, stated in its categorical terminology, may seem a bit too extreme: *never ever get into personal fights with any member of the congregation for whatever reason.*

I am aware that people may say that there are some situations when there are legitimate exceptions, but after all is said and done, there really is no reason why a rabbi should ever be obliged to enter into a fight. There are belligerent congregants who may goad rabbis into bellicose verbal confrontations, but it takes two to tango, and the rabbi should be able to deflect the verbal hype and bring the congregant down to a respectable mode, and to neutralize any attempts to engage in exchanging invective.

No rabbi would have any more reason to engage in personal mudslinging than Moshe Rabbeinu, when he was confronted with the unwarranted and insulting challenge of Korah and his cohorts. Yet even in this instance, when the reaction of outrage would have been understandable, Moshe Rabbeinu instead chose the conciliatory approach and, in fact, went up to his self-declared rivals and tried to make peace with them. This should be the model rabbis adopt.

In the person of Moshe Rabbeinu, we have a clear instance of a leader who did not allow ego to get in the way of community, and instead saw everything in perspective. The destiny of the congregation was far more important to Moshe Rabbeinu than his own position, and he reacted accordingly. This is what is asked of the rabbi.

CONCLUSION

After enumerating many of the pitfalls, certainly not all of them, that a rabbi may expect in congregational life, one may wonder whether it pays to become a rabbi at all. There are so many matters of which to be aware, so many dangers, so many potential crises and disappointments.

This is undoubtedly true, but there is hardly an endeavor in life that is free of dangers. The institution of marriage involves so many delicate considerations, yet it would be ridiculous to suggest that because of this, one should be denied the great fulfillments that come from married life or from parenthood. A parent has so many difficult hurdles to overcome, including sleepless nights, worries about the child, confrontations with the child as the child grows up, anxieties about the child's future. And once the child has become well established and the parent can relax, the anxieties of grandparenthood begin.

What makes it all worthwhile is the fulfillment that comes from being a happy spouse or a contented parent. One is not always guaranteed that this will be the case, but usually, one gets out of a relationship what one puts into it.

Being a rabbi has many potential risks, but as one travels the right road—and the right road is the one that is charted through knowing where not to go because that is where the pitfalls are—there is no end to the potential fulfillments that come from a healthy rabbi–congregation dynamic.

The pleasures that one experiences from steering a couple in the right direction upon marriage, or of uplifting the spirits of someone who is not well, or of comforting someone who is experiencing intense bereavement, are uplifting and ennobling. Other professions may have less problems, but they also have less meaningful human fulfillment.

The rabbi who goes into the rabbinate for the right reasons, and with the right motivations, will eventually, if not immediately, realize that he made the right decision. It is therefore crucial to know the pitfalls, so that one does not enter into the rabbinate blindly. Certainly, entering into the rabbinate blindly is not the way for an individual who is expected to be a "man of vision!"

15

The Rabbi as a Ben Torah

Rabbi Mordechai Willig

Rav Hayyim Soloveitchik has said that too many rabbis believe that they are exempt from the mitzvah of Talmud Torah. In the contemporary rabbinate, the lack of learning on the part of such a rabbi is less defensible than ever. While the demands on his time can be overwhelming, it is surely the case that the rabbi must set aside regular hours for and attach priority to such study—as much for his congregants as for himself, as a Rav and ben torah. At such times, congregants must know that he is not available, save for genuine emergencies. Rabbi Mordechai Willig, rabbi and rosh yeshivah, provides his perspective, advice, and personal example on this fundamental issue.

Chazal have taught that Jewish leadership must be appropriate for the particular needs of the generation. In our times, we are witness to a tremendous increase in Torah learning in America. Graduates of the major yeshivot, including Rabbeinu Yitzchak Elchanan, have been exposed to the teachings of great roshei yeshivah and often continue learning despite heavy professional or business schedules. A spiritual leader can ill afford to lag behind congregants in Torah scholarship or assiduousness.

While this challenge may seem formidable, it should be recognized as a key element in a rabbi's personal growth. In the past, while some congregational rabbis have flourished in the spiritual wasteland of ignorant communities in Europe and the United States, pursuing their Torah studies almost uninterruptedly, many more have languished and stagnated. The image of the rabbi as a glorified toastmaster, social worker, and politician is a direct result of this phenomenon.

This is not surprising. Most individuals, even rabbis, lack the discipline to engage in regular, rigorous talmudic study without any recognition or professional need. One who is never called upon to deliver a high-level shiur or to render a complex halakhic ruling is likely to abandon his serious Torah study. In this sense, today's rabbi, who serves a better Jewishly educated laity, is blessed by the challenge of being a true talmid chakham, a perennial student. Even the higher degree of general education and intellectual interest which pervades the broader society compels the rabbi to raise the standards of instruction.

To accomplish this goal and meet this challenge, a rabbi must establish fixed sedarim for Torah learning. Too often, the daily schedule is filled with other activities, with Talmud Torah relegated to gaps in the appointment calendar which are not appropriate for extended, concentrated study. Superficial learning yields little growth or satisfaction, and simply doesn't meet the emerging needs of our communities.

Ideally, a rabbi should teach in a school setting. There is no substitute for the inquisitiveness of youth. One who is committed to prepare and organize lessons and to answer questions is forcibly involved in serious Torah study. Many synagogues have come to realize that the time spent by their rabbi in a yeshivah setting is ultimately to their benefit.

In any event, the rabbi should prepare thoroughly for a weekly Talmud shiur, ordinarily given on Shabbat afternoon. For some congregants, this is the only Talmud studied all week. For others, the shiur must be sufficiently attractive to be preferred to self-study. In either case, a cogent presentation is essential to attract and satisfy the needs of the congregants. Of course, the problem of heterogenous backgrounds and abilities is a serious one. But if the rabbi is to excel in his primary role of teacher, he must strive to overcome this problem.

The area of *pesak halakhah* is also a wonderful source for growth in Torah knowledge. Rabbis who routinely refer all halakhic questions whose answers they do not know to more learned colleagues are depriving themselves of an excellent opportunity to add to their realms of competence. Ideally, a rabbi should research the issue himself, becoming well acquainted with the primary and secondary sources, and only then consult with others to ascertain that his conclusions are justified.

Indeed, a series of shiurim on topics of *halakhah le'ma'aseh* can be very popular in a synagogue setting. Even those unqualified for, or uninterested in, a purely abstract talmudic discourse usually find the analysis of a practical question, and its relation to the ultimate resolution, to be fascinating. Thus, the need to render a *pesak*, aside from its own inherent value, can assist the rabbi to learn and to teach.

The rabbi's library should conform to his scholarly needs and predilections. If one delves extensively into primary sources, they should be part of his library. Secondary sources, including recent anthologies of talmudic or halakhic texts, are extremely useful. English language works can be valuable tools as well, especially for teaching beginners.

A rabbi's main role is to influence his congregants. The word *influence* relates to the word *flow*, or more precisely, *overflow*. One can be *mashpia* only by virtue of his own *shefa*. A rabbi cannot instill the love of Torah study to others unless he has an overflowing, burning commitment to Talmud Torah. A Rav who is a *matmid* inspires his congregants and earns their respect as he progresses in his scholarship and competence. The rabbinate enables a talmid chakham who loves Torah *lishmah* to merit the many great things that Chazal enumerated (*Avot* 6:1). Such a rabbi, and his community, are indeed fortunate.

16

The Rabbi as Judaica Scholar

Rabbi Jacob J. Schacter

Rabbi Jacob J. Schacter makes a powerful case for the rabbinic benefits to be drawn from a familiarity with modern Judaic scholarship, as well as contemporary literature. While the study of Torah, traditionally defined, is pivotal, there is a growing body of academic research and publication that can serve to deepen one's appreciation and understanding of traditional texts. Such studies can maximize the rabbi's impact as a speaker and teacher, at the same time adding an important dimension to one's own learning.

My heart was always inclined to know [and] to examine worldly matters as well; the [various] nations and faiths, their characteristics and dispositions, their histories and wisdoms, all of whose matters cannot be known from our sacred books. This was also [necessary] in order to know how to respond [to a heretic], to mingle comfortably with people, to know the proper etiquette of each country. . . . All this I yearned to learn from their own books in the original. . . .[1]

The study of Torah is undoubtedly the most important component of Jewish religious life. It is the most central religious imperative binding on all Jews and certainly is an obligation for rabbis who are directly responsible for the accurate transmission of its values and teachings. Nevertheless, this emphasis on the primacy of Torah study notwithstanding, great rabbinic scholars throughout the generations were also involved in a wide variety of extra-talmudic disciplines and acknowledged their value even when they were not directly applied to elucidate specific Torah laws or customs. From ancient through modern times, a large number of universally acknowledged rabbinic authorities recognized the importance of such knowledge and integrated it into their way of thinking and writing. As the quote from Rabbi Emden indicates, primacy of Torah study does not necessarily imply exclusivity.[2]

While secular studies were always valued throughout our history, their importance is even greater today. The moral relativism and intellectual skepticism characteristic of contemporary society have provided an unprecedented challenge to traditional Jewish life. All segments of the Orthodox community have been forced to devise strategies to cope with these new realities. Some advocate complete withdrawal from what is becoming an ever more alien and hostile world. For others, modern or centrist Orthodox Jews, this is no solution. By opting to function wholly within Western society while continuing to maintain a strict allegiance to Torah study and observance of mizvot, we have chosen to confront the challenges of contemporary culture head-on by seeking ways of resolving the apparent conflicts that arise out of living in both worlds. The knowledgeable rabbi, learned in both Torah and secular culture, is in the best position to achieve this goal and thus provide sorely needed guidance in these confusing times.

In addition, growing numbers of modern Orthodox Jews are becoming increasingly more intellectually sophisticated. Many of these have had the benefit of advanced yeshiva education and high level postgraduate professional training. Their level of knowledge is impressive in the areas of secular disciplines as well as in Torah. As a result, rabbis who serve such *balebatim* must also have such broad intellectual interests if they are to be effective. A more literate and educated laity expects its rabbi to have wide-ranging secular and Torah knowledge and to bring these different disciplines together in intelligent and meaningful ways. If Rabbi Emden could write in the second half of the eighteenth century that secular knowledge was important to enable someone "to mingle comfortably with people," how much more true is it for a rabbi today when such knowledge is so widespread among the members of his own congregation. He must speak the language of his community and can only do so if he shares their level of intellectual sophistication. In most modern Orthodox congregations, the more knowledgeable and worldly the rabbi, the more he will be respected and by extension, the greater will be his impact and success.

An openness to and appreciation of the world beyond the Gemara is indispensable for a number of practical reasons. First, it enables the rabbi to express himself in a clear and articulate manner. In the homiletics seminar I took as a semikhah student in Mesivta Torah Vodaath in the early 1970s, our teacher, Rabbi Moshe Sherer, encouraged us to read the editorial page of *The New York Times* every day. It was very important, he said, not so much for its content as for its rich vocabulary and felicitous style. Read it long enough, he counseled, and you will slowly be able to raise the level of sophistication of your own speaking. In a long conversation with Dr. Norman Lamm shortly after I became Rabbi of The Jewish Center, he told me that he regularly read *Saturday Review* for the same reason and also recommended the works of Loren Eiseley, the noted anthropologist. My own favorite is *The New Republic*, which I find most useful for its clever turns of phrase and elegant literary style. Clarity of expression and eloquence of presentation are the first critical components for a successful rabbinate, "all of whose matters cannot be known from our sacred books."

Second, the content of any contemporary rabbinic presentation is greatly enriched by allusions to modern secular literature. The following, taken from my own sermons during the last year or two, are only some examples of how such works can be very useful in illustrating matters of concern and interest to us and our listeners: Thornton Wilder's *Our Town* for an example of the fleeting nature of life, Anthony Storr's *Solitude: A Return to the Self* for a discussion of the introspection necessary during the *Yamim Nora'im*, John Updike's presentation of the conflict between science and religion in *Roger's Version*, Erich Fromm's *The Forgotten Language* on the nature of symbolism, and Harvey Cox's *Religion in the Secular City* on the *ba'al teshuvah* phenomenon. Older and more well-known examples I have also used are Soren Kierkegaard's *Fear and Trembling* on the *akeidah*,[3] Rudolf Otto's notion of *mysterium tremendum* in his *The Idea of the Holy* for a characterization of the transcendent quality of God, and the series of books by Elizabeth Kubler-Ross on aspects of *hilkhot aveilut*. Not only are these works intrinsically worthwhile for the different dimensions and perspectives they provide, but they also enhance the rabbi's level of respect in the community. The ability of the rabbi to incorporate this type of material regularly into his sermons, lectures, and even personal conversations raises his stature in the eyes of his congregants and is thus essential to his success.

A third and more directly useful component for the well-rounded modern Orthodox rabbi is familiarity with the growing world of Jewish scholarship. A historically oriented approach to Jewish texts will clearly enhance one's understanding of many areas of halakhah and hashkafah and enable the rabbi to present this material to others in a more complete and interesting way. For example, a knowledge of Jewish history is indispensable for a full appreciation of the *teshuvah* of the Rosh about the different practices relevant to the recital of *ve-ten tal u-matar* (She'elot u-Teshuvot ha-Rosh 4:10); the cross-cultural influences referred to by the Taz regarding the varying customs in lighting Hanukkah candles (*Orah Hayyim* 671:1); the opinion of Tosafot (*Avodah Zarah* 2a, s.v. Asur) that medieval Christians should not be considered in the category of idolaters;[4] the institution of the "Shabbat goy";[5] the earliest time in the day one is permitted to daven Ma'ariv;[6] or even the perennial struggle against talking in the synagogue during services.[7]

There is a great deal of material in books and periodicals discussing various halakhot and minhagim from such a more scholarly, historical perspective, and the literature is growing rapidly. The bibliography (pp. 172–174) contains just a few examples taken from the literature relating specifically to the *chagim* that I have found to be effective in the shiurim and lectures I have delivered in my own shul during the last few years. The works listed are intended to illustrate the kind of material already available on relatively familiar subjects. I do not agree with all their conclusions, but they all provide interesting perspectives which will undoubtedly serve to enrich any presentation on the issues they address. All the periodicals listed in the bibliography contain any number of articles on halakhic themes from a more scholarly perspective. I suggest that the reader skim through them all on a regular basis and occasionally choose those subjects or areas that are of greatest interest. They will certainly prove to be of great value in the preparation of shiurim and lectures.

Also listed in the bibliography are several books and periodicals that I can recommend as containing many similarly useful presentations.

Furthermore, in any shiur or class I give, I invariably digress for a moment to touch briefly upon some aspect of the life of the particular figure whose opinion I am quoting. For example, I have discussed the Rambam's encounter with the Almohades in twelfth-century Spain, the death of the Mordecai in the Rindfleisch massacres in Germany at the end of the thirteenth century, the maggid of R. Yosef Karo in sixteenth-century Turkey,[8] the Sabbatian controversies of Chakham Zevi in the seventeenth century, and the banking career of R. Barukh ha-Levi Epstein, author of the *Torah Temimah*, at the turn of the twentieth century. Not only do these little excursi present the listener with a more well-rounded perspective on these great rabbinic scholars, they also serve to make the shiur or lecture more interesting and enjoyable for teacher and student alike.

There is one final benefit to developing an interest in secular studies and Jewish scholarship, one that applies equally as much to maintaining a regular program of ongoing Torah study as well. Quite apart from their role in helping the rabbi enhance his effectiveness as a professional, they are also rich sources for personal growth and development. In spite of our best intentions at the beginning of our careers, we very often find ourselves caught up in the daily pressing demands that take up the bulk of our time and tend to neglect our obligation to continue to develop ourselves as talmidei chakhamim and as intellectuals. Even those of us who participate in active adult education programs often find ourselves preparing just to "get by" the class and not learning or studying for ourselves. We are so busy running around nurturing others that we have precious little time left to nurture ourselves. My father, Rabbi Herschel Schacter, often told me that his father used to illustrate this point by reference to the principle in *Chullin* (113a; Rashi, s.v. Ela), "*di-khol zeman she-terudim liflot einan bol'im.*" We are so busy being *polet* to everyone else that we don't have time to be *bole'a* for ourselves. This is a potentially tragic situation and could lead to an unhappy, resentful, and ultimately unsuccessful rabbinate. Torah study and scholarship are critically important because they give us an outlet for our interest and creativity, help us develop ourselves as Jews and human beings, and provide a balance between our synagogue lives and our private lives. Such involvement could take many forms—personal study, working toward a graduate degree, teaching at a local university and/or publishing books and articles. However we choose to pursue them, Jewish and secular scholarship enhance our personal fulfillment as well as our professional effectiveness.

SELECTED BIBLIOGRAPHY

Shabbat

Ta-Shema, I. (1975–1976). Ner shel Kavod. *Tarbiz* 45:128–137. The historical origin and social and halakhic implications of the minhag to light a minimum of two Shabbat candles.

Rosh Hashanah

Bloom, N. A. (1978). The Rosh Hashanah prayers—historical perspectives. *Tradition* 17:51–73.

Gartner, J. (1972). Ta-anit bi-Rosh Hashanah. *Hadarom* 38:69–77.

_____ (1973). Ta-anit bi-Rosh Hashanah. *Hadarom* 36:125–162.

Speigel, S. (1967). *The Last Trial*. New York: Pantheon Books. A treatment of various midrashim on the *akeidah*.

Tabori, J. (1978–1979). Le-Mikomah shel Birkhat Malkhuyot bi-Tefillat Rosh Hashanah. *Tarbiz* 48:30–34.

Yom Kippur

Finkelstein, L. (1938). The ten martyrs. In *Essays and Studies in Memory of Linda R. Miller*, pp. 29–55. New York: Jewish Theological Seminary of America.

Kraus, S. (1925). Asarah Marugei Malkhut. *Ha-Shiloah* 44:10–22, 106–117, 221–233.

Lauterbach, J. Z. (1935). The ritual for the Kapparot ceremony. In *Jewish Studies in Memory*, ed. S. Baron and A. Marx, pp. 413–422. New York: The Alexander Kohut Memorial Foundation. Reprinted in J. Z. Lauterbach (1970) *Studies in Jewish Law, Custom and Folklore*, pp. 133–142. New York: Ktav.

Merhavyah, H. (1984). Kol Nidrei—ben Ba'ayah le-Chidah. In *Sefer ha-Yovel li-Khvod Morenu ha-Gaon Rabbi Yosef Dov Halevi Soloveitchik Shlita*, vol. 2, pp. 1056–1096. Jerusalem: Mosad Harav Kook.

Reik, T. (1931). A theory on Kol Nidrei. In *Ritual: Psycho-Analytic Studies*, pp. 167–219. London: The Hogarth Press.

Weider, N. (1978). Avar ve-Atid bi-Nusach Kol Nidrei. In *Mikhtam le-David*, pp. 180–209. Ramat Gan, Israel: Bar Ilan University.

Zimmels, H. J. (1947). The historical background of the Midrash Eleh Ezkerah. In *Semitic Studies in Memory of Immanuel Low*, pp. 334–338. Budapest: The Alexander Kohut Memorial Foundation.

Sukkot

Newman, J. (1967). Isru Hag. In *Essays Presented to Chief Rabbi Israel Brodie on the Occasion of His Seventieth Birthday*, ed. H. J. Zimmels, J. H. Rabinowitz, and I. Finestein, pp. 301–310. London: Soncino.

Tselnik, N. (1973). *Atzeret*. Jerusalem: Machon Harry Fischel. About Shemini Atzeret, Shevi'i shel Pesach, and Shavuot.

Zimmer, E. (1973). Yeshivah bi-Sukkah bi-Shemini Atzeret bi-Kehillot Ashkenez. *Sinai* 73:252–262.

Hanukkah

Alon, G. (1977). Did the Jewish people and its sages cause the Hasmoneans to be forgotten? In *Jews, Judaism and the Classical World*, pp. 1–17. Jerusalem: Magnes Press.

Ninth of Tevet

Leiman, S. (1983). The Scroll of Fasts: The Ninth of Tebet. *Jewish Quarterly Review* 74:174–195.

Pesach

Tabori, J. (1977). Le-Toledat Hilkhot Leil ha-Seder. Unpublished doctoral dissertation. Jerusalem: Bar-Ilan University.

Yom Hashoah

Baumel, J. T. (1988). Zikhron Olam—Tefillot ve-Yemei Evel le-Achar ha-Shoah le-Zekher Korbanot ha-Shoah. *Sinai* 101:271–284.

Michman, D. (1983). Ve-Emunah Initani—al Magamot bi-Emunah bi-Yemei ha-Shoah. *Millet* 1:341–350.

Yom Yerushalayim

Bialoblutzky, S. (1948–1952). Yerushalayim bi-Halakhah. In *Alei Ayin*, pp. 25–74. Jerusalem.
Werblowsky, R. J. Z. (1973–1974). The meaning of Jerusalem to Jews, Christians and Muslims. *Jaarbericht Ex Orient Lux* 23. Reprinted as a separate pamphlet by the Israel Universities Study Group for Middle Eastern Affairs, Jerusalem, 1977.

Tisha B'Av

Cohen, N. J. (1982). Shekhinta bi-Galuta: a midrashic response to destruction and persecution. *Journal for the Study of Judaism* 13:147–159.
Goldenberg, R. (1982). Early rabbinic explanations of the destruction of Jerusalem. *Journal of Jewish Studies* 33:517–525.
Mintz, A. (1984). *Hurban: Responses to Catastrophe in Hebrew Literature.* New York: Columbia University Press.
Polen, N. (1987). Divine weeping: Rabbi Kalonymous Shapira's theology of catastrophe in the Warsaw ghetto. *Modern Judaism* 7:253–269.
Roskies, D. (1984). *Against the Apocalypse: Responses to Catastrophe in Modern Jewish Culture.* Cambridge, MA: Harvard University Press.

ADDITIONAL BOOKS AND PERIODICALS

Ashkenazy, S. (1977). *Dov Dor u-Minhagav.* Tel Aviv: Don Publishing House.
Hilvitz, H. (1976). *Chikei Zemanim I.* Jerusalem: Mosad Harav Kook.
———— (1981). *Chikei Zemanim II.* Jerusalem: Mosad Harav Kook.
Zimmels, H. J. (1958). *Ashkenazim and Sephardim.* London: Oxford University Press.
Barkai
Ha-Ma'ayon
L'Eylah
Machanayim
Niv ha-Medrashiya
Shanah bi-Shanah

NOTES

[1]Rabbi Jacob Emden, *Megillat Sefer*, ed. D. Kahana. (Warsaw: Shuldberg Bros. and Partners, 1896), pp. 96–97.

[2]I am the editor of a forthcoming book to be published under the auspices of the Torah U-Madda Project of Yeshiva University that will document this phenomenon in detail. It will include essays by Dr. Gerald Blidstein on *tekufat Chazal*, Dr. David Berger on the medieval period, Dr. Shnayer Leiman on the modern period, and Rabbi Aharon Lichtenstein, who will discuss the issue from a more general, philosophical perspective.

[3]See M. Fox, "Kierkegaard and Rabbinic Judaism," *Judaism* 11 (1953), pp. 160–169.

[4]See J. Katz, *Exclusiveness and Tolerance* (London: Oxford University Press, 1961). See also I. Ta-Shema, Yemei Edehem: Perek bi-Hitpat'chut ha-Halakhah bi-Yemei ha-Benayim. *Tarbiz* 47 (1978), pp. 197–215.

[5]See J. Katz, *The "Shabbes Goy": A Study in Halachic Flexibility* (Philadelphia: Jewish Publication Society, 1989).

[6]See J. Katz, Ma'ariv bi-Zemano u-Shelo bi-Zemano: Dugma le-Zikah ben Minhag, Halakhah ve-Chevrah. *Zion* 35 (1970), pp. 35–60.

[7]See M. Hallamish, Sichot Chullin bi-Bet ha-Knesset—Metzi'ut u-Ma'avak. *Milet* 2 (1985), pp. 225–251.

[8]See R. J. Z. Werblowsky, *Joseph Karo: Lawyer and Mystic* (Philadelphia: Jewish Publication Society, 1977).

17

The Rabbi as a Unifying Force

Rabbi Saul Berman

Lincoln Square Synagogue is a unique institution—by virtue of its location and rabbinic leadership. Even so, the rabbinic experience of leading so challenging an institution bears significance for other rabbis in various settings. The benefits as well as stresses, the satisfactions as well as frustrations, the need to draw lines between public and personal spheres, are all concerns that every rabbi can appreciate. Rabbi Saul Berman shares some insightful and deeply personal perspectives from the viewpoint of an academician turned rabbi. While he is no longer associated with the synagogue, his observations remain relevant to our concerns.

The challenges in my own move from Jewish academician to congregational rabbi were clearly enormous: to expand the concept of spiritual achievement so as to more include the ethical as well as the ritual; to provide the stimulus and the opportunity for learned Jews to continue their Jewish intellectual growth; to foster greater religious intensity while keeping the community open to alienated and unaffiliated Jews; to provide as many doorways as possible through which any Jew might enter and taste the sweetness of Torah; to help shatter the sense of isolation and aloneness of singles, of single parents, of newcomers in a city which fosters anonymity; to intensify opportunities for religious expression by women within the structure of halakhah; to lead the congregation to a greater awareness of our responsibilities to both Jewish and non-Jewish needy and homeless; and more.

It is very difficult to say how distinctively my goals are correlated to the size and setting of the congregation, but it is perfectly clear to me that both size and setting impact enormously on the character of my own work and experience. First, as to size, Lincoln Square Synagogue has a membership of approximately 700 families and 500 single persons of all ages. Beyond the membership, approximately half of the 850 people registered in weekly classes are nonmembers; over one third of the 1,200 people who crowd five separate services every Shabbat morning are not members; our outreach and community action programs reach deeply into the Jewish community, far beyond our own membership. For me, it has been very difficult to relate to the congregation as a community — it feels more like a town or even a small city. And if I feel that way, how must lay people feel about it? On the other hand, the exhilaration of being in the midst of an overcrowded sanctuary, of the street being blocked every Shabbat after tefillah by 1,000 people socializing, lends a special intensity and vitality to the sense of being Jewish.

Size makes for another tension. Even with the total devotion of an extraordinary staff of two additional rabbis, a cantor, and outreach and community action professionals — serving a community this large and this diverse is a constantly frustrating undertaking for two reasons. First, programs and services implemented at great pains and with enormous effort to serve one segment of the community or one dimension of its ideology are often perceived by other segments of the community as, at best, wasteful, and at worst, ideologically offensive. Some of my proudest achievements in the four years I have been at the synagogue are the creation of the L.S.S. Lehrhaus providing an opportunity for advanced Jewish study with some of the finest Jewish scholars of America and Israel; the expansion of the Women's Service from an occasional to a regularly and frequently scheduled service; the development of our youth program as a vibrant force for Jewish informal education and experience; the implementation of "Turn Friday Night Into Shabbos" as a national program in which over 4,000 Jews participated in twenty-three synagogues across the U.S. and Canada; the creation of a Community Action program encompassing political action on behalf of Israel and Soviet Jewry as well as food drives, clothing drives, toy drives, and programs and conferences on the environment and on world hunger; and the development of a nonprofessional shadkhen service and the dialogue program between members of L.S.S. and members of Stephen Wise Free Synagogue.

These projects and programs without exception have been sub-ject to both acclaim and condemnation within the congregation. Helping people stretch their ideological tolerance seems to be a constant but thankless task at all ends of the spectrum. Size and diversity seem to assure that there will always be a vocal minority who think that the particular effort is either too expensive, not appropriate for a synagogue, not sufficiently responsive to the problem, too much of a compromise, too fragmenting of the community, or too concerned with keeping everybody happy. I have grown increasingly intolerant of and impatient with this particular phenomenon.

The second area of impact of size and diversity has been the effect on my own intellectual growth and on my relationship to my family. On one hand, the range of halakhic questions with which I am compelled to deal both as individual *she'elot* and as communal policy, is enormous. How should our Chevra Kadisha relate to a deceased who had AIDS? May an unmarried woman plan to have a child by artificial insemination by donor? Is a proper eruv really halakhicly possible in a Manhattan neighborhood? These, and a plethora of questions related to business ethics, medical ethics, and ritual matters occupy a significant portion of my intellectual energies, and have broadened my knowledge of and insight into the operation of Jewish law in the real world enormously. But by the same token I no longer have any time during the year for the sort of systematic research and analysis of problems and sharpening of ideas through sharing with colleagues—which, at one time, were such an essential element of my intellectual identity.

As for the impact on my relationship to my family—suffice it to say that being in the rabbinate while attempting to be an involved, responsive, and responsible husband, and father of four young chil-dren, has been for me, a losing battle. I find increasing discrepancy between my own beliefs, sermons, and teaching on the quality of family life and the reality of my own availability to those I so deeply love. I find it increasingly unacceptable to remember that I used to have friends for whom I had time and emotional energy and have that no more. The issue is not even the unrealistic demands created by the few embittered souls who could never be satisfied with my efforts on

their behalf—indeed, for them, even messianic intervention would
probably not suffice. It is rather the reality of the undertaking,
precisely the size and diversity of the congregation which generates the
need for constant availability, or as one congregant put it, "We need a
rabbi on call all the time." Perhaps this is the Achilles heel of my
rabbinate, but I am not willing to assign unequivocal priority to the
needs of the congregation over those of my children, my wife, or
myself.

How have these four-and-a-half years been? There have been
moments of utter frustration at the intractable nature of certain
problems, moments of despair in my inability to relieve pain and
sorrow, moments of anger at people's stubborn unwillingness to see
the obviously good and right, moments of feeling overwhelmed by the
enormity of the task of shaping souls and forming a community. On
the other hand, there have been moments of utter joy in seeing the
spiritual transformation of people I have come to cherish, moments of
enormous gratification in feeling that I have helped someone through
a personal or religious crisis, moments of great pleasure in seeing a bar
or bat mizvah child for whom the synagogue, its ideology and its
essence, have shaped the soul into the next generation. Most of all,
there are moments when I am overwhelmed with a feeling of gratitude
to God for making possible for me a sense of achievement in my
undertakings unparalleled in my prior experience.

18

The Rabbinate as Family

Dr. Irving N. Levitz

By its very nature, the rabbinate tends to make demands of the rabbi that impinge on his family life. Very often the rabbi himself is unaware of the impact, both positive and negative, on his family dynamic. At other times, the rabbi is only too painfully aware of stresses within his family occasioned by his image, role, and duties within the community. There can be no question that to be most effective in his work, he needs the support, understanding, and cooperation of his wife and children. But at the same time he must be sensitive to their needs. Dr. Irving Levitz explores some of these dynamics, based on studies he has done in the field. Some might argue that his findings are not typical. Even so, at the very least the questions he raises should be pondered by every rabbi—for their ramifications for himself, his family, and the community he serves.

For the majority of congregational rabbis, role-related stress is a significant factor affecting not only the rabbi, but his family as well. Always in the public eye, the rabbi, and by association his family, is subject to constant scrutiny, unrealistic expectations, distorted projections, community intrusiveness, economic insecurity, and frequent mobility. In contrast to the average family, the rabbinic family is not only socially more visible, but psychologically more vulnerable.

The rabbinate tends to encircle the life of the rabbi, engulfing him to the point where he has time neither for himself nor for his family. Rabbis are actually involved in negotiating three separate emotionally interfaced family systems—the individual families which make up the congregation; the congregation itself which functions as a family in its own right; and their own nuclear and extended families.

The rabbi is faced with special problems in marriage. He has taken up a role that conflicts with, and seeks to invade, his role as husband. Reflecting the strain experienced in rabbinical families is the precipitous increase in divorce among rabbis.

The results of a study of divorcing clergy seem particularly relevant to rabbinic marriages as well. Seventy percent of divorced clergymen reported that the primary complaint of their former wives was their inordinate time commitment to career. Thirty percent of a sample of rabbis reported that their wives would prefer that they not be rabbis.

In recent years there has been a mushrooming concern about the impact of the rabbinate on both the rabbi and his family. Nevertheless, there has been no empirical data reflecting the effects of rabbinical life on children of rabbinic families. Systems theory clearly suggests that stress on any family member affects the homeostasis and functioning of the entire family.

Though observations of the impact of clerical life upon children of ministers have been reported, despite their obvious roles as barometers of family life, children of rabbis have not been investigated in any systematic way. The purpose of these studies, therefore, was to determine the impact of the rabbinate on children raised in rabbinic families.

It was reasonably expected that children of congregational rabbis would show many of the stresses experienced by children of clergy in general. The higher standards and greater expectations placed upon children of clergy create for them inordinate difficulties in growing up. Consequently, children of clergy experience feelings of isolation and inner conflict emanating from the strong desire to maintain the family image while being accepted by peers as individuals with an identity apart from their ancillary role. Among clergy children, intrafamilial distress is often reflected in episodes of dramatic rebellion, both as a way to attract attention from the clergy parent enmeshed in congregational life, and as an expression of anger against a way of life often experienced as overly restrictive and coercively imposed.

It is reasonable to assume that children of congregational rabbis have much in common with children of all clergy. With the impact of congregational life on rabbinic families as perceived by their children as the focus of this study, it was my interest not only to learn more about the particular blend of anxieties and stresses experienced by rabbinic families, but to investigate their strategies for maintaining homeostasis and stability in light of these stresses.

The three areas of concern that guided this investigation were the impact of the rabbinate on the developing self-identity of rabbinic children, rabbinic family dynamics, and interpersonal relationships outside the family unit.

METHOD

The investigation took the form of a series of in-depth, semistructured interviews of forty children of rabbis who met individually or in small groups (two to three) for a minimum of one hour.

Children of congregational rabbis who served as respondents were selected in several ways. The subject pool consisted of personal contacts, referrals of one respondent by another, and volunteers who incidentally heard about the inquiry and requested interviews.

Since the purpose of the study was to examine the unique experiences of children of congregational rabbis, children of rabbis engaged in educational, organizational, or other professional careers were intentionally excluded.

Of the twenty-three female and seventeen male respondents, the mean age was 26.7, with an age range of 17 to 52 years. They included twenty-two children of Orthodox rabbis, thirteen of Conservative, and five of Reform rabbis. The interview was in two parts. The first involved structured questions pertaining to the three areas of focus, namely issues of identity, interpersonal relationship, and family dynamics. In the second part, respondents were asked to candidly discuss whatever relevant memories, events, or anecdotes, they felt could best reflect their unique experiences as children of rabbis.

In an attempt to expand the opportunity for data collection, and to solicit as wide a range of perception and memory as possible, respondents were invited to submit in writing any experiences, memories, insights, or reactions that came to mind following the interview. Eight respondents submitted written material.

With assurances of strict confidentiality, the interviews generally elicited candid and often cathartic responses, with respondents invariably expressing gratitude for the opportunity to share what they believed were some of the most salient albeit unrecognized dimensions of their development. The high degree of congruence among this diverse group of subjects suggests that their perceptions are not atypical and may be representative of children of congregational rabbis in general.

What follows is a discussion of the emergent patterns reflected in these interviews.

ISSUES OF IDENTITY

By virtue of every psychosocial definition of the construct "role," "rabbi's child" emerges as a distinct role. There are role expectations related to behavior and attitudes, as well as an overall sense of responsibilities associated with the designation son/daughter of a rabbi. It is an ancillary role not unlike that of rabbi's wife, but one acquired by birth, not volition, rooted in a parent's career choice, often unrecognized and undefined, yet apparently having significant impact on the developing identity of rabbinic children. As one rabbi's daughter wrote:

> I always struggled to maintain an identity of my own. I was always introduced by name, then followed by "the Rabbi's daughter." It was as if I couldn't be whole without having the attachment of my father's profession noted. . . . My brothers had it worse. . . . I used to cringe at overhearing congregants comment on the "little rabbis." Even though I really believe that many of these remarks were well intended, the reality was that my brothers and I felt as if we were stripped of the dignity of being who we were first and foremost.

Another rabbi's child bemoaned the fact that for half of the community he did not even have a name. He was simply "the rabbi's son."

Not all rabbis' children experienced the role as entirely negative. For the most part, rabbis' children looked upon their role as one affording them special status. Vicarious identification with a prominent father, and pride associated with his achievements, were for most children of rabbis the positive aspects of the role.

Figuring prominently among the negative aspects of the role, however, was that of experiencing frequent isolation. Rabbis' children also tended to recall a strong sense of isolation during childhood and adolescence. Feeling both "special" and "isolated" seems to best reflect the ambivalence of rabbis' children to their role. An example of this is the rabbi's daughter who expressed great resentment at being so closely identified with her father's profession but recalls standing in front of her yeshiva day school building when she was 11 and proudly proclaiming to all who would listen that her father was the man who built the school. Similarly, a rabbi's son recalled feeling most privileged to sit next to this father in the synagogue, but resented being a rabbi's son when his friends excluded him from hearing any of their off-color jokes or from participating in any group mischief. Ironically, when his father left the rabbinate in an unanticipated career change, he described the experience as a "sense of profound loss."

One young woman felt especially proud when as a student in a new school, she was recognized as the daughter of a prominent community rabbi. She remembers feeling isolated and resentful, however, when a teacher said to her, following a minor misdemeanor which she committed as part of a group, "I would not have expected this kind of behavior from a rabbi's daughter."

PARENTAL ROLE EXPECTATIONS

It is not only the community whose projections and role expectations children of rabbis have to cope with. Instances of role expectations and required role behavior were often overtly and covertly communicated by parents as well. The expression, "*Es past nisht*" ("It is inappropriate") or "What will people say?" often superseded both reason and personal feelings in determining the permissibility of behavior outside the home. At times, rabbinic children received mixed messages. When a rabbi told his son, "First be yourself, and then you can concern yourself with being the rabbi's son," the young man felt relieved that his father was allowing him his own identity. At a later point in time, when he was told that it was expected that he be the valedictorian of his class, because "How would it look if the rabbi's son didn't get it?" he was confused and resentful.

ADOLESCENCE

Developmentally, the issues of identity reach their peak during the sturm und drang of adolescence, a time of identity crisis and "individuation." Strategies for dealing with identity crisis vary significantly among individual rabbis' children. Observations that clergy children tend to act out normal rebellion or experimental behavior in a more dramatic way than others because they want peers to notice and realize that they are not different, appear to be true for rabbis' children as well. One rabbi's son recalls his conscious and abundant use of verbal obscenities so that others would not suspect him of being the son of a rabbi. More than anything else he wanted to be "one of the boys."

At the other end of the spectrum are those few who fully identify with the role of "rabbi's child," apparently without even the most subtle signs of adolescent struggle. One such young man, the only one in this study who ultimately became a rabbi himself, remembers his adolescence as the time when he first began delivering brief sermonettes to the congregation.

For a significant number of rabbis' children, however, developing a personal identity simply meant telling no one—who did not already know—that their fathers were rabbis, and developing relationships outside of the congregation. "For years following my marriage," noted one rabbi's daughter, "I told no one that my father was a rabbi."

RELATIONSHIP TO THE COMMUNITY

Attitudinally, among the most negative experiences reported by children of rabbis, were those involving congregants. Relationships with members of the congregation tended to be associated with a sense of pervasive distrust, discomfort, hurt, and anger. Sitting among members of the congregation, rabbis' children would often feel offended at cynical references and caustic comments critical of their fathers. Most poignant were the instances when a congregant would appoint the rabbi's son as liaison to deliver a pointed message to his father. One rabbi's son recalls being told to "tell your father not to talk too long today." (He was 8 years old at the time.) More than half of the respondents recalled incidents with congregants that were experienced as either intrusive or abusive. In one such instance, a congregant telephoned the rabbi's daughter after Sabbath to tell her that he noticed that morning that her hair was untidy. "Would anyone ever call a dentist's daughter and tell her that?" she asked bitterly. In another instance, a rabbi's son reported on how the president's son would regularly beat up on him, harass him, seek him out, and tease and bully him. "My parents simply told me to avoid him," he said. "But they themselves apparently felt impotent to stop him because he was the president's son. To this day I can still feel rage when I think about it."

The often fickle nature of a congregation's allegiance to its rabbi, and the turning tides of community politics, were most often noted as a painful, albeit crucial experience for children of rabbis. Congregants were often described dichotomously as either "friends" or "enemies." "The people who enter your home, no matter how friendly or supportive, are never really friends," remarked one young respondent cynically. "They are *balebatim* (congregants)." From an early age, most respondents learned that talking to congregants needed to be guided by caution and vigilance. To protect themselves against the possibility of harmful gossip from the congregational network, rabbinic families tend to enforce an especially strict code of security regarding information about the family or information passing through the family. For the rabbinic family, its visibility and vulnerability apparently require firmer boundaries and greater concealment than the average family. Anything less could jeopardize the family's security or community status. For children of rabbis, this meant special precautions and strict censorship regarding family information. For the average adolescent, telling his closest friend that his father has a temper or that his parents argue from time to time is common, but for a rabbi's child, sharing such information would be unthinkable.

One rabbi's son learned early the lessons of what is permissible to share and the extent to which censorship is required. He was 7 years old when he casually told one his friends that it was his father's fortieth birthday. For reasons still unclear, this was considered restricted information and potentially damaging. As he recalled the incident, he could still feel the tension, anxiety, and anger when his parents discovered that he divulged a family secret.

SOCIAL LIFE

As they grew older, the respondents tended to prefer socializing outside of the community. For many, it would be unthinkable to date a member of the congregation. Not only was dating within the community avoided whenever possible "because things done or said in private could ultimately become public" with embarrassing repercussions, but because children of rabbis wanted to be seen as real people, separate and apart from their designated role. Not uncommon was the experience of one rabbi's daughter who, in fact, had seriously dated the son of a congregant only to terminate the relationship when she came to realize that her being the rabbi's daughter was for him one of her most attractive attributes. "I suddenly felt as if I were only an extension of my father's profession, and stripped of my own selfhood." She never dated in the community again.

RABBINIC FAMILY DYNAMICS

The most dramatic impact of congregational life on the children of rabbis was reflected in the many descriptions of family life and family relationships. A significant number of respondents (70 percent) reported that they perceived their fathers as being overinvolved with synagogue life, and their mothers overinvolved with the children. Twenty percent of the respondents described their fathers as emotionally absent from family life. "He wasn't even there when he was there. His mind always seemed preoccupied."

In several instances, rabbinic children expressed resentment at what they perceived to be differential treatment afforded congregational children in contrast to themselves. Examples included not being called upon by the rabbi/father to perform or give an answer in class in order that he not appear preferential. The issue of time and the quality of time spent with other children in the congregation was also frequently noted. "I would watch my father speak very patiently to other children. He would sometimes spend hours with them, but didn't really seem to know that I needed him as well. I wanted to be loved by my father who was so accessible to everyone else, but had so little time and interest in me."

As many rabbinic children described their families, it appeared that the most stressful role within the family structure was often that of the rabbi's wife. She tended to be the critical link between children and father, often functioning as both mediator and liaison. Paradoxically, even among those who resented their father's aloofness and distance, there tended to be an idealization of the rabbinic father, and a tendency toward warmth and emotional closeness with the rabbinic mother. As one respondent wrote of her aloof father:

> My deep identification with my father . . . has been the cornerstone of my personality. I was both fascinated by and scared of my father. Sometimes he stood in my eyes as the symbol of God with . . . strength and mercy. . . . Sometimes he was the strict judge who inspired my fearful respect. But . . . he was always the rabbi par excellence. Unfortunately, we were never close.

Another young woman reflected on her vicarious identification with and obsessive attraction to anyone who had even the faintest resemblance to her father. Through psychotherapy she became sufficiently insightful and aware that she was seeking the affections of a father whom she adored but who had eluded her.

The rabbinic family as a family entity appears very much to revolve around synagogue life. Most often, at one time or another, all family members are recruited to run errands, take telephone messages, serve at an open house or Shabbat tea, as well as conduct Junior services, read the Torah, and call members for a daily minyan. The congregation is seemingly woven into the fabric of rabbinic family life. As one respondent put it: "The rabbinate is a family business. It is open seven days a week, twenty-four hours a day."

In this vein, respondents frequently noted how the urgent needs of congregants tended to intrude on family life. Family dinners, vacations, and Sunday outings were always subject to disruption or cancellation by a phone call requiring the rabbi to attend a funeral, visit a hospital, or negotiate a crisis. Most rabbinic families learned to accept a reality that congregational needs take priority over their own.

Several factors appear critical to the stability of the rabbinic family and the degree of satisfaction with family life for the children of rabbis. As a general rule, family life and individual self-esteem are enhanced when each family member feels valued and rooted in the family structure, identifying with its ideals, goals, struggles, triumphs, and disappointments. The rabbinic family experience apparently offers many meaningful opportunities for family members to be part of a joint venture where both conquests and frustrations can be shared.

It seemed apparent from the interviews that to the degree that children of rabbis were afforded an opportunity to contribute to the family calling, did they have a sense of family solidarity as well as enhanced self-esteem.

Another factor involved the family's perception of the locus of stress. So long as stress was perceived as emanating from outside the family structure, emotional solidarity remained strong. Where, however, hurt and stress were perceived as emanating from within the family, from a father, for example, whose responsiveness to the congregation was viewed as a rejection of his own family, then emotional disunity, rooted in hurtful deprivation, eroded family life.

In this regard, what appeared particularly critical for most of the rabbinic children was the ability of the rabbinic parent to separate professional role from family life and within the family context to consider interaction with their children important. In those instances where rabbis were able to be parents without the encumbrances of their rabbinic role, their children seemed better able to cope with the many conflicts and stresses that they normally encountered.

Relatedly, it was not surprising to find that in those rabbinic families with the greatest degree of reported stability and satisfaction, the marital relationship seemed strongest. Where children perceived their parents as being emotionally close, spending time together, and apparently content in their marriage, positive ripple effects were felt through the family. Conversely, when the rabbinic father was seen as overinvolved in the congregation and mother as overinvolved with the children, both consequently being underinvolved with each other, negative ripple effects reverberated through the family. This family structure is simply less efficient in being able to buffer its members from the stressful intrusiveness of congregational life.

SUMMARY AND CONCLUSION

Thus, several factors have emerged as critical variables for rabbinic children. Where interpersonal relationships are confounded by projections and expectations related to their being children of rabbis, their developing identity and emerging selfhood tend to be tempered by ambivalence and conflict. The very special status afforded them as extensions of their father's clerical position excludes them from full acceptance among peers. Isolation frequently becomes the price paid for noblesse oblige.

The community, always a significant factor in rabbinic life, tends to affect children of rabbis in several ways. The greater the turbulence, factionalism, and instability a community exhibits, the more stress, anxiety, and insecurity the rabbinic family will experience. Disillusionment with yesterday's supporters who have become today's detractors tends to make many rabbinic children less trustful of allegiances and more wary of relationships within the community. Never too far from consciousness is the realization that the rabbi serves at the pleasure of his congregation, and that job security, financial stability, and a sense of personal well being are contingent upon the good will of the congregation. Children of rabbis grow up in the ever-present shadow of this reality.

Driven by anxiety and insecurity, a significant number of rabbis become overinvolved with their congregations and underinvolved with their families. They are seemingly unable to divest themselves of their rabbinic roles and relate to their families as husbands and fathers. As a result, feelings of loss and separation often remain unresolved for their children even through adulthood.

Several significant implications have emerged from this analysis. For the rabbi's child, self-esteem is enhanced with the experience of feeling valued as an integral part of the family group in its designated work with the congregation. In positively regarding the function prescribed to the rabbi's child by the family, the role itself takes on greater value. Secondly, if the source of stress is perceived by the rabbi's child as emanating from the congregation and not as a veiled rejection by the rabbinic father, emotional support tends to develop within the family.

Third, the ability of rabbinic parents to separate work from family life creates "community-proof" boundaries. Divesting themselves of the trappings of the rabbinic role appears crucial to development of normal life with all the needed support it has to offer.

Finally, there is a reaffirmation of the importance of the rabbi's role as husband. Where the marital relationship is strong, the positive effects are felt throughout the family system.

It is interesting to note that the majority of the respondents in this study were either students preparing for a professional career, or individuals professionally engaged in some form of community service. There is an intriguing possibility that children of rabbis who grew up with the ideals of public service, albeit with the insecurity of dependence on a congregation, have chosen careers or avocations that permit for the fulfillment of the service ideal without the insecurity of dependence on others. In a sense, most of the children of rabbis in this study chose to become secular clergy, independent of congregations, but in the service of others nevertheless.

This study, in its attempt to examine the impact of rabbinic life on children of rabbis, has implications not only for rabbinic families, but for all families where stress, vulnerability, and insecurity exist as a factor of daily life. It underscores the importance of family boundaries that protect a family from outside intrusion while permitting it to develop supportive cohesion from within. It reconfirms the long known observation regarding the centrality of the marital dyad and its ability to either buffer children from external stress or itself become a source of stress.

IMPLICATIONS FOR FURTHER RESEARCH

Though the respondents studied have appeared openly candid about their life experiences as rabbinic children, no attempt was made to study the impact of these experiences on their lives as adults. Further research exploring the effects of rabbinic life on adult identity and subsequent relationships with mates, children, friends, and authority figures, as well as on level of religious commitment, career choice, and communal involvement would be enlightening. Children of rabbis, like all individuals, play out their script of unfinished business throughout adult life. Undoubtedly, discovering the themes of that script would give us more complete understanding of the full impact of clerical life on the children it spawns.

19

The Rabbi as Public and Private Individual

Rabbi Basil Herring

Numerous studies seem to indicate that the rabbinate carries unusually high stress, burnout, and dropout rates. It is without doubt a profession that requires a high level of idealism and selflessness, and the person who enters the field is certainly prepared to make many sacrifices. But at the same time, it is possible to avoid much of the downside that so many associate with the rabbinate, without necessarily compromising one's effectiveness. In this chapter, one approach is described, geared to a particular congregation and a specific rabbi. Its applicability to other situations will of course be a function of synagogue need and precedent, as well as the personalities of the rabbi and his family members. Even so, its major thrust reflects some of the points made in the accompanying chapters.

INTRODUCTION

What follows here is not an attempt to formulate the right or wrong approach to the relationship between a rabbi's public and personal life. It merely attempts to describe, in abbreviated fashion, what works for me, and what I find most satisfying and productive, after fifteen years in the rabbinate.

I start with a premise: it is necessary to draw a sharp line, not always impermeable, but mostly quite definitive, between myself as a rabbi and myself as private person, husband, father, friend, neighbor, and, not least, Jew. Until I learned to make this distinction, I found myself easily frustrated, often resentful of the rabbinate, and a compromised husband and father to my wife and kids.

THE PUBLIC VERSUS THE PRIVATE SELF

For a long time I somehow assumed that being a rabbi is a twenty-four-hour-a-day proposition, that is, not only are you the rabbi when you are on the pulpit and in your study, but also when you sit in your garden, walk down the street, meet your *balebatim* at the theater, and throw a birthday party for your kids. I assumed that I always had to put on my rabbinic hat and mask—because I was different from everyone else, and they had different (read "higher") expectations of their rabbi. *Chalilah ve'chas* they should perceive me as an "ordinary" human being, who could throw a ball or play with his kids; God forbid I should be seen in shirtsleeves without a tie (especially anywhere near the synagogue); inconceivable that my son or daughter should be judged no differently than other kids on the block.

But what is the result of such attitudes? For me it meant continual frustration and resentment. For others it has meant choosing to leave the rabbinate, rather than live on such a pedestal, aloof and exposed. Why is this so? Others may have their own explanation, but for me it is simply this: being a rabbi is, or should be, what I *do*, not what I *am.* Being a rabbi is how I function as a professional, the vehicle that I have chosen to share my love for Yiddishkeit with others, my yearning to perpetuate Torah values and practices among as many of my fellow Jews as I can reach, and the manner in which, for whatever psychological reasons, I express my inner drive to reach a position of respected leadership among my peers. But that does not mean that everything else in my life can only function and be seen through the prism of my rabbinic identity. Much like other professionals (for that is how I see myself, as a professional, albeit one with a sense of a calling in life), I have a private life that is not the business of my *balebatim*—just as long as it does not contradict the law or the ethic of the Torah and of the land.

Thus, the first sermon I gave in my present position was dedicated to making this point—and interestingly enough, the *balebatim* appreciated and accepted its premises. They, especially the younger and more sensitive among them, did not want a super Jew, a stuffed shirt, an otherworldly figure, with whom they and their children would have difficulty identifying. They can and do respect a rabbi who can draw a distinction between his private and public self—without in any way compromising his rabbinic "dignity" or "bearing." And even they can appreciate, with just a little prompting from the rabbi, that he and his family are not owned by the synagogue, not always available to their whims, and are to be treated as they would deal with any respected and accomplished professional to whom they turn for help. Helping *balebatim* understand this has, in my experience, brought more, rather than less, rabbinic respect and effectiveness.

TIME OUT FOR THE FAMILY

Allow me a few illustrations that follow from this attitude and self-image. I am not on call seven days a week, except for genuine emergencies. Thus routine meetings or classes with me are, wherever possible, not scheduled for Sundays (which is my family's time too), or if they have to be on such a day, they are set for a time that will not conflict with our family schedule. The same is true of unveilings. As to the telephone, my *balebatim* know that I have a study number which rings simultaneously at my synagogue and home study locations, where I can be reached, if need be. But it is attached to an answering machine which takes calls not only when I am away from my desk, but also during meals or other family hours. If it is an emergency they can call on our private line (listed in my wife's name), which is an option which most *balebatim* do not abuse. I do not feel the need to justify the hours that I am or am not available for calls or other synagogue business. Were I to keep an accounting of the total time I spend "on the job" it would likely be significantly more than most *balebatim* spend on theirs. Thus I choose to allocate my time at my discretion: if I must be at evening meetings, then I take other times (e.g., afternoons) to be with my family or on private pursuits.

A particular problem is Shabbat and Yom Tov. Most rabbis feel that they have no choice but to compromise their enjoyment of these special days, because they are after all the major times when a rabbi has to "produce" and assume his public functions. If Shabbat is a time when everyone else is relaxed and unpressured, able to enjoy not only the immediate family but the extended family as well, whether at home or in going away for Shabbat—the opposite is true of the rabbi. I do not know if there is a comprehensive and fully satisfactory solution to this problem, but a few suggestions are perhaps in order. I try wherever possible (but not always successfully) to finish my preparations for Shabbat/Yom Tov before these days begin. Why spend the precious *leil Shabbat* preparing a last-minute (and probably poorly thought out) derashah, dvar torah, shiur, or miscellaneous presentations? In addition I intentionally limit Friday night lectures, or activities that require out of home excursions at that hour. There is no substitute for a Shabbat evening table and home atmosphere, neither for my family nor my *balebatim*.

As to the other six days of the week, similar considerations apply. My *balebatim* know (and see) that I play with my kids in the park, ride my bike, enjoy selected movies, wear comfortable and "easy" clothing, if necessary put out the garbage, shovel the snow, mow the lawn, and wash my car. I do not believe it necessary to be invariably dressed in "rabbinic black," although it is important to me that my clothing be tasteful and relatively restrained (in fashion or tone). Certainly good grooming and cleanliness is a sine qua non. The same, by the way, is true of the rabbi's means of transportation: if he can afford a more expensive or attractive automobile, good luck to him! He need not display penury or embarrassment at what some out-spoken *balebatim* might think of his choice as to how to spend his hard-earned money—rather let them (especially the youth) see that a life dedicated to spreading Torah, and one that enjoys reasonable comforts and pleasures, are not mutually exclusive! Thus, when I explain to my *balebatim*, as I often do, that the attachments on top of my car are bike racks for when we go biking as a family, their sense of identification and understanding is invariably palpable. One of the things that I have enjoyed doing is a weekly racquetball workout with a group of my *balebatim*—an activity which I find not only salutary for my health (and therefore halakhicly mandatory) but also a wonderful means of deflating most of my aggressions and self-deluding sense of superiority over my *balebatim*! Yes, I even take my racing bicycle on lengthy exercise excursions several times a week, helmet included. Again I must say that I do not do these things for the approbation of my *balebatim*, or to garner their respect—if they respect or disrespect me it will be as a result of my "conventional" rabbinic accomplishments or failures. I do them because I find them personally important and worthwhile, even as they serve to bridge the distance that is all too often perceived between the life blessed with Torah, and one devoid of it.

FAMILY EXPECTATIONS

My kids' behavior is no different from that of other *frum* kids in the neighborhood, and I do my level best not to put (or allow) any expectations on them just because they are the rabbi's children. Thus, from time to time (including the *Yamim Nora'im*, when all their friends are with *their* fathers) I sit with them for short periods in the front rows of the shul—why should they or I be permanently deprived of sitting together during tefillah? On this particular topic, I refer the reader to chapter 17 in this volume, by Dr. Irving Levitz.

My wife is not referred to as Rebbetsin—by her choice. While she is somewhat active in the synagogue, it is only in those areas where she chooses to be. She has no obligations to the synagogue. She sits in the sanctuary wherever she pleases, and attends Sisterhood meetings at her own volition. My philosophy is that it is I who was employed, not she. Indeed, she was not—and should not be—part of the interviewing process when her husband is hired in the first place. We certainly enjoy entertaining *balebatim* at home, but again at our discretion, not because there is some expectation that the rabbi "has" to have an open house, gathering, etc.

PRIVATE HOUSING

This last point touches on the issue of housing. Other than the financial considerations that might favor a rabbi living in his own, as opposed to a synagogue's, home, there is the matter of rabbinic privacy. Living in the synagogue home can sometimes leave the rabbi at a disadvantage in making independent decisions regarding the quality, conditions, and best interests of his family life. Certainly, in my view, living in the synagogue's home makes it all the more difficult to properly separate one's professional obligations to the community from one's personal, private, and family life.

SOCIAL LIFE

As to friendships, we do have personal friends among the *balebatim*, and yes, with a few we are on a first-name basis. It is after all our neighborhood too—why should we have to cultivate friends only at a distance? As to first names generally, and the use of the title, "Rabbi," I am often angered when getting calls or letters from rabbinic colleagues who personally identify themselves to me as "Rabbi So and So." Why the pomposity? Some even sign their names with the title as if it is their first name. Why the inflated self-esteem? *Yehalelkha zar!* We all love to hear our name and titles (yes, I do have a PH.D. too, but in my rabbinic capacity I use it only on stationery, or study walls)—but I would submit that we gain far more respect and genuine affection from our *balebatim* when we identify ourselves (on the phone or elsewhere) by our first and second names, and let others bestow our titles. In any case, I have found that my *balebatim* always respond with real esteem to such matter-of-fact approaches. On occasion, some, as we get closer to them, do ask me, "Rabbi, how do you want me to address you?" and I generally respond by saying "in private, however you feel comfortable, but in public by using my title."

True it is a very thin line we tread, one that I dare say few of us ever adequately resolve. How do we achieve friendship, social camaraderie, closeness, intimate confidence, and mutual warmth without fatally compromising our effectiveness as role models, leaders, teachers, and representatives who embody higher Torah values and practices, capable of giving mussar and communal direction? The answer to this question can be obvious only to the inexperienced or supremely self-assured, if not arrogant, among us. Yet it is clear that both extremes are somehow to be avoided, through careful and constant self-evaluation, so as to avoid losing the respect of one's *balebatim* on the one hand, or their ability to identify with oneself as a role model on the other.

But insofar as our own personal and family needs are concerned, it is vastly more important that we not inflict upon ourselves the

consequences of burnout, of stress, of wives and children who resent
the encroachments of our public selves, and ultimately our own sense
of identity confusion that is all too often the reverse side of our selfless
idealism.

THE PARALLEL PROFESSIONAL CAREER

It is my considered belief that if it is at all possible, a rabbi should
for a number of very good reasons avoid becoming exclusively occupied with his synagogue responsibilities. At some point in the development of Jewish life, the notion of the congregational rabbinate as an
exclusive occupation became the norm, yet it is time that we ourselves
questioned the viability and desirability of such a model. When I look
at most successful, admired, and effective pulpit rabbis in Orthodoxy
today, they are invariably the ones whose professional interests go
beyond the limiting confines of the synagogue in its strict sense. They
either teach, administer schools or communal organizations, provide
counseling services, chaplaincy, publish, or pursue their own graduate
careers. It is not even necessary to remain within the organized Jewish
community's orbit, as one pursues a legitimate parallel career. The
rabbinate in and of itself can be a stultifying, and no-growth, setting.
Many colleagues with whom I speak tell me how satisfying they find
their outside interests and activities; how much the *balebatim* themselves respect such independence, such expertise, such creativity on
their part. They also, of course, value the added income and security
that such parallel careers provide.

Over the long run, such broadening of one's interests are, I
believe, of immense value. Often we hear of rabbis whose *balebatim*
decide, after twenty or thirty years of devoted service, that they need
a new, younger, more "dynamic" rabbi to turn the shul around, or
some such rationale. Sometimes the *balebatim* may even be right, and
it is time for a rabbi to move on, both for his benefit and theirs. But
what is he to do, especially if he is 60 or 65 years old? Start a new
position at that late point in his life, with all the adjustments he
thought he had left behind? Start a whole new career then? Go to
graduate school, or take a job that he must now learn as a novice?
Many in such situations have no choice but to retire gracefully (or
otherwise) in spite of abundant energies and talents they still possess.

But such rabbis have none but themselves to blame—having selflessly and totally given themselves to communal work all the years, without thought of alternatives and worst-case scenarios. Contrast this with the rabbi who in his younger years cultivates other areas of expertise, whether in the organized Jewish community or beyond.

I surely understand that not every rabbi can find the time or energy to free himself for such parallel activity. Some would consider such an option impractical, given their relationship with their congregations. But for others, such contingencies and alternatives ought surely to be considered. I for one happen to believe that in due course what ought to happen is that a new kind of professional relationship must emerge between many congregations and rabbis, one that will afford rabbis the time and opportunity to cultivate such other areas of competence, and enable them to reach out to many more people, and in more profound ways, than is presently the case. But until that happens, there is no reason in the world why we as rabbanim should not pursue parallel professional careers, to supplement and complement our effectiveness, our self-respect, our *shalom bayit*, our long-term security, and surely not least, our financial income and independence.

IN CONCLUSION

These approaches and attitudes seem to work (more or less) for me. I find that they heighten my own productivity, my self-respect, and my positive relationships with most of my *balebatim* (at least those whose opinions I care to value, knowing full well that no rabbi can ever please everybody, no more than any other professional or businessman can hope to do). Saying all of the above does not in any way diminish the need for, and importance of, effective rabbinic leadership, through one's ongoing and uncompromised commitment to learning, teaching, halakhic expertise, and considered *hashkafah*. But by taking the approach that I have here outlined, I believe that whatever effective Torah leadership I have had to offer has been significantly intensified.

I do realize that not all pulpit rabbis wish to or can take the position that I have described here. Some are temperamentally un-suited to it, others are not blessed with the kind of *balebatim* who would allow it, through their own, or their predecessors' laxity. Nonetheless, it is possible that at the very least some of the ideas herein described can be considered on their own merits, and investigated for their applicability in whatever degree, to any given personality or rabbinic setting.

20

The Rabbi as Wage-Earner

Rabbi William Herskowitz

The popular image of the rabbi, especially the Orthodox rabbi, is one of financial dependence and inexperience. He is perceived as having more important priorities than that of acquiring wealth. To a large extent this generalization is true—and that is as it should be. Nonetheless, even rabbis and their families are entitled to financial security. The problem is that as a class they hesitate to acquire the skills and knowledge necessary to achieve that end, in the belief that such pursuits are somehow beneath their calling. But this perception is changing, as more and more rabbis realize that rabbinic security is a legitimate concern in a world of ever-increasing costs and decreasing financial expectations. Rabbi William Herskowitz has invested significant time and effort over the years in examining this issue, and herein summarizes much of what he has learned.

Orthodox rabbis, by and large, are underpaid, often grossly underpaid. It would be easy to assume that the cause of this condition is that Orthodox *balebatim* are not well-to-do and that Orthodox synagogues are in poor financial condition. However, this is simply not true in the overwhelming majority of the cases.[1] The real problem is to be found in rabbis' attitudes toward earning and handling money. Many feel that it is demeaning to ask for raises and "unrabbinic" to concern themselves with economic matters or doing anything to improve their finances. The truth is that rabbis' wives and families are forced to cope with the problems the rabbis themselves neglect. Eventually, the rabbis end up spending a great deal of time trying to make ends meet with the little they have. This time and effort could be utilized for more productive purposes were they to avoid this dilemma by negotiating a proper salary in the first place.

There are a number of early sources that warn against using a rabbinic position to gain wealth or positions of prominence, especially *Avot* 4:7: "Whoever derives a profit for himself from the words of the Torah is bringing on his own destruction." These words were valid when being a rabbi left sufficient time to earn a living at a trade. Once the demands on a rabbi's services made that impossible, we were told that scholars were entitled to *sekhar batalah*. If a Rav were to figure out what he could earn if he hadn't gone into the rabbinate, he would not be so timid in negotiating for his salary.

When rabbis don't demand proper compensation for their efforts, they are not only cheating themselves and their families, they are also damaging their stature in the eyes of their *balebatim* and community. R. Israel of Rizhyn, commenting on the sentence, "And Abram was very rich in cattle, in silver and in gold," states that Abraham needed the wealth so that people would pay proper attention to him and his message. The Gemara (*Gittin* 59a) points out that the three individuals most responsible for the transmission of Jewish law, Moshe Rabbeinu, Rebbe, and Rav Ashi, were outstanding for their combination of wealth and learning. If Hashem blessed them with both riches and knowledge, there is no reason others should not seek decent wages for their efforts.

EARNING AN APPROPRIATE SALARY

Once a Rav believes that he is entitled to adequate remuneration, there are some basic steps he must take. Rabbis work very hard for their congregations and should be recompensed accordingly. Unfortunately, they cannot accomplish financial security this just by demonstrating how much time and effort they put into their work. Rabbis cannot rely solely on the largesse of their boards. Clergymen going into salary negotiations must prepare properly. They must not only gather and organize all the facts they need, they must also marshal the assistance that is available from board members and fellow professionals, so that these negotiations can be concluded successfully.

One of the problems in seeking the proper salary level is that most Orthodox rabbis do not really know what others in their situation are earning. They are insecure about informing others of their contract's provisions, either because they are ashamed of how little they earn or are convinced that this information is so private that no one else should be privy to it. The first step in acquiring knowledge about someone else's contract is the willingness to share information about your own figures. We could all gain if we would be more forthcoming in this area. In other rabbinic groups, knowledge of salary scales is not only known, it is shared. Surveys by the movements have established not only how much is paid, but what fringe benefits are sought. The Conservative and Reform organizations take an active role in establishing proper salary packages for their clientele.

The first step in raising rabbinic compensation is to ascertain what the current patterns are and then to establish goals for different types of synagogues and lengths of rabbinic service. Rabbis must also define what fringe benefits are sine qua non and which ones are negotiable. They should make available to the congregation's board some sample contracts to help them in their deliberations.[2] Rabbi Isaac Elchanan Theological Seminary (RIETS) at Yeshiva University and the Rabbinical Council of America have begun to become active in these areas. They must be pushed to get more involved and to provide their members with the materials needed for meaningful negotiations.

One opinion is that the Rav should not be his own negotiator. This is not because it is beneath the rabbi's dignity to negotiate, but because the job can be done more effectively by others.[3]

Because Orthodox lay leaders have not been accustomed to dealing with these negotiators, committee members sometimes feel threatened when professionals represent the rabbi. In these cases, the rabbi has two options. He can ask that the negotiating committee at least meet with these professionals to learn what is current and accepted. Failing that, he should get someone, from the board or the congregation, who is well versed in finances and negotiations and is favorably disposed to the rabbi, to meet with these people so that he or she can represent the rabbi more meaningfully in the deliberations. If the rabbi must represent himself, the very least he should do is meet with these representatives personally to prepare properly for the negotiations.

ALLOCATING ONE'S SALARY

While receiving adequate compensation is the first goal, rabbis must also see that the funds they receive are allocated in the most advantageous manner in order to legally minimize their tax liabilities.[4]

Most clergymen in the United States and Canada are familiar with the tremendous benefits of a housing allowance. It can shelter a significant portion of the rabbi's salary.[5] Some, however, do not exploit this allowance to its fullest capacity or use it for items which are not legitimate.[6] The size of the housing allowance is limited only by what is normal and usual to provide housing and its related expenses in your area. A housing allowance not only reduces taxable income while the rabbi is serving the congregation, it can provide important benefits during the retirement period (see the following section, "Planning For Retirement").

In addition to a housing allowance, car expenses, convention costs, continuing education, insurance coverage for health, accidents, and death, and other such items can be paid for by the synagogue, under certain circumstances, without becoming taxable.[7] Some of these benefits will be provided because they benefit the synagogue. Coverage for catastrophic illnesses, accidents, and death should be carried by the congregation so that if, God forbid, they occur, the synagogue will not be burdened with the costs entailed in providing properly for the rabbi and his family, while covering the costs of maintaining the activities and services of the congregation. Other items, such as allocating salary to a housing allowance, deducting the rabbi's portion of a pension payment from a proposed salary figure, or letting the rabbi go in with them on a fuel oil or gardening contract, will be readily agreed to because *zeh neheneh ve'zeh lo chaser*.

Since the laws on these categories may change periodically and each situation can have unique complications, these items should be reviewed by an accountant before a contract is signed. He should be familiar with the rules pertaining to clergymen. The rabbi should use his own accountant, rather than relying on someone from the synagogue, so that the advice will be impartial and he will have greater freedom to discuss alternate possibilities. Be very careful in this matter because some of the methods being suggested are, in the eyes of tax people I have spoken to, extremely questionable.[8]

In the United States, monies received by rabbis from their congregations are salaried income and must be reported on a W-2 form. They are not subject to withholding tax unless both the rabbi and congregation voluntarily agree to this arrangement. Taxes not withheld must be paid on a quarterly basis according to tax liabilities. Even though clergymen are considered employees insofar as their salary from the congregation or institution is concerned, they are technically self-employed for Social Security purposes. Any monies contributed by the synagogue toward Social Security coverage are taxable as income. While a housing allowance is not taxable as income, it must be included in the computation for Social Security coverage.

Rabbis entering the field can opt out of Social Security by offering some religious rationale.[9] According to most experts, they would be making a serious mistake if they do so because

1. Social Security is a forced saving plan and most people do not save adequate amounts.
2. People without Social Security are not eligible for the medicare and disability provisions.
3. The benefits, unlike those of other retirement plans, have been continually upgraded by legislators who consider them a sacred cow.[10] This is especially true in light of the "Graying of America."

PLANNING FOR RETIREMENT

With life expectancies growing, most rabbis can expect to experience, God willing, at least a decade of retirement. To continue living in a suitable fashion, rabbis must put aside a sizable amount of capital. Social Security will not meet these needs. Its benefits must be supplemented.

The first line of additional income should be a pension plan. Pensions are now an accepted part of a business payroll so that there should be little difficulty in having a pension plan contribution made by the synagogue. In addition, the congregation will find it advantageous because it frees them of the responsibility to support their rabbi when he can no longer work. While any type of pension plan can be adopted, my experience is that it is easier to sell the congregation on participating in the Rabbinical Council of America plan for several reasons:

1. Many other rabbis are covered by it.
2. There is an accepted formula for congregational participation in part of the allocation (although many synagogues pay the full amount).
3. It is a solid fund with a good track record, one the congregation can rely on to be there in the future.

The monies paid by the congregation are not taxable as current income. If the rabbi forgoes part of his raise so that the congregation will pay the full amount of the pension contribution, the total contribution is considered deferred income. There is no tax on the monies earned by a pension fund until the money is withdrawn after retirement. Because of the parsonage allowance, much of the money can avoid the tax collector's grasp even after retirement. The congregation can stipulate that they want a certain percentage of their rabbi's pension to be for parsonage expenses.[11] Since the amount that the pension pays may not be much more than what is being received currently as a parsonage allowance, it is possible that the entire amount may be tax free if it meets the usual and reasonable guideline mentioned earlier. This benefit produces another advantage. Since Social Security payments are taxable after retirement earnings reach a certain threshold, the tax-free parsonage payments allow rabbis to earn more money before being subject to taxation.

In addition to Social Security and a pension plan on synagogue salaries, rabbis in the United States can have a Keogh for their outside self-employment income.[12] There are two types of Keoghs, a defined contribution account and a defined benefit plan. In a defined contribution account, the allowable contribution is a fixed percent, currently 15 percent, of the self-employment income. In a defined benefit plan, the rabbi can state that he wants to retire with the same yearly self-employment income that he now receives. An actuary then determines how much the rabbi must contribute each year until his retirement in order to accomplish this goal. This amount, which is usually substantially higher than the fixed percent, can then be deducted from the taxable income[13] and put away until retirement.

Since there is a set-up charge in addition to yearly fees for an actuary to compute the figures, and they may be substantial, one must weigh the advantages against the expense. Amounts up to the entire value of the self-employed income can be set aside depending on the amount of time left before retirement and the level of capital required to reach the desired level of benefits. This plan is especially beneficial to clergymen who did not put away Keogh money in their early years because of high expenses and now want to catch up. Recent legislation has practically eliminated IRA participation for rabbis who have pension plans and Keoghs. Because of the features mentioned above, either of these are preferable to an IRA.

Contributions to pension plans and Keoghs are all tax-deductible. This means that no income tax is paid on them during the high salaried years when tax rates are the most onerous. Instead, taxes become due during the withdrawal period when reduced income results in lower rates. In addition, all the monies earned by these funds are not taxable until they are withdrawn, between the ages of 59½ and 70½.[14] The government, in effect, is subsidizing the cost of retirement through these plans and every effort should be made to take advantage of these breaks. Retirement expenses, especially health care, can be much higher than most people estimate. It is important to save as much as you can during your most productive years.

THE HOUSING DILEMMA

Is it better for a rabbi to purchase his own home or to reside in one owned by the congregation? This question is a matter of some controversy, and the answer depends on the responses to four questions.

The first is how long the rabbi intends to remain with the congregation. If this is an interim position, it is best to reside in a home provided by the synagogue. Having a home tends to make people more reluctant to uproot themselves. Additionally, the chance of making a profit over a short term, with the possibility of pressure to make a quick sale, is not very great.

The second variable is whether the homes in the area are

reasonably priced or are very costly and whether there will still be substantial growth. This is, obviously, a difficult question and, since prophecy today is restricted to children and fools, there is no way to always find the correct answer. By speaking to real estate people in the area, it is possible to get some informed "guesstimates."

The third issue is whether the house is viewed as a source for potential profit or simply as a place to live after you retire. Many congregations will stipulate that the rabbi and/or rebbitzen will have the right to remain in the home as long as they live. Others will agree that housing will be provided for them, but reserve the option of providing an adequate apartment instead of the large home they resided in. Some congregations have turned the home over to the rabbi as a gift upon his retirement.

The last, and probably most important question relates to saving habits and willpower. If you are disciplined enough to put aside each month, in a savings or investment account, what it would cost you for the mortgage payments, taxes, and housing expenses incurred, by living in a shul house you could end up with more money than would have been made by purchasing the home. Remember that if it is the shul's house, they are responsible for all repairs. This usually includes the maintenance of the house and grounds, major appliances, heat and air conditioning, as well as some decorating. Homes owned by synagogues do not pay real estate taxes, while those owned by the rabbi do. These taxes, which are deductible for individuals who file itemized returns, can amount to several thousand dollars a year for most homes. There are some legal ways to buy a home and sell it to the shul thus avoiding these taxes. Such steps legally turn the house over to the synagogue. Different methods may guarantee the rabbi's investment in the home, but all entail some risks.

However, after all is said and done, since most people are not sufficiently disciplined to maintain such a consistent savings program over a period of years, it probably makes sense to own a home. The biggest problem in buying a home, after picking out the right location, size, and room layout, is coming up with the down payment. Many congregations, or groups within a synagogue, will help in arranging this substantial sum. Their assistance may take the form of a personal loan, an advance on salary (in the form of a parsonage allowance) of a multiyear contract, or some guarantee to the mortgage-loaning institution. Make sure that the cost of the house, the down payment, and monthly mortgage figures are affordable. While a shul will often help out if there is a temporary financial bind, chronic financial difficulties invariably give rise to great problems in the relationship between rabbi and congregation. This can spill over to the congregation's attitude to the rabbi's main task, his performance as a religious leader.

There are many advantages to owning a home. Over the years, it has been one of the best investments. While there are no guarantees that the increase in the future will match those of the last twenty or thirty years, Hashem is not making more real estate, and there is a housing shortage in most Jewish areas. Even if prices do not escalate as they have in the past, owning a home is an excellent form of forced savings. For many, it will be the only guarantee that at the end of their careers they will have a sizable sum of equity with which to face their retirement or to leave as a *yerushah*. Owning a home should never be a substitute for a pension, but, unfortunately, most people have not been properly preparing for their golden years and a house may be their only substantial investment.

Currently, home owners have the advantage of being able to write off the interest on their mortgages and real estate taxes on the home. They can also use the equity in their homes to obtain loans where the interest is tax deductible. In addition, clergymen have the benefit of "double dipping," having the mortgage payments come out of a housing allowance that is already tax free, and deducting the interest and taxes included in these payments as part of the itemized deductions. Congress had been threatening to end this privilege, but the tax law of 1986 repealed Revenue Ruling 83.3 and its threat to this unusual privilege.

Another advantage of owning a home is the ability to live more comfortably. Homes owned by a congregation are invariably close to the synagogue, frequently on or adjacent to shul property. They often are not in the location that a rabbi would have chosen to guarantee his family's privacy nor do they always have the proper configuration for the rabbi's family. Alterations usually cannot be made to an apartment and generally are not made to a synagogue-owned home. On the other hand, "a man's home is his castle," and can be modified as he sees fit without shul members having any say in the matter.

Be aware that owning a home entails responsibilities in areas that are not a rabbi's greatest strengths. Unless the synagogue has a good superintendent who is readily available to take care of chores and repairs, the rabbi will either have to hire people to do these things or do some of them himself. Hiring workers is expensive, and they are not always available. If the rabbi is not handy, he may end up waiting long periods of time for suitable tradesmen, or overpaying for what has to be done. Fortunately, necessity is the mother of invention and with a little application of *sekhel*, many of these items can be handled with little trouble.

THE CRUX OF THE PROBLEM

The basic issue of rabbinic security really hinges on how the rabbi manages his money. It is always beneficial to earn more, but, unless there is proper management, a larger income will disappear just as quickly as a smaller one without substantially reducing debts or increasing savings. A person with good money management habits will get by on a meager salary and really flourish on a decent one, while those who do not handle money well will have problems no matter what income they receive.

In order to manage money properly, the first step is to know how it is being spent. Most people do not know what is happening with their money, except that it vanishes very quickly. Part of the problem is that the bulk of their transactions consists of cash payments, often without receipts. Unless receipts are saved for every payment or a written ongoing record is kept of all disbursements, by the end of the day it is impossible to know how the money disappeared. The easiest way to establish a record is to deposit all salary checks and other income, and pay everything by check. When all payments are made by check or credit card, there is a record of what the actual costs are. By reviewing all the checks and charges for a few months, it is easy to see how the money is spent.

There is another advantage to this method. People have a tendency to disperse cash rather freely. When they have to write a check for something, they pause to think a little before spending the money. This is especially true when they see the totals of their expenditures piling up on the check register pages. This is not true of charge account purchases which tend to be hidden until the balances come due at the end of the month, and by then it is too late.

When money is needed for a large purchase and the regular budget cannot accommodate the expense, the best source to turn to is a loan on a life insurance policy. The rates are usually below market costs and, since they own the policy, the life insurance company does not ask for any collateral. Older life insurance policies carry low loan rates of 3 percent to 5 percent. New ones may have rates of 9 percent or 10 percent. These will become very expensive as the new tax law limitations on the deductibility of interest are phased in. A better alternative for short-term debt, such as a car loan, would be a homeowners equity loan whereby interest payments are tax deductible. In an emergency, congregations will often get their local bank to issue the loan using their accounts to back it up.

One of the most highly recommended methods for starting a savings pattern is to "pay yourself first." Pick a sum that is reasonable, start with something small but not insignificant, and put that in a savings or money market account *before* paying any bills. This may cause some anguish as efforts are made to stretch the remaining dollars to cover the bills awaiting payment. Perhaps a telephone bill, dues payment, or utility charge will have to await the next payday when it will be on the top of the list. If a call is made stating that the payment will be a little late, most firms will understand, providing it doesn't happen too frequently. The effort entailed in making these decisions and the follow-up calls may be the necessary ingredient for forcing some budget cuts.

Another way of accomplishing a similar result is to take some minor item of income, such as checks from funerals, fees for lectures, or any bonuses or gifts received, and immediately deposit these funds in a separate account. Make believe that they do not exist and manage without them. Believe it or not, it is possible to survive without these funds. It may take some juggling to make ends meet, but it can be done, and a savings habit will have been established. Once some money has been accumulated, it is possible to have money make more money, but this will not happen until a nest egg is built up.

Most rabbis are not very sophisticated investors. They frequently do not know what to look for in determining the value and the risks entailed in different undertakings. Often they invest simply because they know someone else who made money in that particular field or they turn their investments over to somebody they believe will make the right decisions for them. Be very wary of people who offer advice, especially if they are *nog'im ba-davar*, whether they are money managers, friends, or relatives.

Those rabbis who take the time and make the effort to familiarize themselves with the areas in which they are investing can become quite good at handling their capital. When starting an investment program, it is best to be conservative. I would suggest money market funds or CDs until enough has accumulated to allow certain risks with a part of the savings. The basic rules are "Don't gamble with money you can't afford to lose" and "It is better to be safe, than sorry."[15]

NOTES

[1]Mr. Martin L. Kamerow, CPA, author of many books and articles dealing with clergymen and tax-exempt organizations, has been active in local, national, and international Jewish organizations and has dealt with their tax matters and with salary negotiations for their rabbis and cantors. He not only concurred with the truth of this statement based on his experience, he went on to take exception to the way congregations allocate funds for rabbinic salaries. In a letter to me, he has written, "I take a very strong position that the rabbi of a congregation is the central most important expenditure that the congregation makes in the course of its existence. While there probably are some exceptions, I do not believe that the weak financial statement of a congregation should, in any way, prevent the Rabbi from maintaining a decent standard of living, providing for his current family needs and retirement as is the case with any other professional. I believe that this position had been too long overlooked in Orthodox congregations in particular and it is time to address them fairly. If a congregation is in poor financial condition and the building needs redecorating, the officers want to go to a convention, the gas and electric bills are due, etc., a congregation somehow goes out and raises the money to meet these necessary needs. I cannot see why the circumstances should be any different in arriving at the fair compensation of the rabbi."

[2]RIETS has such a model contract. It is included in this volume as Appendix 4.

[3]Mr. Kamerow disagrees. He feels that the Rav is the most eloquent spokesman for his needs and that he can make the most effective presentation based on his education, experience, and the comparative salaries.

[4]Here again, rabbis would benefit greatly from sharing information. Periodic opportunities to discuss what tax-saving practices are being used by our colleagues as well as suggestions from accountants who deal with rabbis

would be most beneficial. Since most of the tax breaks rabbis enjoy are the result of rulings established for Christian clergy, we could learn from consulting with them also.

[5]The tax laws recognize full-time cantors as clergy and many of the points in this article apply to them as well.

[6]In the United States, housing allowances can cover basic services such as down payments, mortgage payments, heating, air conditioning, electricity, gas, water, taxes, insurance, alarms, gardening, decorating, and other such work. Equipment such as furniture, linens, window treatments, phones, antennas, lighting, etc., are all included. Telephone bills, portable electronics, and business equipment are not eligible. For additional details, see IRS regulation 1.107-1.

[7]If the rabbi is the only full-time employee, these arrangements can be made. If there are other full-time employees, they would be entitled to similar benefits unless there is a legally justifiable method of differentiating their categories.

[8]For instance, giving rabbis' children a tuition break in a school run by the organization he works for is permissible. Payments for their tuition in another institution is taxable as income.

[9]The basis for this is the claim that Social Security is against religious beliefs, a very questionable assertion insofar as rabbis are concerned.

[10]Social Security funds can be drawn upon as early as age 62, but people who start then will only get 80 percent of the benefits they would be entitled to. The government will automatically issue benefits at 70 if they haven't been applied for earlier. In the event, God forbid, of the premature death of a rabbi with children under 18 (in some cases 21), there are substantial death and monthly payment benefits.

[11]This must be done at an official board meeting prior to the rabbi's retirement and can be stipulated long before that date. The form to be filed with the pension plan is appended to this article (Appendix 3). Self-directed plans do not qualify for this provision, but plans such as the one offered by the RCA, in which there is congregational participation, can provide this important benefit.

[12]The classic definition of self-employed income is work which does not have to be done on a regular basis at a time and place specified by an employer. These are positions for which 1099s, rather than W-2s, are issued. Typically, such income comes from part-time work such as chaplaincies, hakhnasah, hashgachah, and consulting positions. An accountant familiar with the details should be consulted to make sure the funds are really self-employment income.

[13]Keogh contributions are permitted only up to the level of reported income in the self-employment category.

[14]If the prescribed portion of the pension is not withdrawn by 70½, there can be a substantial penalty. Currently it is 50 percent of that amount.

[15]I am deeply indebted to Martin Ginsberg and Martin L. Kamerow for reading the article, suggesting corrections, and supplying technical advice and to Nathan Katz and Rabbi Abner Weiss for their assistance in improving the language and style. Without their help, this piece would have been less informative, not as authoritative, and more difficult to follow. They have been most generous with their time and skills and I greatly appreciate their help.

III

VISION
AND
PERSPECTIVE

Parts I and II have dealt with a large variety of rabbinic concerns and priorities. In a profound sense they can be said to share the characteristic of preoccupation with daily details and particulars, routines and efficiencies. But the rabbinate must also be characterized by a larger vision and imagination, imparting leadership, direction, and inspiration, much in the mold of the prophets of old.

In Part III we present several approaches and prescriptions addressed to this side of the contemporary rabbinate. In so doing we hope to effect a balance between these two sides of the rabbi's concern: the ritual and the visionary, the administrative and the inspirational, the dedicated public servant and the respected, if not revered, communal leader.

21

The Rabbi as Policy Maker

Rabbi Immanuel Jakobovits

Rabbi Immanuel Jakobovits presents his own perspective on the need for the rabbi to make his impact on the broader canvas of Jewish—and national—life. He is particularly mindful of the alternate sources of communal leadership to have emerged in modern times and of the need for rabbis to assert their historic responsibilities even today. While Rabbi Jakobovits speaks from a British perspective, his comments are equally valid and relevant to the American rabbinic experience.

With the secularization of Jewish life, initiated with the emancipation in the last century and accelerated by the evolution and consummation of Jewish statehood, the role of rabbinic leadership underwent a dramatic change. This change was brought about in part by the progressive transfer of strategic key positions from spiritual to lay leaders, replacing rabbis by an assortment of politicians, communal organizers, efficient fundraisers, and public relations experts in the decision-making processes governing the fortunes of the Jewish people. To some extent this development was inevitable, as the external pressures of integration into a secular society combined with the internal exigencies of administering a modern state, and I suspect that rabbis, even if they were allowed to resume their traditional leadership role, would scarcely improve on the lay performance in the management of statecraft. Under modern conditions and pending the advent of the messianic age, theocracy is certainly not for us, neither at the national nor at the communal level.

But the displacement of rabbis as policymakers, or even as pacesetters in the progress of Jewish life, is certainly not due only to their ousting or usurpation by their secular rivals. It must equally be traced to the deliberate withdrawal of rabbis from spheres of influence and activity which had traditionally been theirs. In large measure, they have simply abdicated their role in the governance of the Jewish destiny, the definition of the Jewish purpose, and the mobilization of Jewish spiritual resources. Sadly, they represent neither the government nor even the opposition in the leadership of the Jewish people. Meat inspectors and catering supervisors, officials who marry and bury people or who preach to the converted and denounce the rest, or even scholars who withdraw to secluded cloisters to instruct devoted disciples in the intricacies of the Talmud—all these are bound to be marginal in the direction of national or communal affairs.

Even where rabbis occasionally do occupy commanding positions, notably in the United States, they do so usually by virtue of their competence in lay affairs rather than as spiritual leaders.

Of course, most rabbis are deeply involved in every aspect of Jewish life, ranging from Zionism to Soviet Jewry, and from the education of the young to the welfare of the old. But by and large, they merely amplify and embellish the acclaim for policies set by lay leaders and endorsed by the vox populi. They conduct appeals, join protests, march in demonstrations, and generally call on their communities to support accepted strategies and slogans. But they scarcely ever challenge national policies, let alone devise and propagate policies of their own.

THE SIN OF NONCONFORMITY

Not that such nonconformity would be welcome in the prevailing climate of public opinion, as I can testify from my occasional sallies into the political arena. Deviation and dissent are today's cardinal sins as I found out when I dared publicly to arouse the Jewish conscience on the wretched plight of the Arab refugees years ago, or to add "Let My People Live" to the slogan "Let My People Go" in a plea for revising our policies on Soviet Jewry following my visit to Russia, or to question the wisdom of certain policies vociferously advocated in Israel, especially in religious circles, in more recent times. I was told that rabbis should not dabble in these matters, and told this either by those who usually complain that rabbis are not relevant enough in their teachings, or by the very people who constantly ask me to make political representations to the government, church leaders, or the press to support their campaigns. In other words, politics is for rabbis, only provided they sign on the dotted line drawn by others. And most rabbis seem to prefer the dotted line as the line of least resistance.

INTERPRETING CONTEMPORARY EVENTS

What, then, are the imperatives and priorities of Jewish spiritual leadership?

In the first place, I think our people are entitled to expect from the exponents of Judaism the application of Jewish perceptions to an understanding of our contemporary condition and predicament. Rabbis must interpret present events as well as, and in the light of, past history. I am not suggesting that they can explain a unique awesome enigma like the Holocaust, though the subject should exercise them more than it has done, any more than they can fathom why our generation should have been chosen to witness the rebirth of Jewish national independence.

But surely rabbis can and should tell our people something more meaningful and more distinctly Jewish than simply to repeat the bleating of their flock who blame all our travails on others. Who, if not rabbis, should press home on our people that our covenant with God, on which we base our claim to Zion, is mutual, operative only if we fulfill our side of the agreement by observing His law? They should expose the bankruptcy of secular Zionism, which promised that the normalization of the Jewish condition through statehood would "solve the Jewish problem" and eliminate anti-Semitism, a promise now proved one of the greatest illusions in our history. They should proclaim boldly, as did the Prophets, that Jews without Judaism are not viable, and that the future of a Jewish state alienated from the Jewish tradition is both questionable and meaningless.

JEWS MINUS JUDAISM: THE COST

These are not empty dogmas based on blind faith. They can be empirically substantiated by pragmatic facts. Who are the *yordim* and *noshrim*, who opt for other countries by the thousands because Israel can no longer offer them superior security, if not those who do not care about living a fuller Jewish life possible only in Israel? And conversely, what—if not religious idealism—is the major dynamic of Western *aliyah* today? Both factors show that *yeridah* and *aliyah* alike are governed primarily by the religious quality of Israeli life. Or need one point to the absence of a police station in Bnei Brak to prove that there is some correlation between religious observance and the elimination of crime?

In the diaspora, too, what threatens Jewish survival more than any anti-Zionism or anti-Semitism if not the self-inflicted erosion by assimilation, intermarriage, and the low birthrate, all resulting from an abandonment of Jewish values?

RESTORING THE UNIVERSAL PURPOSE

Rabbis, in resuming their prophetic role in addition to their priestly or ritual function, must also seek to restore the universal dimension to the Jewish national purpose. We cannot divorce ourselves from the concerns of mankind and surrender our role as moral pathfinders without betraying our historic trust, however unfriendly the world is in which we live. I am not advocating Jewish–Christian dialogues, let alone Jewish missionary activities of any kind. But our objections to theological encounters do not absolve us from involving ourselves as Jews in the great moral debates animating society. We ought sometimes to take a stand on issues not patently related to Jewish self-interest, but that do impinge on the Jewish moral conscience. These might include issues that range from pornography to the abuse of leisure by idleness, and from the prostitution of entertainment to the invasion of privacy by a sensation-hungry press, to mention only a few topical items on which our voice ought to be heard.

More important still, Jewish spiritual leaders must relate individual and collective Jewish conduct to our universal purpose, in the sense of the verse: "And all the nations of the earth shall see that the Name of the Lord is called upon you, and they shall respect you." What a difference it would make to our standing among the nations if we consciously strove to turn Israel into a model society, to be the one country to have found the elusive formula of how to eradicate the scourges of depravity and broken homes, of selfishness and discrimination! We should induce at least the same national pride in high marks for integrity or a record output of stable marriages as exists for the feats of the Israeli army or the disproportion of Jews among Nobel prize winners.

HARNESSING SPIRITUAL RESOURCES

At the more practical level, the highest priority must be education. There are now tens of thousands of yeshiva alumni. Spiritual leaders, and especially heads of yeshivot, should regard themselves as commanders of this vast army of bnei Torah—to train it, to mobilize it, and to deploy it as the vanguard to a massive religious reawakening. The yeshivot must be made to understand that they themselves cannot survive in isolation if they allow the vast hinterland of large communities, from whom they draw their main support, to disintegrate. They must look upon these communities not merely as a convenient source for financial and moral support, but as essential bastions of a balanced Torah society in their own right, by urging bnei Torah to be trained as competent rabbis and teachers as well as to serve as active lay leaders and members of these communities, thus reversing their present decline. Indeed, rabbis and communal leaders may have to consider steps to ensure that the support rendered to yeshivot is reciprocal, so that the traditional Issachar–Zevulun partnership assures viability and true equality for both. Without seeking or enforcing such an understanding with the yeshivot, I can see no way to restoring a vibrant and potent rabbinate.

More generally, Torah leaders must demonstrate that every Jew, and above all every Jewish child, is their concern. Even our devotions on Yom Kippur are not complete unless we are prepared "to pray with the sinners," based on the dictum in the Talmud: "Any fast which does not include the transgressors of Israel is not a fast." How different would the impact and image of Torah scholars be if, instead of segregating themselves from the wider community or simply writing it off, they would identify and involve themselves with all elements of our people, personally visiting schools, universities, and clubs, or consulting on constructive plans for the gradual introduction of religious instruction and observances into all our schools.

ASSERTING RABBINICAL INDEPENDENCE

In the conduct of religious policies, the rabbinate will have to assert far greater independence from the dictates of both the political interests of the secular leadership on the Left, and the confined special interest groups on the Right. Such independence should enable rabbis to apply objective criteria to spiritual leadership, resisting partisan pressures.

AGREEMENT ON PRIORITIES

High on the list of priorities I would place items on which our entire people ought to be united, notably its spiritual regeneration and its physical survival. Within the first category would feature the intensification and sophistication of Jewish education, the emphasis on moral integrity as the hallmark of Jewish life, and the popularization of a value system consistent with Jewish teaching. Within the second category, I would include a sustained campaign to raise the Jewish birthrate by stressing the gloomy prospects for the Jewish future already apparent from the neglect of Jewish ethical dictates on birth-control and abortion. For such objectives, we might well win far wider public support and respect than by pressing for legislation of interest only to minorities already accepting the sovereignty of Jewish law.

THE ART OF COMPOSING BLESSINGS

The reorientation required in the direction of Jewish spiritual leadership is well illustrated in a beautiful interpretation given by Rav Kook on the composition of *Birkat ha-Minim* as related in the Talmud: "Said Rabban Gamliel to the Sages, is there anyone who knows how to compose the Benediction of the Heretics? Thereupon Samuel the Younger arose and composed it." What was the problem here? Why was it so hard to find a suitable author for this particular blessing when there was evidently no such difficulty in composing all the other benedictions of the *Shemoneh Esreh?*

Explained Rav Kook in his inimitable manner:

All the other blessings are filled with benevolence and love; they beseech the Almighty to grant the bounties of forgiveness and healing, the prosperity of the Land the rebuilding of Jerusalem, and similar blessings for His people. But the Benediction of the Heretics is an exception in that it invokes a curse upon the slanders and evil-doers. Blessings for good can be composed by any Sage worthy of his high station to order fixed prayers for a holy nation, a wise and understanding people. But regarding this Benediction, which contains within it words of hatred and imprecation, and man being only human, it is altogether impossible that there should not be found in him some natural hostility towards his enemies and the pursuers of his people; hence, this prayer can be authored only by one who is completely pure and holy unto God, in whose heart there is no disposition towards natural enmity at all, and who entreats the Lord to cast away the wicked only because through their evil and ensnaring actions, destiny cannot be unfolded. But if there remains in the heart the slightest feeling of hatred caused by natural antagonism, even though he was originally moved by the holiest motives, nevertheless there will develop in his heart also a natural enmity beyond the true intention. Therefore Samuel the Younger arose and composed the prayer, since only he was really qualified, as he constantly taught "when your enemy falls, do not rejoice." He thus removed from his heart feelings of hatred even towards his own detractors, and when he was inspired to compose the Benediction of the Heretics, it manifested nothing but the feelings of the purest heart dedicated to the truest common good.

These precious words indicate precisely the stand we ought to adopt toward our generation and the members of our communities. It is our duty to arrange and formulate the blessings for the peace and success of the House of Israel. Today, alas, the reverse often applies. There is no lack of masters of learning and giants of Torah who know how to compose a Benediction of Heretics, by invoking words of denunciation, abuse, accusation, and blame upon the heads of presumptuous transgressors, and who knows whether all the words of condemnation and castigation in this *Birkat ha-Minim* always really spring from a heart pure of every vestige of hatred, free from the slightest personal or political interest. For not every rabbi is an expert in this like Samuel the Younger. On the other hand, few are they who have no truck with the curse of heretics, but who compose blessings of love and compassion supplicating for mercy on the House of Israel, teaching understanding to those who err, comfort to those broken in spirit, and courage to the faint-hearted.

Our greatest national desideratum today is *Ahavat Yisrael*, bred of tolerance for those who disagree and compassion for those who are spiritually deprived. It is to this ideal above all that religious leaders must consecrate themselves and their work if they are to realize the talmudic definition of their function: *Talmidei chakhamim marbim shalom ba-olam*, "Religious scholars increase peace in the world."

This surely sums up the most urgently needed qualities required in Jewish spiritual leadership today: the wisdom to turn the curses of our age into blessings, by interpreting the cause and meaning of our tribulations as a lesson to secure the regeneration of the Jewish genius in the spirit of the Hebrew prophets; and the gift of compassion and inspiration to inspire the impure of our generation into shining examples of pure integrity, rectitude and piety, as indispensable agents in the moral refinement of humanity.

22

The Rabbi as Contemporary Leader

Rabbi Robert S. Hirt

In a changing world, not even the rabbinate is immune to new realities. The Orthodox rabbinate of the nineties is certainly evolving in ever-new directions, some for the good, and others less so. By carefully perceiving and evaluating such trends and developments, the rabbi—be he a new musmakh or one seasoned by many years in the field—can be vastly better able to maximize his impact and personal growth and fulfillment. Rabbi Robert Hirt here provides a thoughtful analysis of the essential qualities of today's successful Rav.

There are myths that abound regarding all fields of professional endeavor. The Orthodox pulpit rabbinate is certainly no exception. Just as realities often lag behind reputations, so do myths persist despite factual refutations. The oft-quoted statement that "the pulpit is not a job for a Jewish boy" conveys, in a cynical sense, that unless a sensitive, learned, idealistic young person is naive and masochistic, he should not select the pulpit rabbinate as a lifelong professional career. Much, however, has changed in the Orthodox community that has direct bearing on its pulpit rabbinate.

In the past fifty years, Orthodox congregational life has gone through various phases in its transition from the areas of first settlement to more affluent city neighborhoods to suburbia and exurbia. Memberships of congregations evolved primarily from uneducated laborers and shopkeepers with limited higher Jewish or secular educa-

tion, to yeshivah- and university-trained professionals and entrepre-
neurs. The resulting effect on the rabbinate has been for the rabbi to
be evaluated much more by the authenticity of his rabbinic scholarship, than by his oratorical and public relations skills; from speaker to
teacher, from spokesman to *posek*.

As the Orthodox day school movement began to flourish, a new
generation of yeshivah-educated, professionally trained laity with a
passionate commitment to Orthodoxy emerged. The models presented by these young men and women, who were able to retain their
Torah way of life while competing effectively in the open society,
proved to be so attractive, that not only did Orthodoxy begin to
retain its young people, but it appealed to increasing numbers of *ba'alei
teshuvah*, who joined Orthodox congregations.[1]

The rabbinic placement picture in the past decade shows that
young promising talmidei chakhamim in their late twenties and early
thirties are much more attractive candidates to major congregations
than more experienced rabbis who have not established their reputations in rabbinic scholarship. This statement is not to say that the
more recently ordained are more competent to provide halakhic
leadership. It does, however, suggest that an increasing number of
congregations today are seeking the Torah scholarship credential as a
sine qua non for pulpit appointment. If a congregation identifies a
charismatic, assertive young man with such a quality (even if he has
limited experience), it will prefer his election to a rabbi several years
his senior who may have served in congregations whose membership
did not put a primary emphasis on Torah learning.

Today, the Orthodox rabbi has the opportunity to impact on
the lives of people who value Torah learning and observance of
mitzvot. He must devote major amounts of time to high-level study, so
that he may remain current in his halakhic leadership. The memberships of yeshivah-educated congregations are aware if there are gaps in
the rabbi's knowledge. Due to increased opportunities, the first-rank
rabbi today has a bright and challenging future ahead of him in the
Orthodox rabbinate. He presents a model of authenticity in the Jewish
community by virtue of his training, competence, priorities, and the
level of commitment that he inspires in his congregants.

There are gifted young people today who could make it in the
professional and business world, but choose to enter the pulpit
rabbinate because of their desire to spend their day in Torah study,

teaching, and community leadership vocationally rather than avoca-
tionally. For these young men, resolving a halakhic or human
problem is more ennobling than dealing with the challenges presented
by the secular, professional, or business world.

This evaluation is not to say that all is well in the Orthodox
pulpit rabbinate. While the above-mentioned factors have had a
positive effect on the overall rabbinic situation, myths stemming from
the experiences of previous decades continue to persist.

Let's look at some of these myths:

Myth. The rabbi must be a jack of all trades and therefore can be
a master of none.

Reality. While the rabbi must fulfill multiple functions, his roles
as teacher and *posek* have radically changed, for the better, from the
days of his being primarily a preacher and community organizer.
Substance, rather than style, is in demand today. In the 1940s, the
medium was the message. In the 1980s, the Torah message became the
medium. As a result, the gap between rabbinic and lay expectations
has been considerably narrowed, thus yielding a greater sense of
satisfaction for both the rabbi and his congregants. The rabbi who
does not advance in his Torah scholarship will be severely handi-
capped in his desire for professional advancement.

Myth. Rabbis feel trapped with no place to go.

Reality. Frustrations and burnout are common to all professions. There is evidence that, where mismatches between rabbis and
congregations do occur, life crises will be greater for the pulpit rabbi
than for other professionals. Dr. Leslie R. Freedman[2] noted that,
surprisingly, rabbis report a considerably higher level of demoralization than is true for the general public. He states further that, "the role
of expert in Jewish law and teacher – is more often than not discredited
and disregarded by the people a rabbi serves. No wonder rabbis
believe themselves to have so little influence over the events of their
lives." In growing Orthodox congregations, where halakhic expertise
and high-level Torah teaching are prized values, the hardy rabbinic
personality that welcomes the challenge of his chosen profession will
not feel that his future is totally out of his control. He will experience
pressures, but not demoralizing stress. Rabbis who discover that they
will not advance in the pulpit because of their own scholarly or other
limitations, or lack of compatibility with the pulpit, have made
successful adjustments to related fields of Jewish communal service.

There is an increasing need, for example, of rabbi-chaplains in hospitals, executives in Jewish communal agencies, and teacher-administrators in Jewish education. Of course, further preparation to obtain the appropriate credentials and experience in these areas is necessary. These often can be obtained while still serving in the pulpit. It is quite common today for rabbis to avoid burnout by cultivating new interests and engaging in activities outside of pulpit duties. Developing personal hobbies and skills, participating in community and rabbinic associations, and taking well-spaced short vacations with children or only with one's wife can help provide necessary distance which allows for development of a healthy perspective for one's professional life without compromising his sense of devotion to the congregation.

Myth. You just can't make a living in the pulpit rabbinate.

Reality. In the past twenty-five years, I have seen very few rabbis who have left the pulpit because of financial considerations. While it is true that rabbis do not have the same opportunity for financial growth as offered in some other fields, the situation currently is much improved. Today, most pulpit rabbis need only one position to support their families. If they also teach at universities and yeshivot, it is often more for personal fulfillment than for financial need. Increasingly, rabbis are advised to purchase their own homes so that they may build equity. In many instances, they effect such purchases with financial support of their congregations.

It should be noted that newly founded Orthodox congregations with observant memberships are developing in many areas of North America. Despite the inability of these congregations to provide full-time salaries, during the early stages of their growth, many rabbis prefer these pulpits (even if they have to supplement their income by day-school teaching) to full-time pulpits that have lower religious commitment, standards, and aspirations.

Myth. When the congregation elects a rabbi, they believe that they have hired his wife as well.

Reality. Today, it is more the rule than the exception for the Orthodox rabbi's wife to be her own person. Most young rabbis' wives, and more senior rebbitzins with grown children, have professional training and pursue their own careers. Yes, they are expected to be active in their communities, but they are not obligated to assume leadership roles. This fact is particularly true of congregations in mid-size and large cities. Rabbis' wives, while expected to be hospitable and supportive of their husbands' work, are not expected to perform rabbinic-related tasks.

The rabbi's wife will have the obligation to serve as a Judaic studies resource person, especially in smaller communities, because of her expertise. However, she will be free to pursue her own concerns or outside interests as well. Rabbis and congregations generally speak with pride of their rebbitzin's independent, professional accomplishments.

Myth. The rabbi is constantly at odds with his lay board.

Reality. The issue of rabbinic authority impacts on rabbi–lay relations in what is essentially a voluntary association. Incidents of exacerbated relationships between the chief executive officers of major companies and boards of directors, as well as the termination rate, are far more common than in the pulpit rabbinate. It is true that the pulpit rabbi who is in the public arena is going to be subject to public scrutiny. He, therefore, cannot be thin skinned or in constant need of approbation. Pulpit rabbis and other communal professionals who are plagued by fragile egos or expect full agreement will not find satisfaction in their work. Effective rabbis soon learn that criticism need not imply rejection, and that difference of opinion need not lead to polarization. The greater the openness to legitimate differences of opinion, the better the climate for resolving tensions with lay boards.

Perhaps the greatest source of tension emerges when congregations and rabbis seem unable or unwilling to respond to each other's reasonable requests in areas relating to advancing the congregation's communal or the rabbi's professional welfare. It is here that intervention of rabbinic and synagogue bodies should be sought.

Rabbis in their initial pulpits, in small, outlying communities, have the greatest adjustments to make. They expect to elevate the religious practices and commitment of the community, increase synagogue attendance, and inspire participation in organized Jewish life. Responses of congregants, in these areas, are frequently unequal to the rabbi's initiatives. In such circumstances, rabbis will express dissatisfaction and frustration in dealing with their lay people. It is important for young rabbis to strike a healthy balance between the responsibility to lead and the opportunity to serve. In congregations with limited religious horizons, the rabbi may have to direct his energies to concentrate more on meeting the essential ritual, programmatic, and pastoral needs of his people than on intellectual, cultural, or spiritual goals. Lay people, in understanding their relationship with their rabbis, must also be honest about their own lack of commitment that may have been pledged in the interviewing process to attract a rabbi to the community. Upon recognizing the nature of lay commitment, senior rabbis have learned to adjust their approaches and develop long-range plans to meet their own needs and those of their congregants. By establishing meaningful personal relationships with their lay leadership and the rank and file of their congregations, effective rabbis are able to bridge halakhic and educational gaps between them.

Not every rabbi will be able to achieve the optimal fulfillment in his first or second pulpit. The average, successful Orthodox rabbi will make three to four changes in positions during his career. In our highly mobile society, this pattern actually represents a more rooted professional pattern which is a testament to the stability of the pulpit rabbinate.

What I have emphasized to this point does not deny that some rabbis do experience frustrations regarding professional and personal advancement. Rabbis, like other professionals, must assess their strengths and limitations and realize that their futures depend on a realistic determination of their abilities. At one time, rabbis, after initially serving in small towns, distant from major centers of Jewish life, could expect to advance to medium-size congregations in larger Jewish communities. Today, however, as a result of congregational mergers brought on by relocations and erosion of the inner city communities, there is a shortage of Orthodox pulpits in large cities. Pulpits in major metropolitan areas are of three kinds: (1) fledgling and growing, (2) aging and declining, and (3) imposing and sophisticated. A rabbi of modest strengths will confront difficult choices. Competition has always been keen at the top and continues to be so. The rabbi who, in his own estimation, will not be comfortable in a congregation that requires a high-ranking talmid chakham, will have to adjust his sights and aspirations. This adjustment may mean accepting a modest pulpit in a large city that will require him to assume an additional position for personal fulfillment or to supplement his income, or he may have to accept a permanent position in a smaller Jewish community lacking some of the amenities desirable to the Orthodox family. In some cases, it will be best advised for him to leave the pulpit rabbinate. Those who seek guidance of the professional staff of the rabbinic training institutions and rabbinic service organizations can receive the assistance needed to help them to make the necessary adjustments that may still enable them to remain in the service of the Jewish people.

The professional staff at the Max Stern Division of Communal Services of Rabbi Isaac Elchanan Theological Seminary, for example, offers a series of programs that encourages rabbis to consult with their colleagues concerning their professional needs and aspirations. It is particularly those rabbis who isolate themselves from mentors and peers who fail to identify suitable means to cope with the ever-emerging difficulties in a challenging profession that seeks to lead and serve.

Certainly, more needs to be done to provide an effective support system for pulpit rabbis and their families. But the days of properly prepared Orthodox rabbis being harassed victims of a career choice marked by limited economic and professional opportunity, that characterized the Orthodox rabbinate of decades ago, have all but disappeared.

The rabbinic leader since the days of Moshe Rabbeinu has been subject to close scrutiny from within his own family and from the community he serves. And yet, despite the demands of rabbinic leadership for four decades, at the end of his days, the Torah records that "his eyes were undimmed and his vigor unabated" and the people wept for Moshe Rabbeinu when he died (*Devarim* 34:5–8).

The leadership of Moshe Rabbeinu provides the model for his rabbinic successors for all generations. There will always be critics. But a supportive family and community can go a long way to encourage creative, inspired, effective spiritual leadership and accomplishment. In looking to the future, may I suggest that the reality of the current experiences of the Orthodox rabbinate, anchored in historical biblical precedent, should help dispel outdated myths.

NOTES

[1]See Dr. M. Herbert Danzger, *Return and Tradition — The Contemporary Revival of Orthodox Judaism* (New Haven, CT: Yale University Press), p. 328.

[2]Leslie Freedman, "Psychological Hardiness and Demoralization among American Rabbis." Lecture presented at the *American Psychological Society Annual Meeting* (August 24, 1986).

23

The Rabbi as Spokesman for Modern Orthodox Philosophy

Rabbi Shubert Spero

The rabbi, besides everything else (and perhaps prior to everything else), is a thinker whose universe is one of ideas, ideals,
concepts, and values. By training and by disposition, he inclines
toward uncovering them in texts, analyzing them, adding to them,
and finally sharing them with others. He is, properly, a thinking
man. Not least among these intellectual activities for the so-called
"Modern Orthodox rabbi" is the need to articulate the elements of
a centrist philosophy of Torah that he and others can live by in
the contemporary world. Rabbi Shubert Spero issues a call to do
precisely that, by way of an insightful analysis of the American
Orthodox rabbinate, for what it is, and what it might become.

If, as has been reliably reported, we now have a recognizable community of Orthodox Jews called Modern Orthodox, ensconced in an
array of powerful, thriving American institutions, why should it be so
difficult to supply what seems to be the crucial missing link in its
development: an articulated ideology—a philosophy of Modern Orthodoxy? To compound the wonder, we are not talking about the
development de nova of a complete philosophy from the ground up.
We are dealing essentially with Orthodox Judaism in all its fundamental respects, with emphasis on a special approach to four or five
issues. And even these approaches themselves are not new but have
been espoused and defended in the past: by Samson Raphael Hirsch
on the need for general culture, by Naftali Zvi Yehudah Berlin and

Yitzchak Dov Bamberger on cooperation, by Zvi Hirsch Kalischer and Avraham Yitzchak ha-Kohen Kook on Zionism, and on all these issues in the pages of *Tradition* during the past twenty-five years. All that is needed is for someone to bring together the scattered elements into a united, cohesive, integrated picture.

It seems rather strange that from the pulpits of the congregational rabbis of the Rabbinical Council there has not come a steady and consistent point of view that would consciously articulate the Modern Orthodox position to the congregation, a position that over the years would coalesce into a Modern Orthodox philosophy and give a sense of identity and self-awareness to the congregation as Modern Orthodox. Is it possible that we have Modern Orthodox Jews but no Modern Orthodox rabbis?

Perhaps the answer lies in a deeply personal problem that constrains most Orthodox rabbis who in important respects do have views which can be called Modern Orthodox. Rabbi Louis Bernstein, in reviewing the history of the Rabbinical Council in relation to the older Agudas Harabbonim, writes: "Conflicting forces affected the young rabbis. On the one hand they sought recognition from the older rabbinic group, which included among its members recognized rabbinic scholars, yet they were constantly rejected by the senior group."[1]

In a time and place that has witnessed a dramatic growth in traditional yeshivot, in traditional talmudic scholarship, and in the number of *chozrim bi-teshuvah*, it is perhaps unrealistic to demand that Orthodox rabbis, in their educational efforts from the pulpit, concentrate on Modern Orthodox themes—that is, on the issues in which they differ from the right-wing Orthodox. At a time when the culture heroes of the new generation among the best families in the congregation are the roshei yeshivah, old and new, can the congregational Orthodox rabbi concentrate on Modern Orthodox themes that the right-wing Orthodox furiously oppose? After all, the modern Orthodox rabbi himself for a good part of his background and a good part of his present religious allegiance identifies with his teachers, the roshei yeshivah—of past and present. This reflects what Liebman points to as the built-in strategic weakness of the modern Orthodox: the modern Orthodox accord legitimacy to the right-wing Orthodox, who do not as yet return the favor.

As difficult as it may be, the existing situation seems to me to have, nevertheless, created a moral imperative for Modern Orthodox rabbis to, as it were, come out of the closet and give guidance to the many whose outer and inner identities are in unrelieved tension. It is not a question of starting a new movement but of helping an existing group to understand itself. Ours was the generation of American rabbis who went to college and studied at the university, and believed in principle in participating in aspects of general culture. We understood that there could not be a Jewish homeland without Jewish engineers, scientists, lawyers, doctors, and soldiers. We understood that the Jewish people could not discharge its obligation and responsibility as a nation to God and to its own people if it were to separate itself from the dynamics of human progress. Can we now abandon the thousands of bright young men and women who, perhaps inspired by our example, chose the path of Modern Orthodoxy to "live a life of patterned desperation" for want of an ideology?

The truth is that the Modern Orthodox need more than simply a philosophical framework. They need a rabbinical leadership that will help them solve their halakhic perplexities with sympathy and courage. They need teachers to help them develop more inwardness in areas of Judaism like prayer and *gemilut chasadim* wherein the piety and religious passion, no longer squandered in *chumrot*, could be redirected and expressed.

It is not easy for a rabbi today to identify himself as standing more in the line of Samson Raphael Hirsch than in the line of some recent rosh yeshivah, but neither is it easy to ignore the demands of intellectual integrity.

NOTES

[1]L. Bernstein, *Challenge and Mission* (New York: Shengold, 1982), p. 13.

24

The Rabbi as Spiritual Leader

Rabbi Norman Lamm

Rabbi Norman Lamm presents his view of the challenges and
opportunities, the obstacles and the rungs, facing the contemporary rabbi, now and for the foreseeable future. It is excerpted from
comments he delivered at a Semikhah Convocation at Yeshivah
University in 1978.

The following comments refer to those of you who are professionally
involved in *melekhet ha-kodesh*. As one who has been deeply immersed
in this activity for twenty-five years, I think I understand some of the
problems you face. And I specifically address myself to the internal
psychological tensions that afflict a rabbi, tensions that could become
a source of creativity but also are reason for great anguish and moral
torment. If there is one clearly identifiable mood that looms above all
others as a threat to the effectiveness, happiness, and even sanity of a
committed Rav in this last quarter of a century, it is frustration. There
is nothing quite as noxiously potent as frustration in defeating a rabbi,
and in robbing him of his inspiration, his ability to function, and his
idealism.

    I can think of no better paradigm of this dangerous defeatism
than the story of Elijah in the famous passage in Kings 1:19. Jezebel
swears that she will kill the prophet. Elijah retreats into the desert to
think. He sits under a tree—and he gives up: *vayish'al et nafsho la-mut.*
Va-yomer rav atah Hashem kach nafshi ki lo tov anokhi me-avotai. A

spiritual leader who is prevented from leading spiritually sees no point
to life. The emptiness is a fate worse than death. His audience has
evaporated, his admonitions fall on deaf ears, his miraculous achievements fail to impress these obdurate Jews, and now they want to kill
him. Well, let them—his prophetic mission is stillborn, he is a frustrated and defeated and desperate man, and he might as well resign
and give up the ghost.

But God will not accommodate Elijah. An angel feeds him and
sends him on a forty-day and forty-night trek to Mount Horeb. Elijah
sleeps in a cave, and the *dvar Hashem* comes to Elijah and inquires:
mah lekha poh Eliyahu—what are you doing here, Elijah? His pathetic
plaint is poured out, and the gall and the bitterness still affect us across
the centuries: *vayomer kano kineiti la-Hashem Tzeva'ot ki-azvu beritkha
benei Yisrael; et mitzbechotekha harasu ve'et nevi'ekha haragu becharev,
va-ivater ani levadi va-yevakshu et nafshi lekachtah.*

Elijah is then exposed to that most famous of all biblical spectacles. A storm is let loose, and its mighty winds break the very rocks,
but: *lo beruach Hashem.* Then there comes an earthquake, and after
that fire, but: *lo bera'ash Hashem, lo be'esh Hashem.* After this Elijah
hears *kol demamah dakah*—the sound of gentle stillness. He wraps his
mantle about his face, and God repeats the question: *mah lekha poh
Eliyahu?* Elijah is not moved. He repeats the same answer, and
reiterates the same impatience and disappointment with the Children
of Israel. At this, God orders the prophet to go back to Damascus and
get on with his business.

A strange scene, indeed a mysterious one, that leaves us full of
questions. Yet a rabbi can identify with it! Those of you who have
been in the practical rabbinate for a while can no doubt empathize
with the forlorn prophet.

I know, because I felt it and often feel it again. If I were in the
rabbinate today I would see Elijah's disappointments and frustrations
as mine. How often an idealistic young rabbi thinks: Here I am, having
declined other and easier and more lucrative occupations, and I have
dedicated myself to the rabbinate, which means God and Torah and
Klal Yisrael. I can say with the prophet, in my own way, *kano kineiti
la-Hashem Tzeva'ot.* Without zeal and devotion and idealism I never
would have undertaken this as my life's work.

Yet, what is my reward for all this? *Ki'azvu beritkha benei Yisrael,*
"for the Children of Israel have forsaken Thy covenant." I am
preaching a doctrine that they do not want to hear, and teaching a

lesson that they do not want to learn, and selling an item they do not want to buy! When sociologists take the statistics of demography and intermarriage, and punch them into their sophisticated computers, and are told and tell us that if things continue in this way, that American Jewry will in a hundred years be down from five and a half million to some nine hundred thousand or maybe even ten thousand—that means that Israel has abandoned the covenant. So who needs me?

Et mitzbechotekha harasu—Jews have overturned the altar. Under the guise of a misguided modernism, and the impress of a muddle-headed liberationism, they have destroyed *kedushat Beit ha-Knesset* by tearing down the mechitzot, opening the parking lots on Shabbat, counting women in the minyan, transforming the nature of the rabbinate, and enshrining ignorance in the ark. When shall the prophet prophesy and when shall the rabbi teach—if *mitzbechotekha harasu*—if halakhah is treated with contempt, if tradition is branded as Neanderthal, if Shabbat is desecrated, if there are no shuls where sanctity is observed and revered?

Ve'et nevi'ekha haragu be'charev va'ivater ani levadi va-yevakshu et nafshi lekachtah: "Thy prophets they killed with a sword, and I remain alone, and they sought my soul to take it away." What use is there in continuing a struggle that is doomed; when congregations eject loyal rabbis with impunity because they refuse to bend the knee to the *Ba'alim* of suburban America? When school boards reveal an aggressively abysmal ignorance of what Jewish education of children is all about; when a rabbi, tired and weary of the constant friction and misunderstanding and confrontation, feels so painfully alone, so dreadfully lonely, so socially ostracized and spiritually isolated? *va-Yevakshu et nafshi lekachtah!* Of what use is it to be a rabbi, even if they raise my salary and buy me a car and send me and my wife to Israel, if they seek to suck out my very nefesh by denying me those spiritual triumphs and satisfactions for which, and for which alone, I became a Rav in the first place?

And yet, our own outbursts leave us unfulfilled. The catharsis of venting our feelings and seeking to end it all is incomplete. We know in our bones what our conscience hears loud and clear: *mah lekha poh Eliyahu*, what are you doing here? Why are you complaining? Maybe you didn't try hard enough. Maybe you do not have the moral warrant to climb into a cave and vent your spleen against your fellow Jews.

So, we determine to make a last, all-out effort. We become dramatic and heroic. We pull out all the plugs. We call mass meetings and we lead rallies and we organize demonstrations—whether for Israel or against the PLO, whether for Russian Jews or against *chillul Shabbat*. We precipitate communal confrontations with Federations and Centers and non-Orthodox temples. We fly into battle fearlessly, and we make a great deal of noise. And the result is—hardly anything. *Lo be'ruach Hashem, lo be'ra'ash Hashem, lo be'esh Hashem*. And again the *kol demamah dakah* penetrates our conscience and asks: *mah lekha poh Eliyahu*. But we give the same answers. We vent our frustrations and our anger and our impatience and our bitterness. And all we get, finally, is an apparent non-sequitur—"Go to Syria!" *Lekh shuv le'dark-ekha Damesek!*

What does all this mean? I suggest that if the hints in this passage are analyzed correctly, they will yield a message of overarching importance for the contemporary Elijahs suffering the same symptoms of spiritual distress and personal unhappiness.

Let me list a few of these hints: there is a trip of forty days and forty nights; the action takes place at Mount Horeb–Sinai; the locales are a desert, a mountaintop, and a cave; there is a theophany accompanying a series of divinely produced natural outbursts of sound and fire and fury; there is a covering of the face and a reluctance to look; and there is, of course, an irrepressible anger at the obstinate, backsliding, disobedient Jews, and an impatience with their spiritual immaturity. It should be obvious by now that we hear in this passage the echoes of the career of Moshe Rabbeinu. The locations, the time, the setting, and the psychological reactions are all there.

Then there is another set of clues—two, to be specific: the story begins in Beersheba and ends in Damascus, Syria. These two areas are the loci that define the historic mission of our Father Abraham.

I suggest that Providence is teaching the prophet about his own mission, his own task on earth.

Elijah is faced with two great historical archetypes of Jewish leadership, that of Moses and Abraham. Moses, during his first sojourn at Mount Sinai, symbolizes the drama, the power, the spectacle that accompanies divine revelation. He is the impatient leader who, much as he loves his people, cannot suffer fools gladly, and is bitterly impatient with their petty selfishness and their concern for trivia which blind them to the grandeur of their divine mission. He

will make the Heavens tremble and the very earth boil in an attempt
to shake these piddling people from their moral lethargy.

The other type of spiritual leadership is that of Abraham.
Abraham is a man of great patience who never tries the spectacular.
He is forbearing towards a Lot, and he can negotiate endlessly with an
oriental Efron. Much as he is offended by the wicked men of Sodom,
he still is willing to take up the cudgels on behalf of the city in his
famous prayer/dialogue with God. If necessary, he will even mobilize
his troops and fight a war to save the just from the unjust—and he
wants nothing in return. He does not expect any miraculous conversions of his pagan peers, but he never gives up trying by exercising
patient influence and gradual inspiration. His motto is "outreach"—
ve'ha-nefesh asher asu be'Charan. He does, of course, reach dramatic
peaks, as when he offers up his son at the akeidah. But it is all done in
the strictest privacy, and if the Torah did not reveal it, no one would
know it—there are no 600,000 witnesses.

These are the two archetypes of Jewish leadership that stood
before the mind of Elijah. His whole career had been a Mosaic-type
leadership, and had left an indelible imprint on all of Jewish history.
But as with Moses, so with Elijah: not all Jews respond to such
aggressive and dramatic leadership. Hence, like Moses, Elijah is angry
and bitter and frustrated. Like Moses he travels forty days and forty
nights, he climbs Mount Horeb or Sinai, he experiences the *kolot
u-verakim*, he flees into a cave, and casts his eyes aside not to gaze at
the presence of God. But it doesn't work and he is ready to give up, a
defeated man. He has the same complaints against Israel that Moses
had, and his reactions were the same, but he could not succeed where
Moses did. And therefore, twice, God asks him: *mah lekha poh Eliyahu?*
What are you doing here? And Elijah does not understand what God
wants and so offers the same answer twice.

It is then that God tells the prophet to go and return to
Damascus. The whole event began in Beersheba, and now it must end
in Syria. God is reminding Elijah that there is another model of
leadership that he had entirely neglected—that of Abraham, who
began in Syria and ended in Beersheba. God is telling the prophet to
retrace the steps taken by Father Abraham.

> You have followed only Moses, but your generation was not
> ready for it, and it has led you into despair. Now is the time to
> reverse the steps from Beersheba to Damascus, and undertake

your prophetic vocation on the exalted pattern of Father Abraham. Forego the great spectacles, abjure the dramatic actions, forsake the climactic confrontations, and never, never become bitter or recriminatory. Your way must now be the way of slow, patient, gradual action. Throw yourself back into daily life and, even if you can perform miracles, do not expect Jews to be miraculously affected by them. Now is the time for an Abraham-type leadership rather than a Moses type.

This, I submit, is the Torah's message for young spiritual leaders of our times: every prophet, every Jewish leader, must alternate between Abraham and Moses, using either one as circumstance dictates. Do not allow yourself to cross the threshold of frustration too readily. Do not rant and rave against Jews who fail to respond to your idealistic self-sacrifice. Do not put your trust in the shock-action of demonstrations and rallies and mass meetings only. Do not crawl into a cave and lament your bitter fate and look around for another profession while there is still time. Tough it out. Be prepared for a long and arduous journey. Know that in the rabbinate the one thing you must never expect is gratitude. Do not demand or expect that people will appreciate either your learning or your loyalty. And yet, love them because they are your brothers and sisters, pray *for* them and *with* them no matter how low they sink, for Father Abraham did the same for people far worse than they. Do not act only as if you are at the climax of a great endeavor, as was Moses at Sinai; instead, imagine too that you are at the beginning of a long adventure, as was Abraham. Act with fortitude and with forbearance, and if the call of *lekh lekha* takes you away from home and your family and the spiritual comforts of your life in yeshiva, follow your vocation happily and lovingly, secure in the knowledge that ultimately it will lead you into the Promised Land of a Jewish community firm in its commitment to Torah and to the *Ribono Shel Olam.*

Always keep both archetypes before you: Moses, who summoned his people to return to the ways of the *Avot,* who attempted to restore *lev banim al avotam*; and Abraham who, beginning without precedent, and nurturing his vision of a future of *emunah ba-Hashem,* tried to move his generation in the direction that his and their children would ultimately take: *lev avot al banim.*

So, my message to you—those charged with the sacred obligation of continuing the historic tradition of Jewish spiritual leadership which began with Father Abraham and continued through Moses and Elijah—is to choose carefully the appropriate model for your specific condition. Above all, do not despair but be of good courage and take heart. Know that in your congregations and schools there are unexplored islands of human goodness and tenderness, unchartered resources of Jewish love and loyalty and commitment, undiscovered treasures of yearning for Torah and tradition. Never give up on a single Jew! Know that as rabbanim you represent a tradition more ancient than that of medicine, more sacred than that of law, more noble than that of commerce and trade. Know that you are but the latest link in a chain that contains the greatest luminaries in the history of our ancient people, and that the masorah is committed into your hands for safekeeping and transmission to those who will follow you. And know, above all, that your yeshivah stands behind you, your roshei yeshivah stand beside you, and the ideals of Torah you learned here stand before you—to keep you company in your loneliness, to allay your apprehensions, to mitigate your frustrations, to enhance your courage, and to recharge you with the inspiration to succeed, despite all obstacles, in the marvelous and wondrous tasks which you have undertaken to transform a mere congregation to a *kehilah kedoshah,* a mere school to a *makom Torah,* and the Jewish community to the *am Hashem.*

> *Hinei Anokhi sholei'ach lakhem et Eliyahu ha-navi lifnei bo yom Hashem ha-gadol ve'ha-nora; ve'heishiv lev avot al banim ve'lev banim al avotam.*

Appendix 1

Membership Application
Yahrzeit Forms
Membership Work-up Sheet
Membership Interest and Experience
Kashrut
Shabbat Shipping List
Rental Contract
Bar Mitzvah
High School Students
Bar Mitzvah-Chaver Program
Special Programs

MEMBERSHIP APPLICATION

Date _____

We hereby apply for membership in the Congregation Beth Tikvah, Dollard des Ormeaux, Quebec. If accepted, we agree to abide by and conform to its Constitution and by-laws now existing or which may be enacted from time to time. We undertake to make payment in accordance with the present regulations or those which may be adopted in the future.

Family Name _____ Address _____

Postal Code _____ Telephone No. _____

Husband _____ Wife _____

Husband's Occupation _____ Firm Name _____

Business Address _____ Business Telephone No. _____

Hebrew Name _____ Father's Hebrew Name _____

Indicate: Cohen _____ Levi _____ Israel _____

Wife's Maiden Name _____

Occupation_____ Firm Name _____

Business Address _____ Business Telephone No. _____

Hebrew Name _____ Father's Hebrew Name _____

Date of Birth: Husband _____ Wife _____

Date of Marriage _____

Names of Children	Hebrew Name	Date of Birth	Religious Education
_____	_____	_____	_____
_____	_____	_____	_____
_____	_____	_____	_____

Yahrtzeit Information

Full Name of Departed	Relationship	English/Hebrew Date	Hebrew Name of Departed and Father
_____	_____	_____	_____
_____	_____	_____	_____
_____	_____	_____	_____
_____	_____	_____	_____

Date _____ Signatures _____

Additional Information for Membership

The following is necessary for processing your application for membership. This information will be held in strict confidence by the Rabbi only. Please feel free to call on the Rabbi to assist you and you may mail this form directly to the Rabbi.

1. a) Religion of applicant: _____
      By birth or by conversion? _____
      If by conversion, please state details (date, place, Rabbi, certificate): _____
      _____

    b) Religion of mother of applicant: _____
      By birth or conversion? _____
      If by conversion, please state details (date, place, Rabbi, certificate): _____
      _____

2. a) If Married (single, to be added upon marriage)
      Religion of wife of applicant: _____
      _____
      By birth or conversion? _____
      If by conversion, please state details (date, place, Rabbi, certificate): _____
      _____

    b) Religion of mother of wife of applicant: _____
      By birth or conversion? _____
      If by conversion, please state details (date, place, Rabbi, certificate): _____
      _____

    c) Religion of father of wife of applicant: _____
      By birth or conversion? _____
      If by conversion, please state details (date, place, Rabbi, certificate): _____
      _____

3. Name of Rabbi Who Performed Marriage Ceremony
    _____

    Congregation _____
    City _____
    Applicant's Signature _____

YAHRZEIT FORMS

Yahrzeit Information

The Yahrtzeit Observance of your beloved _____
_____ will commence on the evening of _____
and on the following day _____

Evening Services _____ Morning Services _____
Please confirm these times by calling the Synagogue office at
683–5610.

A Memorial Prayer will be recited on _____

If you wish to receive a Torah Honour please identify yourself to
the Parnass at the beginning of services.

Yahrtzeit Remembrance

Yahrtzeit in reverent memory of your _____
occurs this year on the evening of and the following day.

Kaddish is to be recited in the Synagogue at the:
Evening Service _____
Morning Service _____
Afternoon Service _____

A candle of Rememberance is kindled in the home on the
evening when Yahrtzeit begins.

A memorial prayer will be recited on _____

If you wish to receive a Torah Honour please identify yourself to
the Parnass at the beginning of services.

MEMBERSHIP WORK-UP SHEET

Date _____Family Name _____

Husband's Name _____ Wife's Name _____

Parent Age Group: 20–25 _____ 26–35 _____ 36–50 _____ 50 + _____

Children

Affiliated with

Name	Age	Youth Group	H.F.S.	H.A.	Playful Parenting
_____	__	_____	_____	____	_____
_____	__	_____	_____	____	_____
_____	__	_____	_____	____	_____
_____	__	_____	_____	____	_____

Address _____

Postal Code _____ Phone Number _____

Interests _____ _____

_____ _____

_____ _____

Comments

Follow-Up: Next 2 weeks _____ 6 Months _____
           Next Year _____ Never _____

Solicited by _____ Date Seen _____

MEMBERSHIP INTERESTS AND EXPERIENCE

Name _____Telephone No. _____

I/We are interested in the following program areas:

Husband (H)   Wife (W)   Both (B)

_____ Youth   _____ Adult Education

_____ Social Programming   _____ Religious

_____ Men's Club   _____ Membership

_____ Administration   _____ B.T. Players
                                           (drama group)
_____ Fund Raising
                                     _____ B.T. Bowling
_____ Hebrew Academy
      (Afternoon School)   _____ B.T. Baseball

_____ Sisterhood   _____ Other

My Organization Experience Includes _____

_____

_____

_____

- -

For office use only

Received _____ Comments _____

                                         _____

Acted Upon _____   _____

By _____

KASHRUT

Regulations on Hashgachah in Synagogues—Regular and Shabbos Standards

Joint Kashrut Commission: Rabbinical Council of Canada (Montreal Region) and Montreal/Vaad Hoir

The Shipping List

1. All deliveries to synagogues must be accompanied by the shipping list of the Joint Kashrut Committee,, and signed by the Mashgiach of the caterer. This applies to any affair on any day.
2. Instructions with regard to food to be left on the stove during Shabbos must be specified on the shipping list. Any gravies or liquids not so specified or arranged before Shabbos cannot be used on Shabbos.

Hors D'Oeuvres: The enclosed list indicates the only hors d'oeuvres that may be served on Shabbos. These may be heated in ovens only if they have been in the oven for at least ten (10) minutes prior to Shabbos. The Mashgiach at the catering establishment shall do this and so indicate on the shipping list.

New Foods: If a new food item is to be introduced by the caterer, it has to have prior approval by the Joint Kashrut Committee.

Synagogue "Check-In" of All Foods: All deliveries to the synagogue must be made in the presence of the Synagogue Mashgiach. An appropriate appointment must be made for delivery and check-in. For Shabbos affairs, the caterer must make an appointment with the Mashgiach for the time of delivery, not later than 1:00 P.M. during the winter, and 2:00 P.M. during the summer.

The Synagogue Mashgiach—A "Yoitze Venichnas"

1. Must be Yoitze Venichnas as long as food is being prepared or served.

2. Must be in the kitchen on Saturday morning when the food is placed in the oven or on the stove.
3. He is responsible for the kashrut of the drinks served at the bar, as well as any kind of refreshments.
4. He is to see to it that no waiter, waitress, or chef brings along any utensils to the synagogue. It is suggested that a secure and convenient place be provided so that coats and purses can be stored out of reach from time of arrival until departure—this can be a closet or trunk.

   The utensils they use must be either the property of the caterer or of the synagogue. In cases where the utensils belong to the caterer, the Mashgiach of the caterer has to indicate so on the shipping list. It is suggested that synagogue utensils be prominently marked with heat-resistant paint of other siman. The same is suggested to caterers for their trays, pots, and pans.
5. He is to make sure that the florists do not bring any edibles whatsoever into the synagogue.

Stoves: Synagogue stoves must be fully equipped with locking devices for all heat controls, Shabbos blech and inside blech.

Meat: Caterers who go into synagogues must purchase their meat from butchers who have a permanent Vaad Mashgiach on their premises.

Vegetables: Only the following alternatives are permitted for the serving of vegetables on Shabbos:

1. It is preferred that vegetables be served cold–room temperature.
2. Vegetables may be left in a double boiler before Shabbos.
3. Completely drained vegetables may be served hot on Shabbos if the pans are in the oven at least for ten (10) minutes on Friday. The Mashgiach at the catering establishment shall do this and so indicate on the shipping list.

Only Vaad approved establishments are permitted to cater to the synagogues under the MK supervision. The rabbi of each synagogue is responsible for the implementation of these standards and regulations. All Mashgichim in synagogues—Mashgiach A as well as Mashgiach B—must be approved by the Joint Kashrut Committee.

SHABBAT SHIPPING LIST

Caterer _____

To Synagogue _____

Client _____

Date of Affair _____

Hors D'Ouevres

Amt.		Amt.		Amt.	
	Egg Rolls		Karnatzal		Frimps
	Pizza		Latkes		Shish Kabob
	Hot Dogs in blankets		Spanish Triangles		Teryiaki
	Asparagus Rolls		Knishes		Meatballs Dry
	Kreplach		Sou Guy		

MEAT FOWL FISH		SIDE DISHES	
Amt.		Amt.	
CAKES & PASTERIES		DESSERTS	
Amt.		Amt.	
KITCHEN UTENSILS SUPPLIED		ITEMS TO BE DELIVERED BY OTHER SUPPLIERS	
		Items to be placed on stove before Shabbos	

The above items have been checked by me and shipped

_____
Signature of Caterer Mashgiach

Date _____

RENTAL CONTRACT

Family Name _____ Bar Mitzvah Boy _____

Father's Name _____ Mother's Name _____

Address _____

_____ Postal Code _____

Telephone No. _____ Date _____ Time _____

Type of Reception _____

CONDITIONS

- Only the Rabbi of this Congregation and/or an appointee sanctioned by the Rabbi is permitted to officiate at any religious ceremony in the synagogue.
- All official celebrations connected with the contracted religious Service of Bar Mitzvah must adhere to the standards of the Congregation in strict compliance with the dietary laws. Any violation of the above not corrected in sufficient time shall render this contract null and void and all deposits shall be forfeited.
- It is understood that in order for the bar mitzvah boy to participate in the synagogue ceremony, his training and preparation must conform to the minimal requirements of our congregation; subject to the approval of the Rabbi.
- The caterer must be approved by the Jewish Community Council of Montreal and is subject to the approval of the Rabbi and Congregation. All foods must be prepared completely in the Synagogue kitchen under the supervision of the Mashgiach duly appointed by the Congregation or brought in from an approved catering establishment.
- The lessee is obliged to submit to the Congregation in writing, for approval, the name of the caterer *before* he is engaged.
- No cooked foods of any kind that have been prepared outside can be served, nor any utensils be brought into the Synagogue without the express permission of the Rabbi or his appointee.
- Cooking on the Sabbath is strictly prohibited.
- Delivery and removal of any nature to and from the Synagogue during the Sabbath and Festivals are prohibited.
- Smoking on the premises is strictly prohibited during the Sabbath.
- No party favors, souvenirs, gifts, etc. may be distributed at functions taking place on the Sabbath or Festivals.
- All functions held at the conclusion of the Sabbath or Festivals cannot commence earlier than one hour past the conclusion of the Sabbath or Festival.
- The lessee is obliged to submit to the Congregation the proof of the invitation to assure all conditions of this contract are complied with.
- Any form of entertainment is subject to the approval of the Rabbi.
- The halls and furniture and kitchen must be left in the same good order and condition as granted and any damage done thereto will be charged to the Lessee.

BAR MITZVAH

A Message to Parents

Bar mitzvah is a highlight in the cycle of life. Practically at birth one already looks forward to the privilege of rearing the child *"l-Torah, l-Chuppah ul-Maasim tovim,"* and symbolizes family loyalty, growth and progress in a large measure. It represents to the Jewish community the continuation of Jewish tradition and ideals and hence is observed usually in gala fashion as both a personal family simchah and an occasion for communal participation in a meaningful, beautiful ceremony.

Cooperate in Bar Mitzvah Preparations

The preparations for bar mitzvah require a substantial amount of time and effort on the part of your child. A child starting our school at the proper age will be ready for the special bar mitzvah Class during his twelfth year. If he has not completed the necessary years for graduation he will have to work at both.

Good Hebrew Schools do not permit the disruption of the class program in order to accommodate the extra bar mitzvah training. Hence it must be done at other times and frequently involves a disruption of schedules and a sacrifice, both on the part of your child and yourselves. If you want your child to accept these added responsibilites without complaint, it is important that you accept them cheerfully. If you show resentment and impatience, it will be reflected in your child's whole attitude toward his training and will adversely affect both the process of learning and above all, his approach to the goals and purposes of this most important event.

Your attitude may be the determining factor whether this becomes a positive creative experience or an arduous task to be gotten "over with."

The Sabbath Services

Shortly before the bar mitzvah, you will receive a list of instructions in order to help you with the details of the bar mitzvah ceremony. You will also be contacted about the "honors" for the Sabbath services and details. In addition, please feel free to call the office for any help that you may need.

The Future

While it is commonly thought by the bar mitzvah boy that "today I am a man," I am sure you know that your child has by no means reached adulthood. In all probability he has entered upon adolescence. This period marking the transition from childhood to adulthood is a most important one in the development of your child and one that requires intelligent guidance and help on your part.

It is during the coming years that your child will seek to discover the way of life and the philosophy that will make life meaningful to him. During these years his loyalties will be crystallized and become a permanent part of him. He will be confronted with "Jewish problems" as he enters life, seeking employment, making friendships, and obtaining a higher education. He will seek to establish his own personality and will rebel against "domination."

Jewish Living

Moreover, as pointed out, there are goals and purposes to bar mizvah training that are equally as important as the actual ceremony. Obviously, we want a beautiful ceremony and a fine performance on the part of your child. But we do not want an empty mechanical performance. Bar mitzvah means becoming a "responsible" member of the Jewish community. It does not mean the end of Jewish education and participation in Jewish living. Parents are often tempted both by the rigors of bar mitzvah preparation and as bribes to an unwilling child, to promise that "you can quit Hebrew School after your bar mitzvah." Nothing could be further from the true and proper attitude toward this ceremony marking "entrance" into Jewish living than this anticipated "exit."

Attitudes

This same principle applies to some of the actual teachings that your child receives. Since children learn by example more than by precept, it is vitally important that you cooperate to the fullest extent. Your home and your conduct should reflect your own loyalty and attachment to the Jewish traditions of our faith. Under any circumstances, there must be no "cynical" attitude toward these teachings. Nothing can be more confusing to a young person than to find his parents disparaging the teachings of his Religious School. You should encourage your child in the observance of Jewish ceremonial—the rich symbolism of which can be most helpful in giving your child a sense of special personal relationship with God and Jewish ideals.

A Spiritual Experience

The bar mitzvah ceremony and its attendant functions undoubtedly loom large in your thinking and planning at this time. This is as it should be to make a great impression on your child. Strengthening the family bond is certainly a positive factor in Jewish living. Having pleasant memories of this ceremony cannot help but be beneficial to your child in future years.

But with all this, it is important to emphasize the fact that the ceremony should have spiritual meaning. It should be more than just a party. Your emphasis on the religious aspects of the ceremony will help to give it this coloring. The fact that the Kiddush, the Hamotzi, and the Grace After Meals will be part of the bar mitzvah celebration will also contribute to his impression.

Your child should be encouraged to make some special personal contribution to a Jewish charity in honor of this occasion, and a personal pledge of loyalty to the ideals represented by this ceremony.

Etiquette

Bar mitzvah means "son of the commandment," that is, one who is obligated to fulfill the commandments of God.

1. Regular attendance at the Hebrew Academy or Hebrew Foundation School is therefore the first essential requirement for being bar mitzvah. Four years of Jewish education is the minimum requirement. Other educational programs are subject to review.

2. A knowledge of the daily prayers and the Sabbath services

can be acquired only through regular daily practices. the bar mizvah must therefore read his prayers every morning and evening and must attend Sabbath services regularly.

3. The bar mitzvah must acquire a set of tefillin six weeks before his bar mitzvah. During the month before his thirteenth birthday he must attend services at the synagogue where he will be taught to put on the tefillin properly and participate in the services. Our Sisterhood gift shop will help with the purchase of talis and tefillin if you so desire.

4. We usually allow three *Aliyot* to your family. You may choose whomever you wish for this honor of being called to the Torah. However, we urge you to choose only such relatives or friends who are, or who can become, familiar with the *Brochos* and the general procedure to avoid embarrassment. There are three honors in addition to the three *Aliyot*.

5. All receptions and foods related to the bar mizvah celebration must be in accordance with the Laws of Kashrut under the supervision of the Vaad Hoir — MK.

Check with the rabbi or religious committee as to the sources for purchasing foods and all other questionable matters.

6. All foods must be brought into the synagogue on Friday afternoon before candle-lighting time. Nothing may be taken from the synagogue until after sundown on Saturday evening.

7. The bar mitzvah and his father must attend the Sabbath Eve Services on Friday evening. The tallis and book should be brought to the synagogue on Friday.

8. Services begin on Saturday morning at 9:00 A.M. The bar mizvah and his family should come to the Services at 8:50 A.M.

9. The success of a bar mitzvah depends on the young man's attendance at Hebrew School after his bar mitzvah ceremony. Only in that way will he show a respect for our great Jewish heritage.

10. All fees due to the synagogue for the bar mitzvah instruction must be paid to the synagogue office before the start of the instruction.

11. Your guests should be invited primarily to pray together with the congregation and your family and not merely to come to the bar mitzvah part alone. They should be invited to a bar mitzvah and not a confirmation. Please remember that we all exchange pleasantries or greet friends we have not seen for some time before or after the services. We are gathered in the synagogue to pray.

Please preserve the dignity and decorum of our services. We trust you will be enriched by this happy occasion.

His Future Education

It is true that children frequently make such demands themselves, as this has become a most unfortunate widespread practice in our country. It is here that parents can be most helpful. If your child brings up the subject of discontinuing his formal Jewish education, do not order him to continue attendance at his Jewish religious school; rather discuss it with him. Point out that many adults find it hard to forgive their parents for having permitted them to discontinue their Hebrew studies, and that many phases of Jewish learning take on meaning only to the mature mind.

The discussion should be left open so that it can be continued again and again. Experience indicates that usually parents can convince their children to continue their studies, not so much by their arguments, as by their sincerity.

Your Part

This period requires great wisdom and discretion on the part of you, his parents. It is not easy to relinquish the sheltering role of parents. Yet if you do not want him to rebel and receive the guidance that builds his personality from outside and undesirable sources, you must win his confidence as his "friend." The companions he has and the group to which he belongs will play a most important part in determining his attitudes and behavior, and your guidance in this respect is of tremendous significance. His attitude toward Judaism and the Jewish People will, substantially, be determined by this group affiliation. You, more than anyone else, can help him through these difficult years. Certainly your rabbi will be very happy to cooperate with you in this task.

Mazel Tov

We are hopeful that the various points that we have mentioned will receive your serious attention and concern. Children are our most precious possessions and our greatest challenge and responsibility. An investment of time and thought in their future welfare can bring us the greatest returns in *Nachas*. It is our earnest hope that the *Nachas* you may have at this ceremony will be but the beginning of a lifetime of Jewish fulfillment and happiness to you and your son.

HIGH SCHOOL STUDENTS

T 'n T: An Explosive Program for Jewish Teens

T 'n T Statement of Purpose

Teens in Torah (T 'n T) is designed to provide you with an opportunity to apply your accumulated Jewish education to real life. By drawing upon and supplementing your Jewish knowledge, you will grow to appreciate the unique contribution Torah can make to your life, and the contribution you can make to the world.

Open to all Jewish teens regardless of synagogue affiliation. All sessions meet at:

Congregation Beth Tikvah
136 Westpark Blvd.

High school credits can be arranged

Registration by interview only
Contact Rabbi David Levy
683–5610

Session begins Tuesday Evening—October 11th
Concludes Tuesday Evening—December 20th

A Practical Guide to World Repair

PCB's on your mind? How about the Greenhouse Effect? Poverty or prejudice? acid rain? In a few short years you're going to be running the world. What can you do to make your world more comfortable for yourself and others?

Planning and Background Meetings

Tuesday Evenings: 6:15–7:10 P.M.

Project Implementations

Sunday morning following youth minyan and breakfast. Hours to be determined by the project. *Facilitator:* Rabbi David Levy. Open to seventh- and eighth-grade students. *Fee:* $18.

Leadership Training or the Power to Lead

The dos and don'ts of getting things done the way you want. Practical hands-on projects will help you perfect the leadership skills you'll be studying. Topics include planning, delegating, communicating, following-through, evaluating, and more.

Introduction of Skill

Tuesday Evenings: 7:15–8:10 P.M.

Leadership Exercise

Sunday morning following youth minyan and breakfast. Hours to be determined by the exercise. *Facilitator:* Rabbi David Levy. Open to ninth- through eleventh-grade students. *Fee:* $18.

BAR MITZVAH–CHAVER PROGRAM

September 15th, 1988

Dear _____ ,

May we extend best wishes of Mazel Tov to you on the occasion of the forthcoming Bar Mitzvah of your son.

To assure that the religious significance of the occasion is experienced and that we all feel most comfortable with Congregation Beth Tikvah's Bar Mitzvah expectations, we wish to advise you of the following:

A. It is our practice that Bar Mitzvah boys attend morning services on or immediately following their Hebrew 13th birthday. This marks the official start of "putting on Tefillin" and allows him to be called to the Torah to mark the occasion. The assigned date is a day on which we wear Tefillin and read the Torah. Your son's assigned date is _____ . Please confirm this date by calling the synagogue office.

B. To help the Bar Mitzvah boy and his family become more familiar with synagogue procedures, we strongly urge your regular participation in synagogue services. We expect regular participation for at least 3–4 months before the Bar Mitzvah date. In keeping with our discussion at the recent chaver meeting, your chaver is _____ . He will be contacting you to introduce himself and to explain the procedures we would like to follow. The function of the chaver is to assist you during services and to explain various procedures.

We trust that all of these experiences will aid in making your Bar Mitzvah simchah a truly satisfying and totally enjoyable experience.

Sincerely yours,

Rabbi Dr. Mordecai E. Zeitz

SPECIAL PROGRAMS

Hatikvah

| IYAR   5749 | MAY   1989 |

SHABBAT: MAY 5TH–MAY 6TH
Candle Lighting until   7:49 PM
Kabbalat Shabbat   7:00 PM
Morning Services   9:00 AM
Torah Portion – Kedoshim
            – Shabbat Rosh Chodesh
Bar Mitzvah of Mark Reich
Evening Services   7:45 PM
Shabbat concludes   8:55 PM

SHABBAT: MAY 19TH–20TH
Candle Lighting until   8:06 PM
Kabbalat Shabbat   7:00 PM
Morning Services   9:00 AM
Torah Portion – Behar
Bar Mitzvah of Ian Mazoff
Evening Services   8:15 PM
Shabbat concludes   9:15 PM

SHABBAT: MAY 12TH–13TH
Candle Lighting until   7:58 PM
Kabbalat Shabbat   7:00 PM
Morning Services   9:00 AM
Torah Portion – Emor
Bar Mitzvah of Leslie Wiseman
Evening Services   8:00 PM
Shabbat concludes   9:05 PM

SHABBAT: MAY 26TH–27TH
Candle Lighting until   8:13 PM
Kabbalat Shabbat   7:00 PM
Morning Services   9:00 AM
Torah Portion – Bechukotai
Bar Mitzvah of Aaron Cohen
Evening Services   8:15 PM
Shabbat concludes   9:23 PM

SPECIAL EVENTS

May 3rd & 4th	Hebrew Academy Registration
May 9th–10th	Yom Ha'atzmaut
May 14th	March to Jerusalem
May 22nd–23rd	Lag B'Omer
June 2nd	Yom Yerushalayim
June 4th	Community Picnic
June 6th	Siyum Hatorah
June 8th–10th	Shavuot
June 9th	Shavuoton

WEEKLY SERVICES

Sunday   8:30 AM
Monday to Friday   6:45 AM
Sunday to Thursday Evening – same as following Saturday night

Appendix 2

Marriage Registration Form
Summary and Translation of the Ketubah
The Ketubah in Hebrew

MARRIAGE REGISTRATION FORM

State _____ City _____ County _____ Vol. ____

Date of Marriage _____ State License No. _____ No. ____

BRIDEGROOM	BRIDE

English
name _____
     last   first   middle

English
name _____
     last   first   middle

Hebrew name _____

Hebrew name _____

Birthplace _____ date _____

Birthplace _____ date _____

Residence _____

Residence _____

Father's
name _____
     state if Kohen or Levi

Father's
name _____
     state if Kohen or Levi

His Hebrew
name _____

His Hebrew
name _____

son of _____ and _____

son of _____ and _____

Mother's Maiden
name _____

Mother's Maiden
name _____

Her Hebrew
name _____

Her Hebrew
name _____

daughter of _____ and _____

daughter of _____ and _____

Are both parents Jewish by birth?
If answer is **No,** give full details on reverse side _____

Are both parents Jewish by birth?
If answer is **No,** give full details on reverse side _____

Previous marriage: any
     date _____ children _____

Previous marriage: any
     date _____ children _____

How
terminated? _____

How
terminated? _____

If by divorce
give date of get _____

If by divorce
give date of get _____

Rabbi who
issued get _____

Rabbi who
issued get _____

Address
of Rabbi _____

Address
of Rabbi _____

Names, in order of seniority, of brothers and/or half-brothers of the Bridegroom having the same father. (If there are no brothers, this fact should be stated.)

If Bride is childless widow, give full details of chalitzah on reverse side.

- -

_____

_____

I hereby certify that the information given above is correct.

I hereby certify that the informtion given above is correct.

Signature of
Bridegroom _____

Signature
of Bride _____

New
residence _____

_____

I hereby certify that to the best of my knowledge the information given herein is true, and there is no impediment in Civil Law or Jewish Law to the solemnization of the marriage.

     Officiating Rabbi _____

Names of witnesses _____ Address _____
on the ketubah
(please print) _____ Address _____
    Note: The witnesses signing the ketubah should also sign the English translation.

Additional Information
Regarding Non-Jewish Parentage

_____

_____

_____

_____

_____

_____

_____

_____

_____

_____

_____

_____

_____

_____

_____

_____

_____

_____

_____

_____

_____

_____

SUMMARY AND TRANSLATION OF THE KETUBAH

This ketubah states

That on the _____ day of the week, the _____ day of the

month of _____ in the year 57 _____ , corresponding

to the _____ day of _____ 19 _____

the holy Covenant of Marriage was entered into

at _____

between the Bridegroom

_____

and the Bride

_____

The said Bridegroom made the following declaration to his Bride: "Be thou my wife according to the law of Moses and of Israel. I faithfully promise that I will be a true husband unto thee; I will honor and cherish thee; I will protect and support thee, and will provide all that is necessary for thy sustenance in accordance with the usual custom of Jewish husbands. I also take upon myself all such further obligations for thy maintenance as are prescribed by our religious statutes."

And the said Bride has entered into this holy Covenant with affection and sincerity, and has thus taken upon herself the fulfillment of all the duties incumbent upon a Jewish wife.

This Covenant of Marriage was duly executed and witnessed this day according to the usage of Israel.

Bridegroom _____

Bride _____

Officiating Rabbi _____

THE KETUBAH IN HEBREW

בס"ד

ב ...... בשבת ב ...... לחדש ...... שנת חמשת אלפים ושבע מאות
.... למנין שאנו מנין כאן ...... איך החתן ...... בן
.... למשפחה .... אמר להדא בתולתא ...... בת
.... למשפחה ...... הוי לי לאנתו כדת משה וישראל ואנא אפלח
ואוקיר ואיזון ואפרנס יתיכי ליכי כהלכות גוברין יהודאין דפלחין ומוקרין וזנין
ומפרנסין לנשיהון בקושטא ויהיבנא ליכי מהר בתוליכי כסף זוזי מאתן דחזי ליכי
מדאוריתא ומזוניכי וכסותיכי וסיפוקיכי ומיעל לותיכי כאורח כל ארבע וצביאת מרת
.... בתולתא דא והות ליה לאנתו ודן נדוניא דהנעלת ליה מבי
.... בין בכסף בין בדהב בין בתכשיטין במאני דלבושא בשימושי דירה
ובשימושא דערסא הכל קבל עליו .... חתן דנן במאה זקוקים כסף צרוף
וצבי .... חתן דנן והוסיף לה מן דיליה עוד מאה זקוקים כסף צרוף אחרים
כנגדן סך הכל מאתים זקוקים כסף צרוף וכך אמר .... חתן דנן אחריות שטר
כתובתא דא נדוניא דן ותוספתא דא קבלית עלי ועל ירתי בתראי להתפרע מכל שפר
ארג נכסין וקנינין דאית לי תחות כל שמיא דקנאי ודעתיד אנא למקנא נכסין דאית להון
אחריות ודלית להון אחריות כלהון יהון אחראין וערבאין לפרוע מנהון שטר כתובתא
דא נדוניא דן ותוספתא דא מנאי ואפילו מן גלימא דעל כתפאי בחיי ובתר חיי מן יומא
דנן ולעלם ואחריות שטר כתובתא דא נדוניא דן ותוספתא דא קבל עליו ....
חתן דנן כחומר כל שטרי כתובות ותוספתות דנהגין בבנת ישראל העשויין כתקון
חכמינו זכרונם לברכה דלא כאסמכתא ודלא כטופסי דשטרי ...... מן
...... בן .... למשפחה .... חתן דנן למדת
.... בת .... למשפחה. .... בתולתא דא על כל מה
דכתוב ומפורש לעיל במנא דכשר למקניא ביה
הכל שריר וקים

נאום .... עד
נאום .... עד

Appendix 3

Prenuptial Agreement
Final Articles of Engagement
English Translation of Final Articles of Engagement
The Ketubah: A Meaningful English Summation and Translation
  Rabbi Moshe D. Tendler

PRENUPTIAL AGREEMENT

The undersigned hereby agree, promise and represent:

In the event that the covenant of marriage to be entered into this day of _____ , 19 _____ by husband (_____ _____) and wife (_____) shall be terminated, dissolved or annulled in accordance with the laws of any civil court having jurisdiction effectively to do so, then in that event husband (_____) and wife (_____ _____) shall voluntarily and promptly upon demand by either of the parties to this marriage present themselves at a mutually convenient time and place to terminate the marriage and relieve each other from the covenant of marriage in accordance with Jewish law and custom before the Ecclesiastical Court (Bet Din) of the Rabbinical Council of America—or before a similarly recognized Orthodox rabbinical court—by delivery and acceptance, respectively, of a "get" (Jewish divorce).

This agreement is recognized as a material inducement to this marriage by the parties hereto. Failure of either of the parties to voluntarily perform his or her obligations hereunder if requested to do so by the other party shall render the noncomplying party liable for all costs, including attorneys' fees, reasonably incurred by the requesting party to secure the noncomplying party's performance and damages caused by the demanding party's unwillingness or inability to marry pending delivery and acceptance of a "get."

The parties hereto recognize that the obligations specified above are unique and special and they agree that the remedy at law for a breach of this contract will be inadequate. Accordingly, in the event of any breach of this contact, in addition to any other legal remedies available, the injured party shall be entitled to injunctive or mandatory relief directing specific performance of the obligations included herein.

Entered into this _____ day of _____ 19 _____ .

_____	_____	_____
Husband	Witness	Date
_____	_____	_____
Wife	Witness	Date

FINAL ARTICLES OF ENGAGEMENT

נוסח שטר תנאים אחרונים

[ע׳ נחלת שבעה סימן ט׳ וסימן י׳]

מזל טוב יצמח ויעלה כגן רטוב עד למעלה דברי הברית והתנאים האלה שדברו
והותנו בין שני הצדדים בשעת החופה ביום פלוני בכך לחודש פלוני שנה פלונית עיר
פלונית דהיינו מר פב״ב ובני החתן פלוני צד אחד ומר פב״פ ובתו הכלה פלונית צד
השני. ראשית דבר מר פלוני הנ״ל נשא וקידש מרת פלונית הנ״ל בטבעת קדושין של
זהב והכניסה לחופה כדת משה וישראל והיא קבלה הקדושין ממנו. ומר פלוני הלביש
את בנו במלבושי כבוד שבת ויו״ט וחול לפי כבודו ונתן לבנו סבלונות לפי כבודו. ומר
פלוני הלביש את בתו הכלה במלבושי כבוד שבת ויו״ט וחול ובגדים וצעיפים וסבלונות
ומטה מוצעת הכל לפי כבודו. ומעתה הזוג הנ״ל ינהגו יחד באהבה ובחיבה ולא יבריחו
ולא יעלימו ולא ינעלו לא זה מזו ולא זו מזה. שום הברחה בעולם רק ישלטו שניהם שוה
בנכסיהם, והחתן מר פלוני הנ״ל יסח ויוקיר ויזון ויפרנס הכלה הנ״ל כהלכות גוברין
יהודאין דפלחין ומוקרין וזנין ומפרנסין לנשיהון בקושטא. וצבי מר פלוני לזון ולפרנס
הכלה הנ״ל כאורח ארעא כל זמן שהיא סמוכה על שולחנו וכל עת שאינה סמוכה על
שולחנו יהיה מאיזה טעם שיהיה התהייב עצמו שאז תיכף ומיד יתן לה מאתים דולר
לפיזור מזונות כסות ומדור וכן יתן לה כל יום ויום משך הזמן שאינה סמוכה על שולחנו
עד שיצא פסק־דין מבית דין צדק שאינה זכאה מעוכבת מלינשא כפי דת משה וישראל
מטעמיה ומן יומא דנן ולעלם הרשות ביד הכלה הנ״ל או להיות סמוכה על שולחנו או
לקבל ממנו סכום הנ״ל לפיזור מזונות וכסות כאוות נפשה, ואם חו״ש יהיה איזה
סיכסוך ביניהם הן בתשלום מזונות, הן בשום דבר מהדברים שבינו לבינה, הן מהדברים
הנוגעים להחזקת ופרנסת צאצאיהם, אז יעמדו לדין לפני בית־דין צדק של דיינים
מומחים הקבוע בעירם או בקהילתם ואם אין בית דין של דיינים מומחים קבוע בעירם
או בקהילתם יעמדו לדין לפני דיינים מומחים ע״י זבל״א וזבל״א תוך י״ד ימים אחר
דרישת אחד מהצדדים וע״פ יעמדו כל ריב וכל נגע, ופסק דינם יהיה כחו יפה הן בדיני
ישראל והן במשפטי המדינה, ואחר שנתפשרו, תחזור מרת פלונית לבית בעלה וכל
הנותר בידה מן המעות שקבלה מבעלה לפיזור מזונות כסות ודיור וכל בגדיה ותכשיטיה
תחזיר למקומם הראשון. וכל הנ״ל נעשה בפנינו עדים החתומים מטה בק״מ דלא
כאסמכתא ודלא כטופסי דשטרי וקנינא מכל אחד מן הצדדים הנ״ל להצד שכנגדו על
כל מה דכתוב ומפורש לעיל במנא דכשר למקניא ביה והכל שריר וקיים

נאום

נאום

וגם אנו באנו על החתום כדי שתעיד עלינו חתימות ידינו כמאה עדים כשרים ונאמנים
על כל מה שכתוב ומפורש לעיל.

החתן:

הכלה:

ENGLISH TRANSLATION OF FINAL ARTICLES
OF ENGAGEMENT

    May good fortune sprout forth and ascend to the greatest heights even as a well-watered garden. These are the words of the covenant and the provisions which were spoken and stipulated between the two parties at the time of the nuptials on the _____ day of the month of _____ in the year _____ in the city of _____ ; to wit:

    Between _____ and his son, the groom, _____ , the party of the first part; and _____ and his daughter, the bride, _____ , the party of the second part.

    Firstly, _____ wedded and married _____ by means of a wedding ring and caused her to be brought under the nuptial canopy in accordance with the law of Moses and Israel and she accepted the wedding ring from him.

    _____ provided his son with dignified clothing for the Sabbath, festivals and weekdays in a proper manner and in accordance with his status and presented his son with marriage gifts in accordance with his status.

    _____ provided his daughter, the bride, with dignified clothing for the Sabbath, festivals and weekdays, clothing, kerchiefs, marriage gifts and furnished bed, all in accordance with his status.

    Henceforth, the aforementioned couple will comport themselves with love and affection and will neither alienate nor conceal nor lock away, neither he from her nor she from him, any property whatever, but they shall both equally exercise jurisdiction over their property.

    The aforementioned groom, _____ will work, honor, support and maintain the bride in accordance with the manner of Jewish husbands who work, honor, support and maintain their wives in truth. And _____ agreed to support and maintain the aforementioned bride in accordance with universal custom so long as she shares his board and at any time that she does not share his board, may it be for any reason whatsoever, the groom obligated himself that he will thereupon immediately give his wife the sum of 200 dollars to spend for food, clothing and domicile and will give her a like sum every single day throughout the period during which she does not share his board until a judgment is issued by a *Bet Din* declaring that she is not prevented from marrying in accordance with the law of Moses and Israel because of him [i.e., because of the husband's feasance or nonfeasance]. And from this day and forevermore it is the prerogative of the aforementioned bride either to share her husband's board or to receive from him the aforementioned sum to spend for food, clothing and domicile in accordance with her desire. If, Heaven forefend, there be any dispute between them whether with regard to payment of maintenance whether with regard to any marital matter, or whether with regard to custody and support of their issue, they will then present their suit before an established *Bet Din* composed of competent judges in their city or community and if there is no established *Bet Din* composed of competent judges in their city or community they will bring their suit before a *Bet Din* of three qualified judges which shall be composed of one judge designated by each party and a third judge chosen by the two judges designated by the parties, within fourteen days after the application of either of the parties. Any quarrel or controversy shall be settled in accordance with their decree and the award of said *Bet Din* may be entered as a judgment in a court of competent jurisdiction.

After a settlement is reached and the wife returns to her husband's home she shall return the balance of the funds received from her husband for purposes of maintenance, clothing and domicile which remain in her possession as well as her clothing and jewelry, to their original site.

All of the foregoing in the presence of us, the undersigned witnesses through conveyance of a *sudar* (kerchief) and in the most efficacious manner, not in the manner of an *asmakhta* (penalty) and not in the manner of a mere documentary form. We have accepted conveyance in the form of a vessel halakhically fit for the purposes of conveyance from each of the aforementioned parties on behalf of the other party with regard to all which is written and stated and Everything is Valid and Confirmed.

_____ (witness)

_____ (witness)

And we also have affixed our signatures in order that our signatures may attest even as a hundred competent and trustworthy witnesses to all which is written and stated above.

_____ (Groom)

_____ (Bride)

THE KETUBAH:
A MEANINGFUL ENGLISH SUMMATION AND TRANSLATION

Rabbi Moshe D. Tendler

The *Ketubah* has been devitalized by being relegated to the ritual of the marriage ceremony. No attempt is made to inform the groom and bride of the provisions of the *Ketubah,* nor are these provisions ever enforced by our *rabbanim* at time of divorce or death of the husband.

The *Ketubah,* if fully enforced, obviates the need for finding new penalty mechanisms to coerce a recalcitrant husband who refuses to give his wife a *get* even after secular divorce.

The total *Ketubah* package includes *Tosafot Ketubah U'nedunya* as well as the many *Chiyuvei Tenai Ketubah* discussed in *Ketubot* 46, 47, 51, 52, and summarized in the *Rambam* (*Ishut* 12).

This English summation of these obligations is offered to my *chaverim* to revitalize the *Ketubah* as a fully enforceable financial obligation made in full faith by husband to wife, intended by our *Chazal.*

Antenuptial Agreement

This contract is an accurate summation of the obligations assumed by the husband to his wife pursuant to the signing of the traditional marriage contract—the *Ketubah.*

It is added to the *Ketubah* document to assure full comprehension by the husband of his obligations; to remove any ambiguity of intent in the original Aramaic language text of the *Ketubah*; and to underscore the valid nature of this contact, so as to facilitate adjudication in the secular courts of the United States of America.

Article One: This agreement is binding on

_____ ,

hereafter referred to as the husband, and his estate, until all clauses are fulfilled.

Article Two: Upon dissolution of this marriage by the death of the husband or by a legally executed divorce in accord with secular and Jewish law (Torah law), a minimum lump sum settlement equivalent to the dollar value of one hundred pounds of silver or the amount specified in the *Ketubah* document, whichever is greater, is guaranteed to _____ , hereafter known as the wife.

Article Three: Upon death of the husband, or complete dissolution of this marriage by secular and religious divorce, the monies, article of value and real estate contributed by the wife to the joint property, are to be returned in full value to said wife. This is understood to include all marriage gifts from the family and friends of the wife, in addition to all property owned by the wife at the time of the marriage or acquired thereafter by independent means. It also includes that part of the wedding expenses paid by the wife or her family.

Article Four: Any dispute as to the true value of the wife's estate is to be submitted to binding arbitration in a rabbinic court.

Article Five: Until complete dissolution of his marriage the husband assumes full responsibility for the wife's:
  A) Food and clothing budget in keeping with the social and economic status of the husband and the previous economic standard of the wife.
  B) Domicilary accommodations commensurate with the social and economic status of the family.
  C) Ransom payments in the event of her being held captive.
  D) Full medical expenses.
  E) Burial expenses.

Article Six: Dissolution of the marriage because of the death of the husband does *not* void article five. The wife may remain in the marital home and continue to receive from the estate, all benefits under article five, until she remarries or agrees to accept the settlement sum specified in article two.

Article Seven: In case of separation or abandonment by the husband all the above obligations remain in full force until the completion of *all* divorce proceedings and the removal of all impediments to the remarriage of the wife. Any residual restrictions to such remarriage be they secular or religious, maintains the support provisions of this agreements in full force.

Duly witnesses and signed:

on this _____ day of _____ in the year _____

Witness _____   Husband _____

Witness _____

Appendix 4

Standard Rabbinical Contract Form
Rabbinical-Congregational Guidelines

STANDARD RABBINICAL CONTRACT FORM

Suggested by Division of Communal Services
Max Stern Division of Communal Services
An Affiliate of Yeshiva University

Whereas Congregation _____ of _____ has invited Rabbi _____ to serve as its spiritual leader, the following agreement is made between the congregation and the rabbi on (date) _____ .

The rabbi shall devote his time, effort and energy to promoting the spiritual welfare of the congregation and the community.

The rabbi shall be the recognized authority on Jewish Law and practice within the congregation, shall be in charge of its religious services, and shall minister to the religious and pastoral needs of its members.

His alone shall be the responsibility for and freedom of the pulpit, and he shall initiate, maintain and supervise educational programs for all ages and interest groups.

The terms of this contract shall initially be for a period of two years beginning (date) _____ through August 31st, _____, and are automatically renewable for a period of three years. Negotiations for new terms will be held by the end of March of the last year of the contract. Should either party not wish to renew, notice shall be given in writing no later than April 1st in the last year thereof.

The congregation shall compensate the rabbi for his services at the annual rate of $_____ for the first year commencing (date) _____ and at the increased rate of $_____ for the second year, commencing (date) _____ .

The congregation shall provide for the rabbi a suitable and mutually acceptable home *or* housing allowance to include utilities.

The congregation shall contribute to a Retirement and Pension Plan (e.g., the Rabbinical Council of America Plan equal to 15.5 percent of the rabbi's salary) and provide for adequate life insurance coverage to protect the rabbi's family.

The congregation shall also provide regular health and hospital insurance and other fringe benefits, as prevalent in the profession. The congregation shall provide an expense allowance, to facilitate the rabbi's participation in two out-of-town rabbinic and scholarly conventions annually. The congregation shall provide for the complete moving expenses and transportation costs for the rabbi and and his family, from his present location.

The rabbi shall be allowed a minimum vacation period of one month, to be taken during July and August. Any additional vacation period at a time of the year which is suitable to both rabbi and congregation, must be approved by the Board of Directors of the Synagogue.

The Division of Communal Services of the Rabbi Isaac Elchanan Theological Seminary at Yeshiva University stands ready at all times to assist in the resolution of possible disputes between the congregation and the rabbi.

May the Almighty bless and prosper the joint efforts of both rabbi and congregation.

_____   _____
      President   Rabbi

                                 _____
                                         Date

RABBINIC-CONGREGATIONAL GUIDELINES

The following reflect the prevailing guidelines governing rabbinic–congregational relationships:

Rabbi's Office

The rabbi shall devote his time, effort and energy to promoting the spiritual welfare of the congregation and the community. The rabbi shall be the recognized authority on Jewish Law and practice within the congregation, shall be in charge of its religious services, and shall minister to the religious and pastoral needs of its members. His alone shall be the responsibility for the freedom of the pulpit, and he shall initiate, maintain and supervise educational programs and activities for all ages and interest groups. The rabbi shall represent the congregation and serve as its spokesman in Jewish and civic activities in the community at large.

Term of Office and Compensation

The period to be covered by the congregational–rabbinical contract usually begins the first of July or August of the given year and concludes August 31st in the last year. This covers the cycle of the congregation's pattern of activities.

The rabbi should be engaged for an initial period of two (2) years, to allow time to become familiar with the congregation. The first renewal should be for three (3) years and the second renewal for five (5) years. Thereafter, the relationship between the rabbi and the congregation should be considered permanent.

Many variables, too many to enumerate, determine the rabbi's salary. Clearly, the salary should reflect the cost of living in the style the rabbi and congregation deem appropriate, in addition to adequate housing arrangements.

Pension Insurance, and Fringe Benefits

The congregation is obliged to protect itself and the family of its spiritual leader by providing the rabbi with a proper pension plan and adequate insurance. The Rabbinical Council of America sponsors a pension program which the congregation may wish to consider. It is suggested that the rabbi and congregation arrange their agreement on the realistic life insurance needs of the family, so that adequate coverage be provided. Congregations cover the entire or major portion of the pension costs. Other insurances to be provided for the rabbi and his family are Blue Cross, Blue Shield, major medical, and disability.

In addition, congregations provide expenses for the cost of moving and transportation to the new location and for professional rabbinic conferences.

Termination of Agreement

If either the rabbi or the congregation do not wish to renew the contract, written notice should be given no later than April 1st in the last year of the contract period. Should the congregation terminate the agreement, it must provide severance pay to the rabbi. The amount of such severance pay, universally accepted as the norm of the profession, is on the basis of one month's salary for each year of service.

After proper notice of termination, the congregation, in consultation with the Director of Rabbinic Services of RIETS at Yeshiva University, will have the right to invite rabbinic candidates to its pulpit. The rabbi, likewise, shall be free to accept invitations to other pulpits.

Vacations

The accepted minimum vacation period is one month. However, as the rabbi continues to serve the congregation, his vacation should gradually be increased to two months. Most rabbis will prefer to take this vacation during the summer.

Sabbaticals

In order to allow the rabbi an opportunity to broaden his knowledge, intensify his Torah studies, and/or continue his postgraduate studies, congregations grant a Sabbatical leave following seven to ten years of service. The congregation provides full salary for the rabbi during his Sabbatical leave, and engages a substitute at its own expense.

Liquidation

In the event that the congregation is forced to liquidate or dissolve, special severance compensation, considerable more than one month's salary per year of service, should be paid to the rabbi. Priority should be given to the rabbi's severance pay from sale of property and possessions.

Resolving Difficulties

The Division of Communal Services stands ready at all times to assist in the resolution of possible disputes between the congregation and the rabbi.

General Principles

The agreement entered into between a rabbi and his congregation is between a religious community and its chosen leader. It goes beyond the stipulation of a legal agreement; it covers a spiritual relationship. A rabbi is not to be considered as an employee of the congregation. He is a consecrated servant of God called by the congregation to serve the religious, educational and pastoral needs of the membership. His ministry shall not be limited to his congregational duties, but shall be left free to serve the larger community. The sacred nature of a Jewish congregation and the lofty character of the rabbi's office dictate that the agreement between rabbi and congregation be preserved on the highest plane of mutual integrity, mutual respect and mutual devotion to the religious purposes for which the congregation exists.

Contributors

Rabbi Elan Adler

Rabbi Adler received Semikhah from RIETS in 1986 and since then has served as Assistant Rabbi at Congregation Agudath Shalom in Stamford, Connecticut. A major part of his responsibilities there involves the synagogue youth, with whom he utilizes his extensive national and international experiences in reaching out to young people.

Rabbi Saul Berman

Rabbi Berman has been Senior Rabbi of the Lincoln Square Synagogue in New York City, and he teaches in the Jewish Studies Department of Stern College, where he was previously chairman of the department. He has published numerous articles on a variety of topics in Jewish life.

Rabbi Louis Bernstein

Rabbi Bernstein received Semikhah from RIETS in 1950. He is Rabbi of the Young Israel of Windsor Park in New York, a past president of the Rabbinical Council of America, a leader of World

Mizrahi, and a community activist who also teaches at Yeshiva University. He is renowned as a spokesman for Modern Orthodoxy in many forums in Jewish life.

Rabbi Hershel Billet

Rabbi Billet received Semikhah from RIETS in 1975 and is the Rabbi of the Young Israel of Woodmere, New York. He has taught Talmud in a variety of institutions, including Yeshiva University and the Genesis Foundation.

Rabbi Ephraim Buchwald

Rabbi Buchwald, after receiving Semikhah from RIETS in 1975, was for fifteen years Educational Director of the Lincoln Square Synagogue in New York City, responsible for many of the synagogue's renowned outreach and educational programs. He is currently Director of the National Jewish Outreach Program, which he founded in October 1987, and Rabbi of the beginner's service at Lincoln Square Synagogue. He is also the founding president of the Association of Jewish Outreach Professionals.

Rabbi Reuven P. Bulka

Rabbi Dr. Bulka is Rabbi of Congregation Machzikei Hadas in Ottawa, Ontario, and editor of the *Journal of Psychology and Judaism*. He is on the editorial boards of several journals, including *Tradition*, and is author of many books. His interest and training in psychology and his direct involvement in synagogue and communal life have given him a special perspective on mental attitudes within the rabbinate.

Rabbi William Cohen

Rabbi Cohen received Semikhah from RIETS in 1943 and is the Rabbi of long standing at the Beth David synagogue in West Hartford, Connecticut. He has been a driving force in the growth and consolidation of Orthodoxy in his community.

Rabbi Basil Herring

Rabbi Dr. Herring received Semikhah from RIETS in 1972 and is the Rabbi of the Jewish Center of Atlantic Beach, Atlantic Beach, New York. He is on the faculty of Stern College for Women and is the editor of the *RCA Record*.

Rabbi William Herskowitz

Rabbi Dr. Herskowitz received Semikhah from RIETS and has been Rabbi of Greystone Jewish Center in Yonkers since 1962. He is Chairman of the RCA Pension Board.

Rabbi Robert S. Hirt

Rabbi Hirt is Vice President for Administration and Professional Education at RIETS. In this capacity he is in a unique position to perceive and evaluate current trends in the pulpit rabbinate.

Rabbi Immanuel Jakobovits

Lord Jakobovits received Semikhah from Yeshiva Etz Chaim, London, in 1941 and served in a number of pulpits in London, Ireland, and New York City before assuming his position as Chief Rabbi of the British Commonwealth. He holds a variety of positions, both communal and academic, with a special interest in bioethics. He has published sermons, essays, and several books dealing with contemporary social and Jewish issues from the viewpoint of tradition and halakhah. Besides being knighted and elevated to the peerage, he obviously has a special perspective on rabbinic leadership.

Rabbi Israel Kestenbaum

Rabbi Kestenbaum has occupied a pulpit in Wilkes-Barre, Pennsylvania, and has studied at the Geisinger School of Pastoral Care.

Rabbi Norman Lamm

Rabbi Dr. Lamm, distinguished President of Yeshiva University, received Semikhah from RIETS and served in the rabbinate in

Springfield, Massachusetts, as well as the Jewish Center on Manhattan's Upper West Side. He is recognized as an insightful and courageous spokesman of what some refer to as Modern Orthodoxy. Given his rabbinic experience and current position, he is in a unique position to articulate and mold the priorities and prospects of the pulpit rabbinate.

Rabbi A. Mark Levin

Rabbi Levin received Semikhah from RIETS in 1972 and has a Master's Degree in Jewish Education and Counseling. He has served as a rabbi in Memphis, Tennessee, for the past fifteen years, where he also teaches Judaica on the college level. He has earned acclaim for his award-winning, innovative work in the field of adult Jewish education.

Dr. Irving N. Levitz

Dr. Levitz is an associate professor at Yeshiva University's Wurzweiler School of Social Work, where he holds the Carl and Dorothy Bennett Chair in Pastoral Counseling, and he is mentor and supervisor of its MSW Program for Clergy. He is also a musmakh of RIETS and a practicing clinical psychologist in Woodmere, New York, specializing in marital and family therapy.

Rabbi Charles D. Lipshitz

Rabbi Lipshitz received Semikhah from RIETS in 1976 and has served as a rabbi in Reading, Pennsylvania and, since 1981, in Richmond, Virginia.

Rabbi Haskel Lookstein

Rabbi Lookstein, a 1958 Musmakh of RIETS, is Rabbi of Congregation Kehilath Jeshurun in New York City, Principal of the Ramaz School, and Joseph H. Lookstein Professor of Homiletics at RIETS.

Rabbi Jacob J. Schacter

Rabbi Dr. Schacter received Semikhah from Yeshiva Torah Vodaath in 1973 and has been Rabbi of the Jewish Center in New York City since 1981. He is Director of Yeshiva University's Torah

U-Madda Project. This article reflects his academic interests, insofar as he holds a Ph.D. from the Department of Near Eastern Languages and Civilizations at Harvard University.

Rabbi Shubert Spero

Rabbi Dr. Spero received Semikhah from Yeshiva Torah Vodaath in 1947 and was Rabbi of the Young Israel of Cleveland, Ohio, from 1950 to 1983, when he made aliyah. He now teaches rabbinic thought at Bar Ilan University. He has published many articles and several books dealing with Jewish philosophy, halakhah, and contemporary issues.

Rabbi David Stavsky

Rabbi Stavsky has been a rabbi in Columbus, Ohio, for more than thirty years, having received Semikhah from RIETS, as well as degrees in psychology and counseling. He has authored several guides dealing with aspects of synagogue programming and has participated in and provided leadership for the growth and consolidation of Orthodoxy in Columbus.

Rabbi Joel Tessler

Rabbi Tessler received Semikhah from RIETS in 1982 and is Rabbi of Congregation Beth Shalom, Washington, DC, and its suburban satellite in Potomac, Maryland. He holds a Masters Degree in social work.

Rabbi Abner Weiss

Rabbi Dr. Weiss is currently Senior Rabbi of Beth Jacob Congregation in Beverly Hills, California, and has held pulpits in Riverdale, New York, and Durban, South Africa, where he lectured at local universities. He received Semikhah from Yeshivat Kerem be'Yavneh in Israel. Rabbi Weiss is renowned for his oratorical expertise.

Rabbi Mordechai Willig

Rabbi Willig received Semikhah from RIETS, where he is a rosh yeshivah. He is also Rabbi of the Young Israel of Riverdale, New York, and is renowned as a lamdan and talmid chakham, attuned to the realities of congregational and communal life.

Rabbi Mordecai E. Zeitz

Rabbi Dr. Zeitz received Semikhah from RIETS in 1962 and is Rabbi of Beth Tikvah in Montreal and Educational Director of its associated Day and Hebrew Schools. As the founder of both institutions, he has seen his community grow from a few Jewish families into a community center currently serving thousands.

Index

Rabbi Basil Herring, Ph.D., is Rabbi of the Jewish Center of Atlantic Beach, New York, and a member of the Executive Committee of the Rabbinical Council of America. He is Adjunct Professor at Stern College for Women of Yeshiva University, where he teaches Jewish philosophy, law, and ethics. A profilic author, lecturer, and speaker, Rabbi Herring's previous works include *Jewish Ethics and Halakhah for Our Time*, two volumes on Jewish law and contemporary issues, and *The Jewish Imagination*, a book of sermons and discourses on Jewish life.

Temple Israel

Minneapolis, Minnesota

A SPEEDY RECOVERY TO

BARBARA RATNER